Life

Leukemia

THE JOURNEY OF A 23 YEAR OLD MOTHER OF TWO, DIAGNOSED WITH A RARE LEUKEMIA, SURVIVING A BONE MARROW TRANSPLANT & FINDING LIFE'S TRUE PURPOSE

Sheri Nocelli

LIFE, LOVE... LEUKEMIA

COPYRIGHT 2013 SHERI NOCELLI
ISBN-13: 978-0615841878

www.SHERINOCELLI.com

SHERI NOCELLI

Authors Notes

Taking on writing this book has been a huge emotional undertaking, but I feel in my heart that sharing my experience is my life's purpose on this planet. I get emails all the time from strangers all around the world, who thank me for sharing my story through my online Blog, but there are so many details and parts of the story that I wasn't well enough to share during the actual time I was experiencing them. My hope is that my story and experiences can help someone else in my position to get through a similar experience, or to help people who are well to understand what it's really like from the eyes of the Cancer patient. I want to share my story of survival, to spread hope to those who need it – and show the world that you can survive this, no matter how grim the diagnosis – and come out a stronger, better, whole version of yourself. I realized as I started to write my story that it was impossible to tell the Cancer portion of the story without also including the story of my life leading up to that point. So this book became a major project in many ways. It's been a TON of research, about myself. I requested copies of all of my medical records from all of the places I was treated over the past five years, and began delving into the medical lingo I never before was able to understand.

It's been a roller coaster passionate journey writing the story as well, as I dig up vivid memories of moments that often times, I've blocked out completely up until the moment my fingers strike the keys - and when I read back my words on the screen, it's often the first time I've thought of these moments since they happened. It's a process in many ways, more than I imagined it would be, but I want the story to be as truthful and raw as possible. I don't like to sugarcoat things, but at the same time I've approached writing this book just as I would hold a conversation telling you my story, so you can really feel my emotions and experience my life through my eyes.

I made it a personal goal to release this book on July 22, 2013, exactly on the five year anniversary of my bone marrow transplant, as a celebration of life. I feel like I've been drudged through some cosmic therapy while writing this book which has been two years in the making. I often times find myself humbled

3

by my own words; crying and laughing along with the woman I am reading about – myself. It's been a difficult undertaking, but was worth every second of emotion I relived in order to describe detailed accounts of my battle.

Please note that all names of people, places and establishments have been changed to alias names and titles, but everything you will read is exactly how it occurred during my journey. The story is one hundred percent truth, only the names of those involved have been changed.

Thank you for inviting me into your life, and allowing me to share my story with you!

Sheri Nocelli

To all those suffering, healing, surviving and who didn't make it – to all noble warriors against cancer.

PART I
Life, Love. . .

I look to my right

To find that you're not there

The clock has all of the time

But I don't have the patience anymore to wait

I need to make you mine

And search for answers that are clear

It's all in the hands of karma now

The law of nature's way will always get its way

- Lucien Nocelli "My Gift" (Lyrics)

SHERI NOCELLI

August 11, 2013

As I stand here on this August night, my face bent into the swirling steam of boiling water, all I can do is smile in this uncomfortable heat as I prepare some Kraft macaroni and cheese for the kids' dinner. Stirring the hard pasta around to prevent it from sticking, my mind begins to wander. How many moms are standing at their stoves right now, working at a hot pan on a ninety-six degree day, and are actually thankful to be in that moment? My bet – I'm the only one who wouldn't trade anything in the world.

It's easy to look into a family and imagine what you want to about how perfect their life is. From the outside peering in, almost any family can appear to be as perfect as 7th Heaven if they try hard enough. How many Eric and Annie Camden's have you ever met? I can think of a couple families who sure seem like the Camden's, but I'm willing to bet if I took a moment to look a little closer, that I could probably remove each and every one from the "perfect life" category pretty quickly.

Looking at our life, I can see how we could be perceived as having everything, being well off, lucky, living the perfect life. Living the dream. For a short time I think we actually did have that, which was something we had worked long and hard for years to achieve. I think our picture perfect time frame began when our second child, our daughter, was born in May of 2007 completing our family. The stars finally aligned just right for us to enjoy our new home, our children, our career and our marriage. These were all the things we had sacrificed for, worked endlessly for and lived for and here we were, just where we wanted to be.

Nine and a half months later, we almost lost everything. Not to fire, not theft, not to flooding or airstrikes, but to something more vicious, heartless, horribly wreckful and quite simply, lethal. Our picture was shattered by Cancer.
Our story had not been a straight road to that moment. We had endured more roadblocks in our time together than some people experience in their entire lifetime.

9

August 11, 2001 (12 Years Earlier)

I am seventeen years old and driving up to Lake Sunapee, New Hampshire in my mother's red Toyota sedan. This is the farthest I've driven on my own from Manchester ever before, a whole hour alone in the car. I have a passion for photography, especially of live performance, and am heading up to see Beatlemania and to get some concert shots of the off Broadway production for my portfolio. My mind wanders as I drive the granite lined highways.

I was never your typical teenager – heck I was never your typical pre-teen either for that matter. Every memory I have of Elementary school is of being discarded by my peers and having more in common with my teachers than my class mates. While the nineties attire of fifth graders consisted of plaid button down shirts, washed out jeans and sneakers, my wardrobe of choice was aqua and lime striped bell bottoms – complete with matching blouse and white platform shoes. The visual discrepancies are clear. While my school mates were listening to Nirvana, my entire music collection included nothing but The Beatles.

I have a clear memory of my fifth grade math teacher, Mr. Wolfe, calling me to his desk at the beginning of January, handing me the torn off December page from his Beatles wall calendar. I remember sitting at my little metal desk, slouching in the hard plastic chair, staring at John, Paul, George and Ringo laughing together as they posed in their grey collarless jackets.

I'd be greeted in the hallway with remarks, "Hey, Beatle Chick" and I'd be taunted on the bus, "Sheri, are you married to Paul McCartney?" Little meaningless remarks not conveying malice, but hurting all the same, just to know that I was that separate from everyone else.

The funny thing is, I used this as an advantage in later years. Teachers loved that I was into the Beatles; it gave us something in common. It's always better to be friends with the teachers in school – you get way more perks this way. Even on my driving test, the instructor and I were so enthralled in a conversation about The White Album that when I blew through a stop sign on

Oak Street he passes me anyway. Oops! Many times the high school gym teacher would mark down that I did the full walk and run mile around the park, when in reality I was hanging out with him in the shade discussing the meaning behind Revolution Number 9. Beatles were my whole childhood, causing a fair amount of social trauma, but on the flip side of the coin, opening many unique doors along the way.

I end up getting to the lake early, which is nice because I have been in contact with the band members before, and think it would be fun to catch up and meet them in person. The band is here, hanging around waiting to begin their sound check. I introduce myself, and hang around to photograph the pre-show action of course, who doesn't love candid shots? The guys are great to hang with and invite me into their circle with open arms. At one point of the day, I am even invited to join them on a boat for a tour of Lake Sunapee – complete with a tour guide who makes sure to teach these tri-state area visitors to the boonies the incredible history of the community. After all, who wouldn't give anything for the claim to fame of being the filming location of the movie On Golden Pond? Snooze. It makes for some great jokes however, and memories that I know two of us will never forget.

Lucien and I hit it off from, "Hello". According to him, we hit it off well before our first greeting, when he "checked me out" through the band touring van's window. He plays the part of John Lennon in the cast of Beatlemania, tours all over the world playing to thousands and thousands of people in stadiums, theaters and grand concert halls. In a magnificent twist of fate, the tour looped them around to this sleepy New England town, and brought our worlds together. He is amazing on stage, captivating, striking, suave and bursting of virtuosity. He is a dream off stage; polite, intellectual, enchanting and magnificently funny.

The concert is spectacular of course as I expected it to be; the guys are great musicians and portray their respective characters to a tee. They start with She Loves You, I Want To Hold Your Hand and From Me To You wearing the classic black suits with velvet collars and glossy pointed boots, performing the Ed Sullivan set. At intermission they get trippy in their head-to-toe silk Sgt. Pepper uniforms for the psychedelic era for songs

11

including Lucy in the Sky with Diamonds, Penny Lane and A Day in the Life. They wrap up the show with the Abbey Road "crossing the street" look for the best songs; Come Together, Get Back, Hey Jude and Revolution. The show is exactly as I expect; entertaining perfection. I'm happy with how my live shots turn out, especially considering I hung out stage left for the duration of the show which my film proves with 95% of the images being of Lucien. Huh, how interesting? ::: Blush :::

After the show, I should turn around and head home. Yeah, how many just-turned-seventeen year olds do you know who would stick to *that* plan? The cast is famished and decide to head out for a bite to eat when they are done packing up, if they would ever be so lucky to find a restaurant open past midnight in Holderness, NH (a town that I swear must have just 3 residents). Of course after the show, during breakdown, the beers start to come out while they pack up their guitars, amps, costumes and other gear. I decide to hang around, help out, and have a couple beers as well. Looking back, I know, this was not a great idea, and I highly don't recommend this!

Lucky enough to locate a small bar which would serve quasi good meals, we get a table for our midnight dinner – this consisting of myself and the four cast members. They tell stories of touring and the road, including the time their storage unit on the roof of the van fell off mid trip sending silk Sgt. Pepper coats flying all over I-95. They talk about where they're from, where they have played and everything else you can imagine. By the time the revolting meal of rubber burgers and mushy French fries is over, it's reached the ripe time of 1:30 A.M. The guys are heading back to their hotel to hang out for a little while and ask me if I would like to join.

There is nothing like a jam session consisting of a drummer thumping out percussion on a suitcase, one mini backpack guitar strumming and five people bellowing out three and four part harmonies. The sing-a-long goes on for about an hour, one by one, band members yawning and excusing themselves to their rooms to rest up for the 7 hour drive back to New Jersey the next day. As the night gains upon us, it becomes clear that it's not a wise idea for me to drive an hour home by myself after the drinking, long day and given the dark narrow country roads. The decision as to whose hotel room floor I should bunk on is left up to one question, "Who doesn't snore?" Lucien's hand goes up in the air. *Yes.*

We stay up until around 5:30 in the morning. The room has two double beds, and we each sit on one, facing each other, telling each other every detail of ourselves leaving no stone unturned. Doing nothing but chatting till the sun starts to come up, nothing is off limits. I tell him that I am a Junior in High School, live in Manchester with my parents and my brother, play bass guitar, am an aspiring photographer, an advanced country line dancer (it's way more fun and less corny than it sounds!), a pointillist artist, my hopes, my dreams and any other detail I can think of. He tells me all about his life, his career as a jazz musician, a rock artist, an author, his touring career, his two children, his current living situation (married but living separate lives, waiting for the right time for a divorce) and anything and everything else.

I tell people all the time, and although it is the most cliché idea in the world, I can say without a doubt that it was love at first sight. It was completely an instant mutual infatuation which neither one of us could explain or deny, we just knew in our hearts it was right. We fell asleep in each other's arms that night, both knowing that was where we belonged. We had found our missing halves – we were finally whole.

Fall 2001

Lucien starts visiting every weekend, making the 6 hour trek up the east coast from Brick, New Jersey to Manchester, New Hampshire to visit me. Sometimes we only are able to be together for four hour intervals at a time, but our love has become our drug with us craving a fix, no matter the length of time. Many weekends we spend locked away in the Motel 8 in Tewksbury, Massachusetts doing nothing but eating deviled eggs, Cheese It's, watching bad basic cable and falling in love more every minute. We spend countless hours laying tangled in each other's arms, staring, studying every line and plane of each other's face, every freckle, every scar, every detail, neither one of us daring to speak a word for fear of waking up from this precious dream.

Sometimes we stroll through the local Market Basket supermarket just for fun. We go down to Marshalls to poke fun of misfit clearance products marked with red discount tags. We roll over laughing at a candle missing its wick marked for $14.99, or hideous home décor that you couldn't *pay* us to take – who buys this stuff? Other weekends, we stroll around the local mall holding hands and embracing while shoppers look our way with a smile - without judgment. No one here knows he is 36 and I am 17, all they know is that we are in love – and that's all that matters. We often have dinner at the I-Hop attached to the front of the hotel, hanging on to each other's every word, sharing our dinner of pancakes with Butter Pecan syrup; memorizing each other's eyes, mouth, dimples, and tucking that memory into a safe spot.

When the weekend winds to an end, we drive back to Manchester, holding hands tight in the car the whole drive, dreading that our time is over until next week. He drops me off secretly down the street from my house on Sunday night, and we start the long five day countdown until we see each other again next Saturday.

From the very first night we met, it was impossible to live apart.

In between visits, we absentmindedly drone through everyday life chores. Every day I go to school, trying my best to look interested and pay attention to keep up my so-far-so-good grades. Every day I leave school at 2:30 and go right to work at the restaurant (the most famous restaurant in southern New Hampshire... US Presidents eat there shrouded in Secret Service... Adam Sandler worked there as a kid... etc.) where I work in the Ice Cream and Take Out areas. Every night I get out of work around 9:00 and rush home to shower and do homework. Every night at 11:00 my lime green phone rings. Just to hear his voice, hear him breathe, hear him ask me how my day was, just to know we are connected is the moment I wait for all day for. We talk, laugh and share our thoughts for hours – sometimes 4 or 5 hours at a time. Often times I lay under my covers, cuddling with the big stuffed penguin we bought together (who we named Pecker) and we just "be". Some of the time we don't even talk, we just listen to the sound of each other breathing.

We wish each other sweet dreams. Sleep. Wake up. Start again. Repeat.

Our weekends together are complete and utter heaven on Earth. We lie for hours and stare at each other, sometimes not speaking a word for what seems like an eternity. We spend countless hours just caressing each other's cheek, falling deeper into each other's eyes and soul with each passing second.

He always brings his big body sunburst Fatovich acoustic guitar, which sometimes we bust out for a quick singing session. Several times he serenades me with a newly written heart felt ballad he'd written for me during the week; my own personal concert. He expresses his longing through masterpiece poetic lyrics that never fail to hit the nail of emotion on the head. My favorite song from this time which always brings back those fluttery feelings of falling in love, and the pit that grows in your stomach when you're separated by your soul's other half. It always reminds me of the life we led when we had to Make Believe.

Make Believe

My baby is so far away
Sometimes don't have much to say
Can't be with her everyday
My baby is my morning light
When I wake up my head and think how she shines so bright

I can still make believe with you
I keep closing my eyes
To see you and wanting to be with you
For the rest of my life

We lay here and talk for a while
While knowing the time will come
To end this with a sad smile
So far yet so close to the heart
This time that we share today
In one breath we'll be apart

I can still make believe with you
I keep closing my eyes
To see you and wanting to be with you
For the rest of my life

In time this will all come to pass
The time that we had to wait
The days will count down at last
I make believe you're here right by my side
When the wind calls your name to me
And all I can do is sigh

I can still make believe with you
I keep closing my eyes
To see you and wanting to be with you
For the rest of my life

Of course, with our age difference, a lot of the dating is in secret. How many fairy tale stories starring a 17 year old girl who says she's in love actually end with it being "the one" in the final chapter of the story? Exactly my point. But when I say I really knew, I mean it with every ounce of my being. I wake up Monday mornings, head off to high school and tell my friends about the amazing weekend. They all think I am crazy of course for dating a man in secret who is 19 years older than me, but support me none the less. They can see in my eyes, and hear in my voice that it is true.

It is a whole other story when it comes to my parents.

My mother has always been my best friend. She understands me, listens, offers advice that I can actually use and relate to. There is nothing I hide from her. It is no different this time around, and while I don't share *every* detail, she knows that I am dating Lucien and she has even met him twice. She has always trusted me to make the right choices in my life and knows that I am mature beyond my years emotionally, so it is no different this time around.

One day she notices a ring on my finger, gold and silver supporting a pretty emerald stone in the center. She asks me, and I tell her the truth, that this is our "for now" ring. We know we belong together and we want to get married.

This is the tipping point. I come home from work one Wednesday night to find my parents sitting on the living room couch. My father has his arms crossed across his chest, he is shaking his head slowly which is never a good sign. The whole scene feels like it is plucked directly from some corny, over acted Lifetime movie. They proceed to tell me that my father knows everything. They lecture; I need to end this relationship. I am a child. He is a grown man. If we try to contact each other, they will get a restraining order. They are taking my phone away. They tell me I can call him right now to tell him it is over.

They are calm and assertive, but deathly serious.

I stand on the other end of the living room, still in my rancid work clothes reeking of chicken tenders and grease, my heart pounding, the blood draining from my face. I scream at them that they don't understand! I scream at the top of my lungs, "I'm not a kid!" The ponytail in my hair feels like it is pulling tighter as my face turns beat red. I scream louder, "you don't know what you're doing, I love him!" The tears burn as they seep from my eyes. Screaming, "You don't understand! I love him! You don't believe me!" My body gives out; I fall to the floor into a helpless pile of emotion. "I love him!"

In the end, they take my phone away, and allow me to call Lucien from their phone to tell him everything that has transpired. He keeps his voice calm, reassuring. He is telling me through the tone of his voice alone that we will find a way. You can't stop true love. You can't stop fate.

A week after this blow up, I become an expert at hiding this relationship. I have another phone hidden away that I hook up to my phone line. At 11:00 at night I routinely take the phone into my bed, cover it with a pillow, turn the ringer down so no one can hear it ring except me. We whisper into the night, hanging onto every word, not knowing when we'll be able to hold each other again. I come up with an idea to film a video of myself to send to him. I film myself playing guitar and singing a song for him, eating a to-go dinner from Boston Market (he loves to watch me

SHERI NOCELLI

eat), and just gazing into the camera proclaiming my love. I package up the VHS tape along with 2 of his favorite candy bars (Nutrageous) and send it off to New Jersey.

A few weeks later he sends a tape of himself around his house, speaking gently to the camera, playing a new song he's written for me "Lord Answer My Prayer". He mails it to my friend Layla's house so that my parents will have no chance of seeing it. I watch this tape countless times, taking in every second. Soon enough, video tapes are not enough, and it is time to plan a secret visit.

I beg a friend of mine, Tilla, to help. She and I were always going on crazy road trips to see bands including excursions to Ohio, Delaware and Virginia. I know she is going to be heading down to Connecticut for Thanksgiving and I beg her to let me hitch a ride. I tell my parents I'm spending the holiday with her and her family. They believe me. I'm not going to lie, it hurt to misuse my parents trust, but I have no regrets in this circumstance. My friend drops me off at a hotel in Connecticut, and there he is, Oh My God how I have missed his beautiful face!

The Red Roof Inn hotel room is small, monotone and just dank. It doesn't matter. We walk to the gas station across the street to pick up some food, finally deciding on Stouffers frozen macaroni and cheese and chicken nuggets which we heat in the gas station microwave. Carrying our dinner back over to the hotel, we set up in front of the TV and eat our gourmet Thanksgiving feast – I don't think either one of us even taste the food, it just doesn't matter. When we are done, Lucien tries to put on the classic Thanksgiving Day Dallas Cowboys football game, which I hate! We wrestle over the remote control until finally I fling it across the room, "Ah ha! I won! No football!" Then we kiss. We lay and take each other in, inhaling each other's scent deep into our core. This time is a gift, we knew it then how lucky we were for every second we were able to hold each other, a lesson we have never forgotten.

Imagine hearing your 17 year old daughter telling you that she's in love with a 36 year old. I get it. I'd be freaking out too! And it's always the same old story… teenager thinks she knows better… but the whole world can see she's just in "puppy love"… blah,

18

blah, blah. This is different, and I am no fool. I know exactly what I have found – my soul mate. There is no way I'm letting this go.

Even shrouded in complete secrecy, our dating becomes more and more adventurous with each week. Some weeks he drives 6 hours to pick me up, and we head 8 hours right out to Buffalo, New York for a Beatlemania show. He does the show, we sleep, turn around to drive 8 hours back to New Hampshire, say our long sappy heart wrenching goodbyes and he heads the lonely 6 hours back to New Jersey.

Every weekend brings new doors to open as we fall deeper into love. As our relationship becomes stronger, so does the invisible force field which separates our reality from the ever growing list of battles we would to have to conquer. Does it really matter what the world thinks of you, as long as you know you've found honest, real love? Not at all.

After a couple months of whirlwind dating featuring a string of hotels, mall walking, Olive Garden dinners, thousands of miles put on the Nissan Altima and being that this was before the "everyone has a cell phone" era – after hundreds of dollars' worth of phone card minutes, Lucien decides to move to New Hampshire to be with me. He empties his belongings from his efficiency apartment he has been renting while he is getting divorced. He loads the Altima to the rim with 4 guitars, a stack of clothes and a really ugly furry fake house plant; all of his worldly belongings. We rent a little apartment on Somerville Street in Manchester (not the best area of town) with a bedroom, bathroom and fire engine red painted living room where we move in all of our furniture... a mattress and a vintage console record player we picked up at a yard sale – for free no less. I move into the apartment two months before I turn eighteen and spend many nights doing high school homework sitting Indian style at our foot locker dining room table. I sit there hashing out chemistry work, occasionally glancing over to the galley style kitchenette where Lucien is whipping up something amazing for dinner.

Daily life is insane. I spend the days in school, then work full time at my new job, a day care center near the Manchester airport,

19

then get up and do it all over again. We are paying our rent and child support for his children, and that's about it. We travel and tour with Beatlemania on the weekends. This is a dream life because it means we are together. Everyday feels like it is the two of us versus the world, mostly because that's exactly what it is. It isn't easy to start completely from scratch for us, owning minimal possessions including a couple guitars, a 13 inch television, a rundown computer and the clothes in our closets. It isn't easy going to sleep each night hoping that the car won't be repossessed before sunrise. It isn't easy making ends meet, landing us at the food pantry getting a box of fruit, veggies, cereal and mystery meat while trying to maintain some personal pride. It isn't easy to live 6 hours away from his two young sons, at the time 6 and 2 years old. It isn't easy for my parents to accept the fact that I am living with a man 19 years older than myself. It isn't easy to get anywhere and survive in a world that doesn't understand what is so crystal clear to the two of us.

Every day is an epic experience. What battles will we face today? What bills will we pay this month and which will we skip till the late notice? How are we going to grow from here? Does it all really matter, as long as we're together? From the day we move into the apartment together, we never sleep a night apart from each other for years – until February 2008 to be exact.

February 2008

The paint samples at Home Depot are starting to blend together. Luckily we know we are aiming for a deep purple for the living room, ideally something to help us relax when we finally get to rest at ten o'clock at night. Working from home, you'd think that we have the best situation, but in reality it can make personal time hard to come by. After sitting in the waiting room at my reception desk for 9 hours a day, the last thing I want to do is go rest in the living room to unwind and see the same generic builder-code tan wall color.

Business has been doing great for us recently. We've even had to extend our daily schedule of students from 1:30-9:30 Monday through Friday (that's right, no breaks either). I must hear the same line at least once a week from a different client, "Wow!

This must be a dream to work from home! You guys are lucky."
We are lucky, a lot of people would love to work from home.
There's also a lot of grind involved. Things have to be spotless
all the time, no clutter and very professional. Just because the
phone rings at 10:13 in the morning, doesn't mean you don't
answer it even though you don't "open" until 1:30. Work never
ends when your office is your home.

I love working with my husband. I run the main office including
phones, billing, scheduling, advertising, website and anything on
the front side of the curtain. The magic happens in our renovated
basement studio. It's a dream teaching environment for Lucien
(as it would be for any music teacher) with two large lesson
studios, one for piano and one for guitar and bass, as well as a
big recording studio. I love our clients, they are all so amazing,
and so many of them have become my friends over time.

Owning your own business has it's perks, and it's downfalls. It's
nice to have no commute, it's nice to control your own hours, it a
blessing to be home with my children while I'm working. Our son,
Adrian, is now in preschool, I don't know how he grew up so fast
and is already 4 years old. Our daughter, Luciana, is new to the
family. She's already 10 months old and rules the castle, as does
any little princess who's the sole feminine sibling in a family with
three brothers. Downfalls? No down time, no personal space,
lots of overhead and business expenses, health insurance is a
joke and more which I try to blacken out of my conscious mind
as best as possible.

Therefore, when I start to get a nagging ache on my left side
under my ribs, I do what I always do and ignore it. Most of the
time going to the doctor to dish out a couple hundred dollars
makes me feel worse than when I went. Most minor ailments
eventually repair themselves naturally, so why should this little
ache be any different? It's a funny little pain too... I don't feel it
all the time unless I take a deep breath, try singing or laugh.

My "injury" as we dub it gets a little worse daily for another week
or so. Man, I must have really pulled something! Maybe lifting
something, or carrying the baby around the house... yeah, that
must be what caused it.

As we start setting up the drop cloths and moving the furniture around to paint the living room, Lucien makes full advantage of my handicap taking every opportunity to crack some stupid joke, causing me to literately double over in pain. In all truth, I probably spend more time holding my side in agony than I do painting anything! It is a joke to us, some pulled muscle that will surely heal soon enough.

February 27 2008

Mondays are so slow. Thank goodness the phones are quiet for the most part today. I feel horrible and I can't believe how much my side hurts right now! 3:30 p.m. Adrian's bus drops him off and he's up stairs watching Noggin (Thank God for Little Bear! Hopefully Franklin is on next). Luciana is in dreamland, lounging in her vibrating sling back chair next to my computer monitor. She looks so content, she's such an angel. 5:00 Maybe I should feed Adrian some dinner. Wow, I can barely walk without clutching my side... I guess he'll have to settle for Spaghetti O's tonight (the commercial did say there's a full serving of Vegetables in every can!) Okay... a couple more students and the night is over. I can't wait to get to bed, I haven't been sleeping right since I've been having these annoying night sweats. The last two nights my temperature has spiked to 102.8. Maybe I have a virus or something. it's getting so painful to breath. 7:45 Kids are tucked in and sleeping... maybe if I sit at my desk and just try to relax this pain will go away. It's getting so painful just to say "Hey! You can go down to the studio, he's ready!" as the 8:00 student comes in. Maybe while they're in their lesson I will just close my eyes and concentrate on short shallow breaths. 8:15, I can't take this anymore... am I even getting any air? Should I go downstairs, interrupt Lucien and his student? No, no, no, I can't do that. Oh, but it hurts. I'll intercom him and tell him... but it's so hard to speak without a knife slicing through my side... Lucien answers the intercom downstairs, "Hello?". "We have to go to the E.R..." I manage out in a barely audible whisper (Did I actually speak those words out loud?). Lucien comes upstairs, and my mind is a blur. He scribbles a note and tapes it to the front door for the rest of the night's students, "Emergency, Lessons Cancelled". He calls someone who lives down the street, the parent of a student to come be

*here with the kids. I move so slow to the van to avoid the knife
jarring under my ribs, I want to breathe! We get in the van and
start to leave behind our house, our children, our home, our life
as we knew it.*

Emergency rooms can best be described as a melting pot with
four main ingredients: Insanity, pandemonium and tribulations
are staples, but the fourth is the variable. Resolution or
commencement. The funny thing is, as you enter the rotating
door into the ER, you're not entirely certain what your fourth
ingredient will be. While we all hope for a simple dose of
resolution so we can get back home and sleep in our own beds,
many of us get side swiped with a serving of commencement
(with a spice of uncertainty).

Sitting across from me is a teenager with their foot wrapped in a
bath towel and raised on some kind of plank looking thing
attached to a wheelchair. In the corner is a homeless woman
sleeping (I thought that was only something you see on the show
E.R.). There are parents rocking infants, and some elderly
couples reading magazines. There is a husband raising his voice
at the nurses' station, "But you don't understand my wife is about
to pa..." "Oh my god!" a voice screams out in the hallway, as a
crush of medical uniforms rush to where a woman has passed
out and hit her head on a wall. I watch as they lift her up on to a
gurney, then go back to their previous positions, leaving the
woman alone with her disgruntled husband tending to her.

I can't watch this commotion; it's making me ill at this point.
Lucien is taking in the unfolding play in front of us (in these other
people's eyes, are we part of the play?) as he rubs my back and
tries to comfort me. My side feels like it's splitting open, I can't
breathe and feel like I'm going to pass out. Hours are passing.
Where is time going? Where is this play script heading... I don't
think I want to come see this show again.

"Nocelli..." a nurse calls in the stereotypical nasal tone. She
leads me into a little room that's not near the rest of the patients
who are separated by thin white curtains for privacy. The room is
small, the size of a closet, with just enough room for a gurney
and a chair. It is completely tiled from ceiling to floor. In the

corner there is a shower head... I can't help but wonder if this is what all E.R. patient rooms look like or if this is the twilight zone?

I swear the pain is getting so much worse by the minute. My lips are getting cracked and sore from my lack of proper breathing, now that short shallow breaths are all I can manage. Even sitting on the bed proves to be impossible. Sitting folded in half with my arms wrapping as much pressure around my abdomen as possible is the only somewhat comforting position. Remember to breathe...

Sometime later, a male nurse rolls in a little machine and asks Lucien to leave, which I am petrified of. We don't do well with any amount of separation, and right now is not a great time to try it out. He leaves and tells me he'll be right outside the door, as the male nurse starts getting his supplies out to perform an EKG. All I can wonder is if there are any needles involved. I've never had an EKG, how do they do it? Isn't this a heart test? I'm clueless, I feel helpless, and I can't even get the words out of my mouth to ask because of the pain. I'm happy to see no needles coming out as the nurse starts putting little sticky electrodes on different part of me, my ankles, my chest, everywhere. It's embarrassing, and I feel gross with all this crap all over me. No sooner does he have them all on, does he glance at the machine then announce that it's over. He removes all the electrodes and wheels out of the room.

Lucien comes right back in the room and rubs my forehead. All I can do is close my eyes and concentrate on breathing. Soon another nurse comes in and tells me that they need to run blood work, start an IV, take X Rays and run a CAT scan. My selective hearing takes effect and all I hear are the words blood work and IV as I start to panic.

I will be the first person to stand up and admit the fact that I have a mind blowing, ultra severe, fear and anxiety when it comes to needles in any situation. When channel 7 news comes on at five talking about the flu epidemic and flash images of screaming children and blank faced elderly receiving vaccines, I cringe and cover my eyes with my hands. Every time I went for blood work during my pregnancies I cried like a colicky baby. Even on the nights before the scheduled appointments with the OBGYN and knowing I was getting blood drawn would have me lying awake in a panic for hours. I've always said it, and I mean it when I say, I would have had 10 children if there were no needles involved (and if I wouldn't have ended up with 10 kids to raise too I guess). Pain is not the issue, I have a very high tolerance for pain, I mean look at me... it took me to the point of looking grey in the face to come to a doctor for this pain in my side. But needles are a whole other story.

I start to whimper at this point, since full on crying is out of the question; I can't even get the tiny blubber of a noise without the knife in my side twisting. This nurse carries in a little pale blue tackle box looking thing, places it on the gurney revealing all of her blood related paraphernalia smashed inside. She starts grabbing at vials and tubes and tape and cotton and all I can do is turn my gaze towards Lucien, staring into his eyes for comfort. He holds my hand, continues rubbing my forehead and almost inaudibly lets out a soft, "Shhhhhh"

The nurse fills up what seems like a hundred massive vials with my blood, then cold heartedly calls for transport to come. I then get rolled away for a CAT scan (which is always fun getting directed to not breath and stop moving, when you're gasping for whatever air you can muster up), then a chest x-ray. Finally, what seems like hours later, they bring me into my very own little slice of the emergency room experience; a curtained off cubicle. They start pumping in some heavy duty doses of painkillers into the IV. As the warm sensation crawls through my veins, up my arm and into my chest, a let out a small groan from pain, and take one last glance over at Lucien sitting to my right, offering a calming nod, before I fall into a deep narcotic induced sleep.

Every hour or so, my eyes drift open to survey the room while my mind tries to remember where I am. Lucien is trying to sleep in the small plastic chair, nurses bustle about their business, machines chime together in an orchestra of beeps and dings, and in the distance is the sound of "Baaaaa, Baaaaaa. Baaaaa, Baaaa" a patient lying on a gurney in the adjoining curtain cubicle channels her inner sheep. "Baaaa, Baaaa". I fall back asleep.

25

Somewhere in the middle of the night I wake up to a Doctor standing at the foot of the bed. Lucien stirs awake and we anxiously await the diagnosis. He does his routine of checking my heart beat, listening to my lungs, reading the machine which is all probably unnecessary and unrelated to what he is about to tell us. Then he blurts out, "Okay, so you have Pleurisy. It's an inflammation of the lining of the lungs. That's what's causing the pain in your side. So, we're going to prescribe some Tylenol with Codeine, and you can get home and get some rest." He pats the end of the bed with his hand two times and leaves our curtain room.

Lucien and I look at each other with relief. Great, I should be feeling better in no time with this painkiller and some rest; thank goodness it isn't anything more severe. We gather our belongings and wait for the nurse to come in to give me the prescription, have me sign whatever I have to sign and get me released. As part of the discharge paperwork they give me a copy of my blood work results which might as well be written in ancient Sanskrit since all of these numbers don't mean a thing to me. There is a bunch of numbers on the paper, but some of them have an asterisk... I notice that all of the ones with the asterisk have numbers that don't fall within what they're showing as the "Reference Range". There are a fair amount of results that are slightly higher or lower than they are supposed to be, but since the doctor has not mentioned anything about this, I come to the conclusion that the numbers are off because of the Pleurisy and my body fighting it.

CHEM PROFILE	REF RANGE	02/25/08
CO_2	24-31	23*
WBC	4.5-11.0	3.3*
RBC	4.10-5.10	3.72*
HEMOGLOBIN	12.0-16.0	11.4*
HEMATOCRIT	35.0-48.0	32.8*
PLATELET CNT	150-450	102*

I can't wait to get back home and out of this damn hospital. This emergency room thing is for the birds and I have no intention of returning any time soon. We fill my prescription at the 24 hour CVS Pharmacy and I start taking my Tylenol with Codeine religiously to try to kick this Pleurisy crap in the rear end. I expect to start feeling improvement at least within a day, I mean codeine is supposed to be good stuff; it should be if you need a prescription. By Friday though, I am absolutely no better. My skin is still a greyish blue tint, my lips are cracked, walking is difficult and breathing impossible. We think it is best I return to the hospital for a reevaluation.

We call a babysitter and endure self-induced torture by reentering those rotating doors to the Emergency Room. A whole new cast of characters greets us in the waiting area; a woman sits in the corner rocking a screaming toddler, an elderly couple look over a crossword puzzle in the Asbury Park Press fighting over the answer to 5 down "Creatures with heads of lions".

"It's the Sphinx, Martha", the old man says in a raspy smoker voice.

"No, no, no, Gerard, Sphinx doesn't fit, it's a Chimera. I saw it on the ancient channel", the old lady whines back at him.

"Martha, look, Chimera doesn't fit, it doesn't line up with the other answers", he rebuts.

I swear they go on for 20 minutes. I want to blurt out "C'mon guys, it's a Griffin! Didn't you see the Mythology special on National Geographic channel? No that's right; you were watching the channel that doesn't exist!" All the while the same homeless man from Monday lay plopped in the corner again... or still.

Finally the nurse calls me in, this time straight to my own little private curtain room. For real, here we go again. I'm all for avoiding the medical world whenever possible, but I also am for the idea of being able to breathe again. After maybe 40 minutes of sitting there, a young doctor enters with a metal clipboard. He doesn't fuss around like the guy I had seen Monday, instead getting right to the point.

"Mrs. Nocelli, after looking over your chart, I see here that you have Pleurisy, an inflammation of the lining of the lungs. Your lungs are clear with no fluid; the CAT scan is negative as of Monday. So, in all honesty, all we're going to do today is redo all of the same tests you had a few days ago, and we're probably going to come to the same conclusion. So, if I were you, I'd just sign myself out, go home, and take the Tylenol with Codeine and rest. The outcome will be the same." He nods at each of us and disappears behind the curtain.

Lucien and I sit there for a minute contemplating our next move. I am still in a fair amount of pain, but if what the doctor said is true, then why should we waste 6 hours of our life and pay for unnecessary testing? So I sign myself out and go home to rest.

May 2002

Finally my eighteenth birthday rolls around in May, and Lucien and I can shake off the extra weight from our shoulders of my age. I am finally legally an adult, even though in all honestly, I've been one for years. I was always very mature for my age. My best friend growing up was my mother. She and I were amazingly close. We shopped together, country line danced together, joined Weight Watchers together, I mean everything. Our big excitement for the week was when Wednesday night would roll around and we'd attend our weekly dinner at Blake's restaurant where we would meet up with Francis and Ursula, our older friends. I could tell my mom anything, and she would always have an understanding, never judge and always support. She was my confidant. In my early teenage years, she would cover for me and my best girlfriend Tilla when we would take off for a road trip to Ohio with nothing but the cash in our pockets and a fabulous wardrobe to wear to whatever concert we were planning on crashing.

Point being, I've lived a lot of life before I turned 18, and was already an adult before the day actually ever came around on paper.

The night of my eighteenth birthday we have a Beatlemania show in Ocean Grove, NJ. I know nothing about the town, but love it when we arrive. It is a quaint town that looks like it was plucked out of a renaissance painting, sprinkled with magic dust and came alive. The Victorian houses and Inns are adorned in ornate wooden detail and painted in a delicate palate of pastel pinks, blues and yellows. In the center of the town is an old fashioned main street complete with a florist, artsy café, cottage design home goods, cramped antique gifts and many more fanciful boutiques.

The show is being held in the main dining hall of an impressive 3 story Victorian building called the Ocean View Inn, located on the very last street which overlooks Asbury Park. What is individual to this venue is that we will be staying in a gorgeous Bed and Breakfast in the same building as the performance. We settle into our room in the back of the building which is adorably decorated with dainty painted white antique furniture, specifically placed nick-knacks and pronounced floral wall paper. This really is the most cheerful place we've ever traveled to for a show.

The show goes great, or at least I think it does when I tune in through my rum and coke induced stupor. After the 40 millionth time you've seen a show, it admittedly starts to lose the "wow" factor. It is finally over, so we pick up the gear, wipe down the guitars, brush the wigs, put the costumes away and decide to take a walk.

It is about a one block walk to the beach, so we head in the direction of the ocean. It's a freeing feeling to walk down the street with your soul mate and not have to worry about life's complications in that moment. It's just the two of you and the rest of the world may as well melt away into nothingness.

At 1:00 in the morning, the beach belongs to the two of us alone. It's a chilly May night and we are the only two people anywhere to be seen. We take off our shoes, toss them to the boardwalk and enter the sand with our bare feet, the cool sand filling the space between our toes. We stroll for a while before settling down to stare into the dark ocean, cuddling under the moonlight, burrowing into each for comfort revealing to no one but the moon and the sand our incontestable binding love. I leave Ocean Grove that weekend with a new perspective towards our future... and a pocket full of beach sand and shells.

I am finishing up my Junior year of high school in June and excited for the summer so that I can work another full time job to get some more income flowing. When school wraps up in June, I assesse my transcripts to discover I have accrued 39 ½ class credits. The total needed to graduate? 40. I have been a dedicated student (having a sever lack of a normal social life will do that to a person). Freshman year I had bypassed the usual Study Hall, opting instead to cram in another course. Also as a Freshman I had placed directly into the Concert Choir, which had consisted of 99% upper classman and 1 % freshman (me). I had worked hard at my schooling, struggling of course on my weaker subjects, but never the less working my butt off to impress the teachers however I could. What I'm trying to say is, I was a model student, the teachers loved me – I made sure they did, and I was hoping for a favor.

I call up the school in June and explain everything. My case is built and I am ready to deliberate. I'm eighteen, I have an apartment to support, I have bills to pay, I need to start working more hours, I was a good student, never caused any trouble, so I need a favor. Can I attend a summer class or come senior year for one class for half a year so I can graduate early? No. They shut that down pretty quickly. They refuse my request with an iron gavel, and demand that I would have to return for a full schedule for the entire senior year. Insert some choice four letter words here.

During the summer I pick up a second job, and start working like nobody's business. I fly from one job to the next, never having a minute in between to do much but sleep and shower. The summer drags on with working, traveling to Lucien's shows, and trying to squeeze in visits with his sons when we make it down to New Jersey. I am so delighted when the boys are able to visit us for an entire week during July. Lucien picks them up and makes the 6 hour drive to New Hampshire with them. We don't have any extra sleeping space, so we give them our bed and we sleep on the floor for the week. I take some time off from working to spend with them and we have the time of our lives. I do painting projects with them, we take them to Livingston (the community pool), we bring them to a country line dancing retro night at a local eatery and so many more amazing memories that I still cherish to this day. They are the most amazing two little boys and I fall head over heels for them instantly.

After the visit is over and they go back to the garden state, the void is apparent. I start to realize that this arrangement isn't working out so well.

I haven't mentioned it before this point, but when I met Lucien he was an alcoholic out of necessity. The living situation he was immersed in before we met was rocky and led him to pop a can of Fosters by noon every day, starting the regimen of beer and rum from that point on. When we would travel to shows, I would join into the drinking and we had some really good times – a lot of havoc – but good times none the less. It started to become a problem when he moved to New Hampshire to be with me and the economy didn't accept him with open arms into the work force. In New Jersey he had taught private guitar lessons for years, but he left his full schedule of students to come to live with me. He brought his resume to the two local music stores and they both had the same reaction. "Lucien, if we could fire the 4 teachers we have and hire you, we would be ecstatic. We've never seen a resume like this for a teaching position before, and to not hire you would be the biggest mistake for our business. But... we can't fire our teachers, I'm sorry."

So while I went to school and worked my jobs, he was working on writing music and recording, which was great, except for the fact that by the time I got home at 2:00 he'd be passed out already for the day in smog of ginseng vodka and rum.

This cycle isn't working anymore. It all comes into play for me one afternoon in August... I come home, sit Lucien down and lay it all on the table. "This isn't working. We have to move closer to the boys, I can finish high school in New Jersey, I really don't give a crap about graduating with my class, that really doesn't matter in the grand scheme of things. We have to pack up and go, but there's one condition. You have to stop drinking."

He never drinks again after that day.

So begins the process of moving which is easier said than done when you have no credit, no money, no resources, but what we do have outweighs everything else. We have our love, our determination, we have each other. We call up the owner of the Ocean View Inn in Ocean Grove where we had played and ask her if we can stay there while we get on our feet. She welcomes us with open arms, even offering for me to work for her in the Inn.

So we pack up our U-Haul with our guitars, clothes, salvaged computer desk (rescued from someone's trash pile) and the ugly fuzzy fake plant and we head south to begin our life.

March 7 2008

Why isn't this pain going away? The ER doctor said the Codeine would start to help, but it's not getting better at all, if not worse. Everyone says to never Google a medical condition that it will only make you self-diagnose the wrong condition, but something in my gut says to look it up. I look up Pleurisy on Web MD and a whole page comes up. "An inflammation of the lining of the lung"… yeah, yeah, I know that part… "May develop as a result as inflammation from pneumonia or tuberculosis"… well I don't have either one of those, they checked already… "You cannot get pleurisy without an underlying condition such as rheumatoid arthritis, sickle cell crisis, pulmonary embolism, lupus, anemia or leukemia". Maybe I should get another opinion; I might have another problem that I don't know about.

I sign into the front desk of my normal doctor. The receptionist gawks at me with a look of alarm and says "Hunny, come right in, we'll see you right away". She looks startled, like she's seen the ghost of Elvis or something. Then there she is opening the door to the back open and starts shuffling me into the belly of the beast, into a room and on an examination table. My breaths are short, shallow, gasps for air.

A nurse comes in, she is talking to me but I can't hear her. Asking me questions, I can't answer. She takes my blood pressure, temperature, listens to my heart and lungs. The doctor comes in now; she gently guides me to lie down. The crinkly paper on the table is annoying me, it always does. The doctor places an oxygen mask over me and guides, "Deep breaths… breathe… breathe…"

I can't.

I see out of the corner of my eye, the nurse has brought in a yellow tackle box full of tubes, gauze and syringe's... oh God, not again. Please, don't do blood! I start crying. What is going on? I want to go home.

The doctor comes over and holds my hand while I sob through gasps for air as and they take several vials of blood. "You need to go to the emergency room right away, we'll call an ambulance." She calmly and slowly explains. But I can't go back to the Hamilton ER... they have sent me home twice with pain killers which obviously at this point aren't doing shit.

"No, I will go myself. I won't go back to Hamilton, I want to go to Metro Medical Hospital," ... small breath, small breath, small breath, "I'll go right now." I manage to finish.

She hands me a pile of prescriptions. "Ultrasound Abdomen STAT (with focus on spleen) DX: 289.4", "CT Head with & without contrast. DX: 784.0" and one that is more of a note than orders, "ER: Please evaluate patient WBC low, platelets low, neutrophils low. Patient having fevers at night, please see attached blood work". She nods and helps me up, Lucien gets the van and swings it around for me to get in. I slide into the passenger seat, and off we go with purpose, apprehension and hope.

Before we head to the ER, I think at this point that it would be wise to swing by the first hospital and get the records from the first two emergency room visits. Maybe if the new hospital sees the tests, results and diagnosis (or lack of diagnosis) it could help them figure this out. We swing over to Hamilton where I have to ask 6 receptionists before someone can direct me down to the basement to the records department. Once there, I have to show my license and wait around for 20 more minutes before they hand me an envelope about a quarter of an inch thick and adorned with colorful medical tabs and such.

It feels like an eternity to travel the five exits on the Garden State Parkway, the mile markers go by my window at snail speed. Lucien holds my hand, gently massaging me with his thumb in slow, even strokes. Every bump in the road sends the knife in my side deeper, it's excruciating, it's miserable, it's not fair.

Everything feels like it's sped down into a slow motion making each second more torturous.

We finally arrive at Metro Medical Hospital. We pull up to the gigantic swirling door which is consuming people left and right into the dark abyss of the Emergency Room. I get out of the van, and am immediately swept into the invisible current flowing towards the entrance. Before I know it I am swept in and deposited at the main desk where a short, stubby woman with curly soccer-mom hair, a deep voice and a name plate that reads Lorraine hands me a pen and dryly tells me to sign in and have a seat. I do as she asks.

Not 30 seconds later, I am called behind a curtain by another short and stubby nurse (are they clones or close relatives?). She weighs me, takes my temperature, blood pressure, and asks me a long interrogation of questions. She reaches into a drawer and pulls out a long stick looking thing in a white medical wrapper. She opens it up... it looks like a gigantic Q-Tip... and tells me to sit in the chair and look at the ceiling.

"We're going to test for the flu." The nurse states like I don't have a choice – I don't after all, do I? Then she starts shoving this stick up my nostril... it's painful, I squirm... she's taking FOREVER. "Well, well, well," she starts, "You have a deviated septum, huh?"

If I didn't have a stick up my nose I would have rebutted, "I don't really care right now since I'm pretty sure that's not affecting my PLEURISY". But considering the fact that even as this thought crossed my mind, I am still being prodded by a stick shoved up my nasal cavity, she never gets to hear my piece of mind about her revelation regarding my defective nose.

She eventually gets bored of torturing me, finishes up the flu exam and guides me to a little curtain cubical. Seeing the green and white paper hospital gown on the bed, I proceed to change out of my civilian clothes, stripping away myself to become just another generic patient. I neatly fold my jeans, underwear, bra and sweater, and place them carefully on the plastic chair with my grey clogs.

My mind begins to wander. I love my grey clogs. Ever since Lucien surprised me with them for Christmas, I've been wearing them with every outfit, every day for every occasion. They're from Kohl's. I had bought a black pair in November, and I loved them so much that I wanted the grey. I must have tried 5 different stores to find the grey, and no one had the size 8. I gave up. Then on Christmas morning, I unwrapped the large box, opened the lid and beamed with the transparent joy of a child when I held in my arms, the beloved grey clogs!

The white curtain flies open and in comes a young doctor and two nurses toting along with them a score of supplies. The nurses start grabbing my arms, poking around, feeling for veins I guess. My heart starts to race and the anxiety of a needle is building a flash flood of emotions in my mind. I have to work hard to focus when the doctor starts to talk.
"I'm Doctor Moradel, I looked over your records and I can assure you we are going to get to the bottom of this and see what's going on. We're going to admit you, so we're going to get an IV started with antibiotics and fluids. We're also going to schedule tests. We're going to figure this out, hang in there kiddo." He smiles a half-grin, pats the foot of the bed and disappears behind the curtain leaving the nurses to fuss over me.

My CBC results come back with bizarre readings of low red cells, dropping white cells and few platelets to speak of. It is a strange mix of, well, plummeting levels. This is alarming, since essentially I've been walking around everyday life with absolutely zero immune system. I've been cleaning poopy diapers, grabbing germ infested shopping carriages and traveling in elbow to elbow crammed elevators without realizing how vulnerable of a state my body is in.

Immediately the doctor has me removed from the Emergency Room where I am at such a dangerous risk of being infected by any number of mystery illnesses all around me, and they relocate me to the oncology ward. It is explained to me that this is an area of people with no immune systems, and that it is a sterile environment to keep me guarded from catching anything. Wouldn't that have been the icing on the cake to catch another illness on top of one that NO ONE COULD FIGURE OUT?

Once I am relocated to my double occupancy room, sharing with an old man who hacks up a lung once about every 35 seconds, things start to get interesting. Since these odd blood counts are exposed to public knowledge, a whole new flood gate of specialists starts visiting my nook of the hospital. Each one rattles off their name, credentials, hands me their business card, explains what they are going to test for, etc. They test me for everything from lupus, to anemia. Infectious disease comes in and tests me for Tuberculosis. I feel like every one of these doctors are grasping at straws for answers, and yet they all come up empty handed.

The days are filled with tests, white coats, thermometers, IV drips, blood draws, and the old man coughing behind the thin geometric patterned curtain that separates us. The nights are filled with a nonstop bustle of nurses' sneakers whispering around the hallways, machinery beeping steadily, muffled voices over intercoms and the damn old man with the croup – all of these elements joining together creating a melancholy symphony.

Two days are a whirlwind of tests. I go from the MRI machine twirling around me, to the CAT scan humming a soft ballad, to X Rays and blood tests galore. I go from never having any tests before, to having them twice in two weeks.

No sooner is the cleaning lady leaving the room in her cloud of Lysol, on the third desolate morning of my hospital stay, do I get my next visitors. A male doctor who introduces himself as a Hematologist (a blood specialist) and a female Oncology doctor (a cancer specialist). The male doctor does most of the talking. He explains to me that at this point every test has come up negative, and due to the blood counts being as worrisome as they were that they really need to go to the source of everything. The bone marrow.

The bone marrow is the fatty sponge like matter that fills the cavities in our bones. The marrow is like the factory of our body, it contains stem cells which are immature blood cells. When the stem cells mature they become red cells, white cells and platelets. If there's a problem with production of blood cells you can usually find the answer in the marrow.

The male doctor starts to explain to me what the procedure involves, but once I hear the words "local anesthetic" and knowing that means needles, my mind fuzzes out. His words become mush and his mouth moves in slow motion until finally he nods, offers fake smiles, pats the bed and exits the room.

The old man next to me snorts and hacks up his other lung.

I lie down in my hospital bed, pulling up the thick white over-bleached sheet to my chin and just take it all in. I am alone again, for now at least. The doctors are preparing what they need for the bone marrow biopsy. I close my eyes, trying to zone out. The phone rings. On the other end of the line is a familiar voice, my good friend Mya.

Mya and I were always destined to cross paths at some point in our lives. She grew up in Derry, New Hampshire just around the same time I was growing up in Manchester, literately a few miles apart. As adults we had both moved to Monmouth County New Jersey, again settling our roots only a few miles apart; her in Tinton Falls and me in Lincroft. When we met, it was like we knew each other all along. We both grew up watching Punky Brewster and spent our weekends crashing the Mall of New Hampshire (the *only* hangout in the southern part of the state at the time). Our shared upbringing experiences makes for many laughs when we reminisce about the unique and often quirky memories we share from growing up in New England. She's one of the few people who know what I'm talking about when I refer to Frappes, Grinders and use the term "wicked"!

Mya works in the Psychiatric ward of Metro Medical Hospital, so as soon as she hears that I was admitted, she calls to see how I am feeling. We chat for a few minutes, but as soon as she hears that I will be having a bone marrow biopsy she offers to come down to be with me. Her timing is impeccable; right behind her is the bone marrow biopsy crew with all their medieval looking gear. It's time for this biopsy.

Bone Marrow Biopsy: a procedure in which the soft tissue, called marrow, is removed from inside the pelvis bone and examined under a microscope to look for the presence of abnormal blood cells.

Procedure: First the skin around the area of the pelvis bone is cleaned with alcohol or an iodine solution. Sterile towels are placed around the area. The area is then injected with local anesthetic (lidocaine) with tiny needles around the site. There may be stinging and a burning sensation. After a few minutes the area will become numb. A needle is then placed through the skin and penetrates the bone. There may be a pressure sensation. A small amount of bone marrow is pulled through a syringe. Next, a somewhat larger needle is then put in the same place and a small sample of bone and marrow is taken up into the needle. The wound site will bleed. Pressure is applied for a few minutes before a sterile bandage is applied.

That's how it goes from a medical perspective. It's different from *my* perspective.

The doctor starts by instructing me to turn on my left side, facing the ugly foam green curtain separating the room. Mya is sitting in the chair right by my bed; she offers to hold my hand, to talk me through this. I start crying; I have no idea what the procedure entails since I really hadn't paid much attention, all I know is that there are needles. Probably a lot, and probably big.

The doctor starts cleaning the area with some kind of a wet alcohol wipe that sends shivers through my body with its cold sensation. He then announces that he's going to start numbing the area. I look to Mya, my eyes filling with fiery tears. She calms me, speaks to me – I can't hear her. The pinching starts, one after another like I am being attacked by a hive of provoked bees. This is just the numbing? When the hell is it going to end?!

By now I am sobbing vast tears which fall over my cheeks like a stream over boulders. My head is throbbing; I tighten my grip on Mya's hand. She tells me to keep squeezing as tight as I have to; she tells me it's almost over. Is it? The doctor isn't talking anymore to me probably since he finally got the message that I don't hear a word he is saying. Instead he barks instructions to the hoard of nurses who surround him. All of a sudden there is an intense sharp sting that starts in my hip and slices me in half in horrifying agony. It is the larger needle, breaking my hip bone, forcing into my pelvis with the force of a stampede and sucking out marrow from the depths of my body. I squeeze my hand so hard trying to release this all-consuming pain.

It takes me a while to realize that it is over. The doctor places a bandage on the area, removes his plastic gloves, cleans up his equipment and exits the room. I don't know if he pats the bed on the way out, I have been in my babbling trance the entire time. I finally release Mya's hand from my kung fu grip revealing a bright red mark where my thumb nail succeeded in piercing her skin. "I'm so sorry! Look at the thanks I give you for comforting me, a wound!" I apologize whole heartedly.

"Please, don't even worry about it. I'm a nurse, I get kicked in the face by patients, this is nothing!" she comes back with her calm, cool, comforting tone. We both smile and for the first time in a few days I laugh a little.

A nurse comes in soon after the procedure and offers some pain meds through the IV which I take her up on immediately. The spot of the biopsy is not only sore to the touch, but has affected every muscle in the area. To get to the bathroom I have to limp and drag my feet for the rest of the day. I try every position, but sitting, standing, laying, balancing on my head – it doesn't matter, the throbbing pain is relentless. I guess this is to be expected after having your pelvis drilled into. I beg for more pain meds and allow myself to fall into a narcotic induced sleep. With the help of my IV dripping my magical concoction I am able to sleep through the night for the first time since I've been here, and not once do I hear the old man.

The next morning the doctor comes in with news I'm not expecting, "You can go home today. We'll send you home with some pain medications and someone will contact you as soon as we have the results of your bone marrow biopsy. Until then, go home and rest up."

Seriously? Just like that? Oh my God, I can go home today! This whole nightmare is OVER! Right away I start limping around the room to gather my things, dragging the burden of the IV pole around with me as I go. I'm completely packed up in a grand total of 7 and a half minutes, then I settle on the bed and proceed to wait, wait, wait. It takes a whole hour of Good

Morning America and almost a full episode of The View before the nurse comes in with a white baggie full of medicine, and a packet of discharge instructions. I go to put my feet down and realize that my shoes are nowhere to be found... my beloved grey clogs! I search around, with a limp, and finally give up. I sit in my wheel chair chariot which has just arrived for my grand exit, ride through the hallways, past the scores of patients, through the lobby, out into the crisp winter air, lower my socked feet to the pavement, maneuver into the van – and release a sigh – I am free.

August 2002

Driving down to New Jersey in the Altima, following close behind the rented U-Haul Lucien is driving is actually a very liberating experience. I'm petrified though, don't get me wrong! In all the traveling I've done I have always been co-pilot. I'm better at maps and switching CDs than actually doing any of the physical driving. So for me to be cruising (in the lamest sense of the word) down the east coast is an untouched experience by far. After six and a half hours of highway, our caravan of two finally arrives at Exit 100A off the Garden State Parkway to the quaint little town of Ocean Grove.

Pulling up to the front porch of the Ocean View Inn I find myself holding my breath with pure anticipation of this new life we are grasping in the palms of our hands. We park our respective vehicles, and meet on the sidewalk. Lucien wraps his arms around me and I tuck my head in under his chin where I fit like a puzzle piece. He kisses my forehead and we hold each other tighter as we take in our new neighborhood.

Our living quarters in this three story bed and breakfast is located in the back of the building's basement. Our 300 square foot "apartment" consists of one room separated into imagined sections. On the far end of the room is our bed (one that has been slept in be hundreds of jersey shore tourists). At the foot of the bed is a sleeper sofa / loveseat which faces a small entertainment center housing a 20 inch TV. Shoved in the corner next to the entertainment center is a small plastic desk which Lucien uses to house his recording equipment. At this point there is a half wall which leads to a refrigerator, and a counter about 4 feet long. There is a "kitchen sink" about a foot squared, and a microwave smeared with remnant drips of former guests quick meals (looks like some kind of a tomato soup perhaps?). We purchase a cheap plug-in model single electric burner to cook with and TA-DA... we have a kitchen. Off of the kitchen is our tiny three piece bathroom. Welcome home.

We make the best of our living space immediately. I paint the whole area to make if fresh, to make it ours. We purchase new laminate tiles and spend one Sunday afternoon resurfacing the kitchen floor with a faux stone look. Slowly it becomes our comfy little corner of the world.

Lucien immediately gets work teaching music lessons again in Red Bank with a store which he is friendly with the owners since he's known them for ten plus years. He spends his days teaching at the store until 6:00, then traveling to private lessons in the mansions of Colts Neck late into the night. While he is away I start working for the owner of the Inn. I spend my days doing touch-up paint in the hallways where tourists overstuffed suitcases have scratched and dented the pale yellow color away. I spend many hours doing laundry in the basement laundry room. I wash all of the guests' towels and sheets. I love washing the bedding which comes in a variety of patterns ranging from sage colored bamboo print to mauve floral and cranberry plaids. Opening the drier, pulling out crisp meadow scented sheets, spreading my arms wide to send each one bellowing into the air for folding and sending the dryer sheet plummeting to the cement floor, folding the sheet up with military precision is the highlight of my work. Every room in the Inn has a different theme making it an adventure behind every door. Washing, drying and folding each set is like a mini getaway vacation to a foreign land.

By the holidays, we learn that we are pregnant with our first child. We have been trying to get pregnant for a month or two so we are elated by this news! Since I am home all day working in the Inn, I would love a little companion to tote around with me. I can't wait to meet our little Lucien & Sheri blend!

Christmas rolls around and I am a few weeks pregnant. I decide that this is not the time to share the news with anyone, so I don't spill the beans not even a little. We travel up to New Hampshire so I can spend the holiday with my large extended family as I've done every year since I was born. When I was young, all the Christmas festivities were help at my Memere and Pepere's house. All of my uncles, aunts and cousins would gather around the big tree in the living room while Pepere would sit under the tree announcing whose gift was next. He'd hand the shining package to the lucky recipient and all eyes would watch to see what was in the wrapping. Afterwards, we'd all cram around the tiny kitchen table for a feast of French dishes, and a large slice of pork pie for everyone. Eventually Memere and Pepere had to sell their house which saddened everyone, but we all knew it was best. From that point on, Christmas celebrations were held at one of their four children's house, rotating every year to continue our family traditions.

Christmas of 2002 is being held in Uncle Dicky and Aunt Bonnies house. Lucien drops me off outside and drives back to the hotel we are staying. He is not welcome here. My father is barely speaking to me since I've moved out of the house, and especially since I've moved to New Jersey. He still doesn't agree with my relationship with Lucien. No one asks me any questions about Lucien, New Jersey or anything all day; everyone pretending it isn't happening, choosing to not acknowledge my new life. Nonetheless, it is wonderful to see my family. I glide around on cloud nine all day, knowing that our little love seed is nestled safety inside of me, reminding me of the truth no one else seems to believe.

That night I go back to my parents' house for a little while to visit. The last time I'd been through the door there was leaving with my bags of clothes and important belongings. I pull my mother into her bedroom to talk, but she knows what I was going to say well before I open my mouth.

"Mom, I have something exciting to tell you," I start.

"You're pregnant. I can tell from the way you're glowing... and the way you had your hand over your stomach all day." She catches me off guard with this. I guess I inadvertently had been hovering over my stomach all day; a plate of turkey, pork pie, mashed potatoes and corn in one hand, and protecting my little munchkin with the other. I hadn't even realized it until she pointed it out. She gives me a big enduring hug and tells me how happy she is for me. She tells me she is happy as long as I am happy.

I decide to keep this from my father a little longer until I am ready. I ask her to keep it a secret as well, because I want to be the one to tell him. He deserves to hear it from me.

As the winter months crawl on, and my abdomen starts to grow, we begin preparing for our baby. I start spending a good portion of my days lounging on the loveseat, watching redundant morning talk shows and crafting plastic canvas baby projects to decorate with. I make wall decorations in pastels of yellows, greens, blues and pinks including a little patterned sign, simply readying "Baby". I hang it with a green ribbon on the wall where I plan to put the crib. Nesting much? Oh yeah!

Ocean Grove gets hammered with a massive blizzard one weekend. The snow is so high; you can barely see the roofs of the cars peeking through the mounds that cover Ocean View Ave completely. Lucien gets bundled up to go help shovel and to dig out the car, but I am not about to hang out in here gawking out the window; I want to get out there too! So I bundle up in a big fuzzy hat, mittens, scarf, boots and my plaid maternity coat and out we go. I feel like a snowman that just got my feet out there, the snow is so high it's impossible to move my legs through the depths of it. Eventually I waddle over towards the car where Lucien is starting to clear an area exposing the pavement below when I slip and start sliding around on my back. I am laughing hysterically. Lucien starts laughing too as he jumps over towards me. I feel like Winnie the Pooh floating on my back in the Hundred Acre Wood river, with my big belly protruding towards the sky.

Lucien and I are laying in the middle of the snow covered one way street, laughing and slipping around when we hear a voice coming from the porch of the Inn.

"Get her out of the snow, she's pregnant!" shouts Carmen, the owner of the Inn. "You two are crazy! Lucien, get her out of the snow and back inside. You crazy kids!" She throws her hand in the air like she is giving up as she turns to get back inside. We find this hilarious. We both laugh deeper until we are crying icy tears down our faces.

In the spring, we find out that we are having a little boy. I spend whole afternoons hanging out at Barnes and Noble pouring over baby name books. I make myself at home in their worn out leather reading chair with a pen and notebook, jotting down boy names that speak to me. I come up with Mateo, Elton, Alton and a few others, but my list is short. None of the names are feeling right. Eventually, it comes to me. I want to name him after my Pepere who has been sick and in the hospital for a few weeks. I come up with the name Francis. I love it.

I finally decide it's time to tell my father about the baby. We drive up to New Hampshire formulating how the plan will go. I want this to go a certain way, hoping that my dad will come around to accept everything. I'm not too confident I can pull this off though. My father is very head strong; it's where I get my immense stubbornness from in all honesty.

I let myself into the back door of my parents' house which enters directly into the kitchen. My mom is working on something at the stove which she abandons to come give me a hug. I ask her if I can have a talk with her and dad, so she goes over to the basement door, pulls it opens and calls down, "Bob, Sheri is here and she'd like to talk to us."

My parents sit on the couch side by side and I sit on the coffee table in front of them, still wearing all my winter gear and bulky winter coat; keeping my secret hidden for the moment. "So…" I start, "There's something I really want to tell you guys".

"You got married?" my dad interrupts.

"Well, no…" I continue as I start to open a small box I brought with me. I show them the contents of the box, which is adorned in blue ribbons centered on a pile of cotton; the cloud upon which a tiny ceramic statue of a baby boy sits, giggling harmoniously. Above the baby I have placed a banner with cursive writing proclaiming the baby's name: Francis Robert named after my grandfather and my father. I proceed to unbutton my coat. I finally manage the final button and dramatically open my coat wide open to reveal my big belly, and a maternity shirt that reads in big maroon block letters BABY. "I'm pregnant!" I exclaim with an all-consuming grin.

After a long dramatic pause my father says "Well, I guess I have to meet him then." I jump up and hug them both. I can't believe this is going so well, I'm in complete and utter joy!

We decide to go out to dinner for the dual purpose of celebrating and for Lucien and my dad to meet. Lucien drives up their street for the first time without having to hide and parks in front of my parents' house. My father comes outside, head held high, and extends his hand out to Lucien. They shake hands with a quick interdiction before the four of us pile into my father's conversion van.

Arriving at the T.G.I Friday restaurant, mom and I get dropped off at the door to go put our names in for a table. Lucien and my father go to find a parking space. Once the van is in park, dad turns to Lucien and says bluntly, "So, when do you plan on marrying my daughter?"

My mom and I sit across from each other in the booth and my dad is across from Lucien. Everything starts out pretty quiet as we order our dinner of medium-well burgers and greasy fries. The waiter leaves the table and the conversational flood gates open. Dad starts asking Lucien about where he's played, who he's shared the stage with, etc. He seems impressed by his career (there are a lot of big names and venues saturating the resume after all).

Their conversation continues as we eat. In between bites they continue to talk. They shift to topics they are both interested in; science, ancient civilizations, extraterrestrials, etc. Mom and I glance at each other in disbelief and smiles in between each bite of burger. This moment is the start of a wonderful relationship between dad and Lucien, and is the beginning of years of great conversation, friendship and mutual respect. It's a beautiful thing to witness. It's the way I have been hoping today would go.

March 12 2008 - Wednesday

On my first morning home after days in the hospital, a bright hopeful Wednesday morning, the world seems calm. The bus has just picked up Adrian for preschool, and I am feeding Luciana her morning bottle on the couch. Lucien is pouring me a cup of coffee which I am thankful for after three days of the hospital variety. My hip is sore from the biopsy still, but being home makes me forget about the pain.
The phone rings interrupting my utopian bliss.

"This is Dr. Topolski's office calling for Sheri Nocelli," a distant woman rattles off like a pre-recorded automation.
"Speaking" I answer just as dryly.

"Dr. Topolski would like to see you in her office as soon as possible to go over the results of your bone marrow biopsy tests. You need to come in right now." the secretary continues with her cold tone.

I hang up and tell Lucien that the doctor wants to see me immediately. I don't know who this doctor is; I am assuming she's one of the ones who gave me their card during my stay. What kind of doctor is she I wonder? Maybe she's a hematologist since my blood counts were low? I wonder this during the entire car ride to her office in Shrewsbury. Pulling in to the parking lot, I see the sign "Dr. Topolski – Oncology". Oh, okay, I think oncologists specialize in bone marrow. This is good; maybe we'll get a real answer finally.

I sign into the front desk and sit in the waiting area. The room is stuffy. It's poorly decorated with fake plants and generic posters of Renoir paintings haphazardly mounted in poster frames. On the coffee table there are a box of ultra-thin tissues, magazines including US Weekly and National Geographic and a pop-up display holding brochures about some wonder Cancer drug for men over the age of 65.

I am called out back. Lucien follows me carrying Luciana in her pink and grey car seat. Her hanging butterfly toy rattles as we walk into a small examination room. Lucien places the baby carrier on a seat and he sits next to her. I assume my position on the exam table. My hip is still sore so I wiggle carefully onto the table while that damn paper crinkles – I hate that, it drives me nuts! The nurse who led us in begins by taking my temperature and blood pressure. She then opens the cabinet and gets out an eggshell colored tackle box full of tubes, ties, bandages, etc. Blood work. Just dandy. I lie on the table and start my now expected routine of crying hysterically while they take blood. Finally she finishes and with a firm voice jokes, "That wasn't so bad, now, was it?" I stare at her blankly as I wipe the tears away and struggle to get my body sitting up again. My hip is throbbing at the biopsy site from all this up and down commotion.

By the time I sit up, the nurse has left the room with the tubes of my blood. Two seconds later a woman walks in wearing a white coat. Dr. Topolski introduces herself, shakes both of our hands then goes over to coo over Luciana who is playing a game of "spit my binky on the floor for daddy to pick up, wipe off, give back to me, repeat". The doctor tells us what a beautiful baby we have, then she turns to us wiping the fake smile from her face.

"So listen, hunny, you have Leukemia," she clasps her hands together in front of her. "The results show that it hasn't blast yet, but is about to any moment. You have to pick a hospital right now. You can go to Guardian Medical Center in north New Jersey to the oncology ward or you can go back to Metro Medical Hospital. They don't have an adult cancer center, but since you're under 25 you can be treated in the pediatric ward. I'll leave you two for a minute to decide which one." She leaves the room.

Lucien and I stare at each other for a few seconds. Luciana spits her binky on the floor. I start bawling and curl into myself. My mind is racing. Leukemia? What does that mean? Is it serious? What is a blast? What the hell does this all mean? Is this cancer? I don't even know. I don't think so, but I have no idea. Pick a hospital? For what? What is going on here? My head is spinning. Lucien wraps his arms around me; rubbing my arms, "Shhh"… he is trying to calm me down, "Okay, try to breathe, we'll figure this out together, sweetie." We rock in this embrace, I don't know for how long.

Dr. Topolski comes back in the room. "Okay, where did you decide to go?" She is cold. She is robotic. She has no soul as far as I can tell.

I speak, words coming from my mouth, but it's not me controlling it. I'm on autopilot trusting that it will guide me right. "I have children. I'm not going to go be surrounded by sick children. I can't do that. I guess the one in north Jersey. If I have something, I might as well get the best care I can." My voice is quivering, my face is beet red, my eyes are burning and I don't know how I am still sitting up at this point.

The doctor doesn't seem to notice any of this, and comes back dryly, "I'll call to tell them you're coming. You have three hours to pack a bag and get to the hospital to be admitted." She exits the room leaving Lucien, Luciana and I staring at the binky on the floor.

We let ourselves out and walk slowly towards the van. We are holding hands tight, afraid to let go for even a split second for fear of losing each other. Once in the car, I kick into survival mode without even realizing I've made the transition. I pick up my hot pink cell phone and dial my mom at work.

"Hello," she answers. Her voice is distant, small and scared. I can hear it even though I know she is trying to disguise it.

"Hi Mom," I am calm and even toned, "I just got the results of the biopsy. The doctor said I have Leukemia." My voice cracks and I am now sobbing into the phone. Big miserable tears fall onto my jeans leaving dark blue puddles of devastation.

"Okay. What do you need me to do, just tell me and I'll do it." Her voice is steady now, a pillar of strength.

"Can you come?" I manage through my emotional breakdown.

There is no pause, she immediately answers, "I'll be there as soon as I can."

Once home, I fly around the house taking care of a million things. In our family, I am the one who takes care of all the finances. I also do all of the scheduling for our music lesson business. It is my top priority to explain how all of these things work so that Lucien can run the house hold smoothly. Once we've gone over everything, I pick up the phone and dial one of our piano student's mothers, who I have become close with and ask her if she could come by to watch Luciana and to get Adrian off the bus when he gets home in a few hours. I finally swing around the house gathering things for my hospital bag – but what exactly am I supposed to be packing? I have no idea how long I'll be there... a few days or a week at most? I toss my phone charger, a note book and pen and some snacks into a bag and we are off. It dawns on me in the car on the way to north Jersey that we are out of baby formula for Luciana, so I ask Lucien to pull into an A&P Supermarket hoping to find what we need in this foreign shopping ground. As we park, Lucien reminds me that the doctors specifically instructed that I have absolutely no immune system right now, and told me to avoid any crowded places. But we need this formula. I put on my mittens and wrap my plum fleece scarf tightly around my head, covering my mouth and nose completely. It's like this that I walk through this unfamiliar grocery store, locate the formula, ward off ogling stares from strangers, pay for the formula and exit the store with a sort of sigh of relief that I didn't have to get too close to anyone.

We continue the drive to the hospital. Our hands never separate the entire journey which feels like an eternity. I slip into a peculiar state of numbness showing no emotion, becoming shut off to the overwhelming emotions that subconsciously I know I can't handle right now.

Guardian Medical Center is a massive hospital set right in the center of a bustling mini city. It is unnerving to drive by these people living their everyday life, not giving a second thought about a thing. It all starts to piss me off; the lady in the black trench coat hailing a taxi, the college students grabbing lunch at the hot dog stand, the business man purchasing a train ticket and the young couple giggling as they enter the tavern for lunch. They are all living normal lives, while mine is being taken away faster than I can even realize it's happening.

Entering the main foyer of the hospital, there is a large "Admissions" sign that we follow to a large waiting area. There's an elderly man waiting at the entrance, a Spanish family with a screaming toddler off in the left corner, and a mix of people filling the rest of the room. No one looks sick here, so they must be like me... have an illness that is invisible to the outside world. It's not very long before we are called into one of the cubicles off to the left. We both take a seat at the gigantic oak desk while the admissions woman starts asking me a volume of questions; Last name, first name, date of birth, address, phone number, social security number, spouse's name and address, spouse's social security number, etc. She starts making some phone calls. I can see she is running into problems when she calls our insurance company. What else is new? She is on hold forever with the insurance company, rattling off medical jargon that I don't understand, tapping her lethal looking zebra print nails on the computer's keyboard.

Eventually she hangs up and excuses herself. I can see her in another cubical asking an older woman with salt and pepper hair for help, showing the older woman all of my information and insurance cards. They both have a baffled look on their face. Like I need this right now?

After about an hour of phone calls, she finally says to us, "I'm sorry this is taking so long dear, but we stopped accepting this insurance about a month ago. We're trying to figure out how to get you admitted so you can get treated." She starts flipping around massive 5 inch bound books which I'm guessing contain the commandments of the insurance company or something to that effect.

At this point, I am crying. Lucien is trying to calm me down, but he's just as frustrated as I am. The woman looks alarmed that I am a basket case asks me if I am feeling sick. I explain to her, "No, but I just left a doctor 3 hours ago who said I need to be admitted and treated right away because something about blasts. All I know is that I really need to get in." She makes some more phone calls and keeps trying to figure this mess out. Her phone starts ringing on her desk, so she answers it, listens for a minute and then hands it to me, "It's for you." I'm perplexed, who's calling me?

"Hi Sheri, My name is Dr. Ayers," he has a soothing, reassuring tone to his voice, "I'm going to be taking care of you. We're going to get you admitted right away, don't worry about anything." I nod and start taking calming breaths as I listen to his voice telling me these hopeful words. "Since we're having this insurance issue, what we're going to have you do is leave the admissions area, and go to the Emergency Room. They have to admit you there regardless of what insurance you have, and it is urgent we get you in and treated. Don't worry about anything, I'll make sure someone down there knows you're coming and we'll get you right to a room." His voice remains steady and comforting. I trust him already. I trust him with my life.

I hang up and tell Lucien everything Dr. Ayers has just explained, Lucien seems to take a deep breath and relax his shoulders a little too. We thank the receptionist for all her help and we make our way to the Emergency Room. I wrap my scarf tight around my head again, blocking access to the smog of ER germs I am about to enter into. To my pleasant surprise, they *are* expecting me in the ER and the whole process seems smooth. They take me into triage right away to do the routine temperature and blood pressure which I am accustomed to by now.

The triage nurse goes through all the normal steps, including weighing me and measuring my height. She mumbles as she enters the results into the computer, "148... five foot two inches..." (insert the sound of screeching tires here). I thought I was five foot FOUR inches, which is what it says on my driver's license. So you're telling me I'm shorter than I thought? Ugh! First I get Cancer... then I lose two inches... this day is going downhill fast.

I'm now expedited out of triage, down a sterile ceramic hallway, past the rows of curtain cubicles and led into a room with a blue door. I assume my position on the gurney while Lucien settles in on the lone chair in the opposite corner of the room. A nurse starts prepping me for an IV, which sends me plummeting through my routine needle reactions. As she is working, parts of the room come into focus; the peeling white paint on the walls, the scuffed up ceramic floor – is this part of the ER? I ask the nurse this question. She explains that it is a part of the ER, but is specially equipped with a self-contained air system meant specifically for patients, like myself, who have no immune system. She smiles, proud to have given us the information, and leaves the room.

Hours go by. Lucien and I are both exhausted. He looks so tired sitting in the little plastic chair, my suede winter jacket folded in half on his lap, every time I glance at him he is biting his lower lip, and nods his head – silently telling me it will be alright. He is my rock through this; thank goodness he is here with me.

Doctors continue to flow in and out of the heavy blue door like an open faucet. They come in clumps of two and three. Usually there is one fellow with a med student or two trailing behind him, frantically jotting notes on their clipboard, smiling and nodding along with their mentor, then exiting the room like ducklings obeying their mother. After the seven hundredth time, the door opens and a doctor with a long white coat enters.

"Hi Sheri, I'm Doctor Ayers, " he introduces himself as he walks over towards the mini sink in the corner where he continues to talk while he scrubs his hands. "I'm sorry it's taking a little time to get you upstairs, we're just waiting for a bed to open. I'm using this time to go over your blood work and your files so that we can start coming up with a plan of action." He wipes his hands on rough bark-like utility grade paper towels, then takes two steps back over towards the bed, extending his hand for a shake. "I'm going to take care of you." His hand is cold, clammy but incredibly gentle and caring. I truly believe with all my heart that he really is going to take care of me.

August 17, 2003

I am bouncing around in the ocean like a buoy, swaying with the natural ebb and flow of the waves. My legs have been swollen like tree trunks for weeks; dead weights beneath me. The saltwater is lifting me up, providing much needed relief for my ailing joints. I'm a week overdue with the baby, my abdomen bulging more unnaturally swollen by the second.

"Keep swimming!" my mother yells from her circa 1983 beach chair. "You have one more day to have this baby before we leave back for home!" she broadcasts from her station under the rainbow beach umbrella.

My parents had planned a trip to visit us after my due date so that they could meet the baby right away. No one counted on the fact that I would be so overdue at this point. They are staying in the bed and breakfast where we live. I asked the owner to have them stay in the light house themed room; it's extra spacious and overlooks the water, easily making it my favorite suite of the Inn. They are leaving tomorrow... and still no baby. We've tried spicy food, walking through town, bobbing in the ocean and multiple other failed attempts at inducing labor.

The next day rolls around and it's time to say our goodbyes. We all huddle around the outside of the Inn; it's a glorious Sunday morning with the sun beaming amply over the Victorian planter overflowing abundantly with a waterfall of pansies and geraniums. We share farewell hugs and kisses and my mom rubs over my stomach one last time while she wishes me well. They drive off into this perfect picturesque scene... and I feel my first contraction.

Lucien and I spend the next five or so hours watching Trading Spaces on HGTV, while I plant myself in my office chair. I wrap both of my hands on the metal support beam which is in the center of our basement living room (only room), and I sway side to side with the precision of the pendulum on a grandfather clock. I sway like this through every contraction. Eventually, it's time to depart for the hospital – there's a little boy who wants to get out – now.

I love the name Francis for our son, but it didn't take long before I started hearing from people, "Oh how cute, Frankie's a great name!" or "Oh Frank will be a musician for sure!" Don't get me wrong, Frank is a great name too, but I don't want my son's name to be Frank, I don't feel like it goes with our last name. It's Francis – not Frank. So we start keeping an ear out for more name options. One lazy night we were watching one of our favorite shows which is about a detective who struggles with his over bearing OCD (Obsessive Compulsive Disorder) while on the job. We get such a kick out of this since so many of his issues mirror ones that Lucien has every day (granted, on a much smaller scale than the detective). The lead characters name is Adrian Monk – we're sold immediately and our unborn son is renamed Adrian Robert. Perfect.

Adrian is born on August 18, 2003. He is a content little man; loves hearing music, rocking in his teddy bear swing and is obsessed with Maisy the Mouse. He fits right into our little family like he's been with us all along.

At five days old, we pack up his things and he is on the road for the first of many Beatlemania concerts. There's no time to waste when it comes to work, so I strap him into a papoose and resume my job as stage manager right away. As an infant he travels to cities all over the east coast; Binghamton, NY, Rehoboth Beach, DE, Fairfax, VA – he goes everywhere with us, our own personal groupie.

The owner of the Inn, Carmen, gives us an extra room across the hallway from our current one for us to spread out during the winter months when bookings are slow for her. We are able to now have our living room and kitchenette in our original space, and a separate bedroom shared with Adrian across the hall. Every night we leave our living space, lock up, take two steps across the hallway, unlock our bedroom door and head to bed with our lil' man. It's difficult to have our living quarters separated by a public hallway – but it is more space than we've ever had so we are elated.

Things are calm enough now that we feel like we can begin planning our wedding. We had discussed getting married right before we became pregnant, but upon learning that Adrian was on the way I put a halt on everything… I did not want to be a pregnant bride! The timing doesn't matter to me, we have known we were going to marry from day one.

We set the date for the fall of 2003… giving me just enough time to drop some baby weight. Throughout the summer I start planning our wedding. The budget is extremely limited so I find ways to be creative with my resources, using my time at home with Adrian to map every detail out. We've decided to hold the wedding in Manchester, New Hampshire in a banquet hall. My parents are amazing and cover the cost of the hall and food, which I am able to keep at an affordable rate by choosing a buffet dinner of BBQ style food. I visit all the local dollar stores amassing a supply of silk flowers in periwinkle blues, deep violets and ivory. For hours I sit in a hurricane of flowers, candles, ribbons and hot glue. I spend an entire week handcrafting a veil hand edged in ribbon with 200 individually glued mini faux pearls. I create my custom bridal bouquet from 30 long stem silk roses, and the bridesmaids' bouquets out of silk hydrangea. I hand make everything myself to save on the budget. My dress is an off-the-rack $79 blowout from David's Bridal and our best man is doubling as our DJ. The whole wedding budget comes in at a mere $2,000.

The wedding weekend is everything I could have ever dreamed of. Everything falls into place amazingly perfect. The morning of October 25, 2003 we gather everyone in the wedding party at my parents' house. Lynda, a longtime family friend and beautician, has volunteered to do all the hair and make-up as her gift to us. My friends Tilla and Layla are my bridesmaids, while our band mate, Jim, and my brother Scott are our groomsmen. Lucien's parents watch over as little Loosh's cheeks puff to blow up a balloon as Justen is hitting more balloons around the room. Adrian is contently laying on his infant play matt, kicking his legs at nothing as he sucks and slobbers his entire left hand. Everyone is under the same roof, all equally excited for the day.

The wedding itself is intimate, doting and utterly stunning. Our vows are simple yet profound and we proclaim our devotion surrounded by our close friends and family. We incorporate the boys into the ceremony where we all take part in a family vow. Our unity candle is surrounded by two ivory pillars, one for me, one for Lucien; and three smaller pale blue pillars – one for each of the boys. At one point, Lucien and I have a seat off to the side where we have a guitar and a percussion shaker waiting for us. In the middle of our ceremony we perform together Make Believe, as well as a comical number, I Got You Babe. We rejoin under the white floral arch where the Justice of The Peace proclaims us husband and wife. Afterwards, we sway slowly for our first dance "I Do"; a song we wrote and recorded ourselves for our wedding day, a heartfelt ballad where my lead vocal is punctuated by subtle acoustic guitar riffs. Our family gathers around taking pictures, smiling, approving. Everything is perfect in our fairytale.

I Do

On this day we will become one
Waited for so long, now it's come
Joyful tears I cry. I know why
Ready all this time, love of mine.

Pronounced man and wife
Union of love
Devote all my life
Will you vow to? I do, take you as mine
'Cause I will always love you for the rest of my life

Walking down the aisle, meet your eyes
Share our wedding vows, hold hands tight
Put this ring on her hand then say
You may kiss the bride, for always

Pronounced man and wife
Union of love
Devote all my life
Will you vow to? I do, take you as mine
'Cause I will always love you for the rest of my life

Dancing with you now, we are wed
In loves warm embrace, our lives we'll spend

Pronounced man and wife
Union of love
Devote all my life
Will you vow to? I do, take you as mine
'Cause I will always love you
Yeah I will always love you
I will always love you for the rest of my life

This chapter in our life has finally arrived after so many trials, tribulations and turmoil. We have clawed at the edges of life's difficult walls to climb triumphantly to the mountain peak, rightfully claiming our victory. We are married. Our love is exemplified for all to see via the tiny golden circle we wear boastfully on our fingers. Our passion blazes brightly for all to see, no hiding, no questions, so clearly. Cloud nine is an understatement – but it sure didn't last long.

One day Carmen asks to speak to us. She explains that the health department came around, discovered the crib and gave her a warning. Legally, we should not have been living in the bed and breakfast since it is zoned as a hotel. "I'm so sorry you guys, but you have to leave, you have to be out in 30 days." Carmen and her husband have always been so generous with us; we have nothing but love in our hearts towards them for giving us the opportunity to get our footing as we began our life together. We completely understand the position they are in concerning us living there, and know that we have to do what we can to move.

We begin our search for an apartment in the area. It's difficult to qualify for anything due to my lack of credit, Lucien's ruined credit (divorce sure will do that), and our self-employed status. Finally, we meet a very sweet and understanding property manager at a complex in Bradley Beach. She fudges our application details a tad and we are in!

Our new apartment is like living in a 5,000 square foot mansion, albeit smaller by some degree. We have a decent size bedroom, a cramped but suitable sized kitchen… with an oven! In the massive living room I am able to partition off a corner for a desk for my home office. We go out a purchase a futon and a small stand for the T.V. area. In the far corner, I create a nursery for Adrian. I use a dresser and a room divider to concoct a little room for him.

Every night Lucien gets home at 9:30. He sits on the lumpy futon, cradling Adrian, rattling a little plush football and humming little ditties. At 10:30, I give Adrian his night bottle as Lucien goes around the room shutting off each light before heading for the bedroom. I leisurely pace the length of the living room, snuggling Adrian against my chest, holding his head in my hand close to my face. I sing in a whisper; "Hush little baby don't say a word, mommy's gonna buy you a mocking bird." I flip the switch on the boom box I keep on Adrian's dresser; it goes right to the A.M.

station that doesn't come in creating a soft hum of static fuzz to sooth little man to sleep. I resume, "and if that mocking bird don't sing, mommy's gonna buy you a diamond ring." I lay his little body down in the crib and creep out of the room. I tiptoe into our bedroom where Lucien is waiting, I lay next to him and we nod off to sleep cradled in each other's arms knowing our family is together; safe and sound.

March 12 2008 - Wednesday

The bone marrow transplant unit of the hospital is a world of its own. There are two sets of air tight doors you must be buzzed through in order to enter. The unit itself is tiny with only 11 beds, reserved for patients undergoing allogenic transplant or receiving high-dose chemotherapy with the intent of preparing for stem cell or bone marrow transplant. The nursing ratio in the BMTU is 1:1 being that everyone here is high risk needing high doses of chemotherapy, blood products, biotherapy, antimicrobials, stem cell rescue, and are often on immunosuppressant drugs. In other words; it's a highly staffed, terrifically orderly and meticulously implemented specialty wing of the hospital. It is explained to me that due to my severe lack of an immune system, and the projected plan of high-dose chemotherapy treatments to come, this is the safest unit of the hospital for me to be in for the time being.

My room is a good size, featuring all the typical hospital room amenities. There's the bed, two nightstands, a recliner, an navy blue plastic couch that folds into a bed, a TV with a DVD player and a mini fridge. My room is all the way on the end, furthest away from the nurses' station presumably because I'm the least sick patient on the floor at the moment.

It's so late by the time I get to the room, that Lucien has to head home to relieve the babysitter. We sit on the bed, embracing, crying, and squeezing for fear of letting go. After some duration, we know it's time. I sit helplessly on the bed watching as he backs out of the room, stands at the door for a long last glance before whispering "I love you" and closing the door behind him. At the click of the door closing, I let out a loud, deep sob and cry through the lump in my throat. I gasp through my tears, turn on my side into the fetal position and burrow into the pillow with tears full of pain, releasing my angst as I fall asleep out of sheer exhaustion and heartache.

Sometime later I am awakened by a delicate presence as a nurse floats around the room. She heads towards the dry erase board and adds her name to the top right hand corner. Turning to me, "My name is Cara, Sheri, it's so nice to meet you. I'll be taking care of you tonight. If you need anything at all, all you have to do is ring your buzzer to the nurse's station and I'll be right in. Is there anything I can get you sweetie?" I shake my head and muster out a "No thank you."

Nurse Cara smiles and perches on the edge of the bed. "Dr. Ayers will be in soon to go over a few things with you, then we'll bring you down to have your port put in. The rest of the night will be slow, so you can get some rest. Tomorrow morning Dr. Ayers will come back and talk to you about your treatment plan. Tomorrow will be testing, but for tonight, you just rest, sweetie." She floats back over to the door and disappears into the hallway.

I have no idea what she was just talking about. What is a port? What the heck does that mean? As these thoughts swim around my head, I wait patiently to see what happens next.

There is a knock on the door a few minutes later, and Dr. Ayers enters followed by two young medical students. I sit straight up in the bed, eagerly waiting for what he has come to tell me. "Okay, we have a few things planned for you tonight," he starts in his calm, even tone. "First you're going down to special procedures where you're going to get a central line inserted. I've decided against the port for you, since it's placed under the skin, I don't want to leave you with any scars since you are so young. The central line will be on the outside, but will make it much easier for us to administer medications and do blood draws without having to use an I.V. while you're inpatient." He pauses a minute and nods, checking to see if I'm getting all of this before continuing.

"Try to get some rest tonight, tomorrow's a big day." He reaches over, handing me his business card. "Call me anytime you have a question or concern, okay?" He nods his head again, and starts towards the door. "Hang in there. I'll see you later on." I glance down at the business card where he has crossed out his office number in sharpie, and on the back of the card scribbled his cell phone number. I feel like I could not have been sent to a more caring or devoted doctor. I am filled with a calming sense that I can trust him with my life.

As I'm staring at the glossy business card, there's a quick knock on the door before a tall man in green scrubs enters, announcing he is here from transport to bring me to special procedures. He asks me if I am well enough to get myself on the transport gurney he has, and I nod as I make the move to the bed on wheels. It hits me once I am on this thing, that I'm going to have this "line" put in, and I start to panic as I realize that presumably means needles are involved. I'm heading into a state of panic, when I notice that Nurse Cara has swiftly appeared at my bed side holding a small Dixie cup and a bottle of water.

"This is some Ativan; it will help to calm your nerves for the procedure. When you're back up here afterwards, I'll get you some Tylenol for the pain." She smiles reassuringly as I am wheeled through the double locked doors of the BMTU and towards the elevator. As the transport worker tries to manhandle the gurney into the elevator, he bumps the thing around a good three or four times hitting every wall possible. The roller coaster finally ends when we're safely inside the elevator.

"Sorry," he looks towards the floor. I tell him it's okay, and laugh at the situation. He looks at me, "So, you play guitar, huh?"

"Yeah... how did you know?" I'm shocked... I mean, it's not like I have a six string hanging off the back of my gurney or anything. How on earth would he have known that? The elevator beeps, and he starts to wheel me down another long white and blue hallway.

"You have your nails cut on your left hand, but not your right hand, so I figured it was so you could play chords. And your right hand, well, you don't need to cut your nails to hold a pick." He looks me right in the eye and smiles, proud of himself. "Okay, this is special procedures." He tucks my gurney up to a wall in the hallway behind two others in line. I hang tight, observing the blond gurney-bound-woman in front of me as she taps her nails on her metal IV pole in a hypnotizing beat. I patiently wait to feel some kind of a sensation from the Ativan. It feels like two hours go by and I'm still sitting in this medial queue waiting for this freakin' procedure.

Eventually a nurse comes over with a clipboard. "Just read over this and then sign below that you consent and understand that you're having the procedure done to install a central line and you understand the risks involved. I'll be right back." She leaves me with this dingy stock clipboard with a pen attached by a string and tape, and this discouragingly long form that stretches on for 4 tedious pages. I glance over the whole thing in 3 seconds before signing my name at the bottom. Does it really matter if there are risks involved with getting a procedure done, if there are Cancer cells swimming through my bloodstream taking over my body? Not really. I signal for the nurse that I'm finished and she comes over, takes back the paperwork and tells me it will be fifteen more minutes and I'll be up.

I freak out. It hits me that this Ativan did conclusively diddly squat for me and that I'm about to have a procedure done involving needles and God knows what; then the tears start to flow. I start sobbing uncontrollably as I notice that I'm next in line. There's no other gurney in front of me in this dreary hallway waiting line, only new patients waiting behind me. The nurse notices immediately and rushes to see what's going on, asking me if I feel sick or am in pain. I explain to her that I can't do this, the antianxiety medicine did nothing. I can't do this. Get me out of here! She hightails it into what looks like a storage closet with a desk and mumbles something into her phone.

Not five minutes later, Nurse Cara is standing next to me with another Dixie cup of pills, "Here you go Sweetie, this will help calm you down. You have a high tolerance for medicine, don't you?" I gulp down the pills, hoping they work this time around. They tell me they'll give me 10 more minutes for the Ativan to kick in before starting. Gosh, does ten minutes crawl by.

Finally, the nurse starts wheeling my gurney around a corner and into a tiny room that looks more like a medical storage room than an operating room. The closet doors are bulging open with towels, paper gowns and plastic bags full of tubes. Medical paraphernalia is strewn all over the place in an insane organized chaos. I feel like I am in some sick horror movie.

A doctor wearing scrubs, blue latex gloves, a hair cap and a paper face mask approaches me as a nurse lays me down flat on the bed. They guide my head to face to the left, leaving me staring at the white cement block wall. I am violently crying, my body jerking and teetering with every sob. They are speaking to me, but I don't hear a word they are saying, all I am aware of is the pain in my side, growing with each lurch of my body. A calming voice breaks the cycle, and a lady nurse appears on my left side. Her kind eyes peek over her mask sharing compassion and comfort through her gaze. She gently reaches for my hand, cupping it between both of hers. Her hands are warm, soothing and compassionate. She promises to stay with me; to help me through this.

"Okay now Sheri, I'm going to start the procedure. I need you to stay very still and calm through this and it will be over very soon," the doctor's muffled voice announces. "Take deep breaths and concentrate on staying very still." He starts rubbing some kind of alcohol on my neck with a piece of gauze. Streams of alcohol trickle down my neck, staining my skin and the stark white sheet beneath me.

They start to unfold and place large blue sterile paper sheets all around me, covering my shoulders, chest and head; leaving exposed only a small square section of my neck, which now has a burgundy red hue coating it from the alcohol. I feel disgusting, contaminated... I feel violated.

A gloved finger starts poking around my neck, prodding in search for the internal jugular vein. After jabbing around, he seems to find the right spot... and pushes on it harder a few times; just making sure, I guess. "You're going to feel some pinching as we administer the local anesthetic," the doctor informs, causing me to cry harder. The lady nurse tightens her grip on my hand, and instructs me to squeeze her hand as hard as I have to, to keep calm, and to stay still.

The needles start. They pinch and torment me as they penetrate my skin in a million places; I swear they poke relentlessly, seeming to go on forever. When the piercing finally stops, I am deep in the grips of an emotional hurricane.

A nurse rubs a sterile ultrasound wand around my neck working with the doctor as a team. The doctor uses his scalpel cutting an incision just smaller than 1 cm into my neck, revealing tissue and my defective Leukemia rich blood. Nearby, a nurse is cleaning and flushing the Hickman catheter with saline, and cuts it to the right length for my specific size. The doctor picks up his 18 gauge micro puncture needle and with the assistance of the ultrasonographic guidance punctures the jugular vein. He advances the guide wire and begins to snake the catheter through my veins. I feel every slither of tubing as it pushes its way through my insides, forcing its way through my bloodstream, making room for itself within my body.

They ask me to stop breathing for a few seconds, as they remove the inner dilator and wire. A plastic square contraption anchors the line, and is then sutured to my skin with three stitches. Protruding from the plastic anchor are three clear tubes, each two inches long, one with a yellow tip, a blue and one with a red. The nurse flushes the three lines out with saline, cleans around the whole area and covers the whole device with a clear plastic bandage. I feel like a ragdoll being sewn together; my floppy, tattered body remaining broken. Tears continue to trickle down my cheeks, even though the nurse holding my hand has been reassuring me that it is over.

By the time I am being wheeled back to my room, back to my little corner of the BMTU, the adrenaline has subsided allowing the Ativan to finally kick in. I am practically sleeping when I am pushed past the nurses' station. I'm afraid to move my head; my neck is stiff and immobile. I have to slide off of the transport gurney and onto my bed, where I am frozen in the position I land in, for fear of this unnatural mechanism protruding from my neck.

I am alone. For the first time in years, I am laying in a bed – alone. Since Lucien and I have lived together, we have never once spent a night apart. Realizing that my worst nightmare is a seemingly becoming reality more and more every second, I close my eyes and cry myself into a restless sleep.

Summer 2004

Life is hectic during the summer months when the Beatlemania tour is in full seasonal swing. We navigate up and down the east coast every few days playing to massive crowds at summer resorts, beach band shells, festivals, amphitheaters and theaters in cities far and wide. We hop on planes flying to Sacramento, California and Milwaukee, Wisconsin to perform for four and five night runs in historic theaters. In between shows, Lucien maintains a full teaching schedule and in his "spare" time has begun writing acoustic songs for his newest album.

With all of this madness we are blissfully happy. The manager of the apartment comes to us one day to ask if we would be interested in moving into a two bedroom unit in the same building. It's more money monthly, but we sure could use the space so we sign on the dotted line immediately. Now we have a bigger kitchen and separate dining room which opens up into a massive living room. We save up some money from the shows and buy a beautiful Broyhill couch and chair set. I pick out my dream L-shaped desk for my work station making my daily tasks a million times easier. I decorate the entire space in an old world, Italian theme with grapes, wine bottles, candles and an old velvet picture of a wrinkled man in a tacky gold frame who once watched over Lucien in his parents parlor.

Adrian finally has his own bedroom and the timing could not be any better now that little man is starting to explore his world on all fours. I decorate his room in an ocean theme – done on a budget of course! At the craft store I pick up little sponges in fish shapes which I use to stamp paint on the walls. Adrian seems to love his new digs. He plays on the floor with his little toys while the Hard Day's Night soundtrack drones on in the background – his favorite Beatles album at the time, of course!

Life feels legit now, like we are a real family, with a real home.

The summer tour dates continue to wrap around the country landing us one weekend in Lucien's hometown of Clifton, NJ. His boys are living there now, so we are able to pick them up before the show, grab them some wholesome White Castle burgers and chicken rings for dinner and get over to Memorial Park where we are playing. They haven't been to a show in a while so it's a great opportunity to pose our three little men behind the Beatlemania drum set for a photo op! The day is perfect, we couldn't ask for anything to be different. At the end of the night, we drop them off at their apartment and start the journey southbound on the parkway. It's a nice short commute home for once, and we enjoy the ride reminiscing about the day.

Before we know it, we're getting off the Bradley Beach exit onto Route 33 with only five minutes left before we arrive at our cozy little apartment haven. There's no one on the road, except for one other vehicle heading towards us on the four lane roadway. As we pass by the Days Inn on our right, the other car decides to turn right into our lane, trying to pull into the hotel driveway as though we are invisible. Lucien throws his arm over to protect me as he screeches the Altima out of the line of connecting with the other car. We skid across the roadway, jump the curb and he miraculously lands us dead center between a telephone pole and a large metal Days Inn sign (the kind you see from the highway). Our car comes to a screeching halt, smoke bellowing from the engine, engulfing the hood in rising smog. Adrian in the back seat starts to cry, and as Lucien turns his attention back to the baby, I look in the opposite direction and spot the other car – unharmed – driving behind the hotel to the parking lot. Primal instinct takes over and I throw the car door open breaking into a jog towards the parking lot. As I run, the sound of my flip flops echoes through the buildings; disrupting the evenings silence with a steady clicking pattern. I reach the back of the building, spot the car which by now has been abandoned and turn back towards Lucien and Adrian. It all starts to hit me what just happened as I take in the image in front of me. Lucien is rocking Adrian in his arms, thank goodness they are both okay. The cloud surrounding the car is cumbersome and there are mere inches on either side of the car between the telephone pole and sign – it is a miracle we didn't hit either one of these head on.

When the police arrive I'm able to guide them to the other car. The officer walks over, feels the hood which is still warm, then heads to the main office to investigate. A few minutes later, the officers are knocking on one of the hotel room doors to question the driver. Sometime later, they inform us that the driver was underage; driving a rental car which he did not rent and was under the influence of alcohol and narcotics. The officer brings us home in the cruiser and we tow our trusty little Nissan Altima to the nearest auto body place. We find out the next day that our car was totaled in the accident since jumping the curb ripped out the entire under carriage.

For a few days we use my little 1984 Cutlass Sierra clunker around town, but we cannot travel with this to gigs, so we are forced to trade it in and enter into a cycle of car payments. The Toyota Sienna minivan is our best option, so we tie into a lease with that. At this point, I have no car anymore – nor do I care. The whole event has scarred me so much with driving in this insane state of New Jersey, and I officially give up on driving. Stick a fork in me – I'm done! For years after this (eight to be exact) I never drive – ever.

Life goes on with us enduring the same insane schedule of the crazy teaching hours sprinkled with the insane touring schedule. The running around is starting to ware on Lucien, but not as much as having to deal with the inadequate teaching environment at the music store he's working in. The rooms are the size of your average bathroom with just enough room for a piano, an amp and two chairs. He's not able to teach properly with all of his sheet music, lead sheets, backing tracks and tools that he generally likes to incorporate into the lessons. I make the suggestion that perhaps it's time for us to start our own music lesson studio where he can have all of his teaching materials and adequate space for him to give proper lessons. I start looking into home rentals in surrounding areas for us to make this big move in our life.

Since Lucien currently teaches in the Red Bank / Colts Neck area we figure that this should be the target area to aim for. I spend hours searching through the classifieds, jotting down the listings which show promise. It's a tricky search to find a home rental in a town where home business is permitted; the property is on a busy street (to avoid annoying the neighbors) and to find a landlord who is okay with us working from home. Finally, in the spring of 2005 I find a great property on West Front Street in the River Plaza section of Red Bank. The owner loves the fact that we're musicians, and is totally open to the idea of us working out of the property. We sign the lease, and get ready for this next big chapter of our life.

Moving in to this house is so amazing. Half of the living room is taken up with my gargantuan L-shaped desk which faces our couch and chair, which will double dip as our living room and waiting area for our clients. We buy a roll of clearance carpeting from Home Depot and re do the entire basement space to be Lucien's teaching studio which we affectionately nickname the "Lesson Laboratory". It quickly snow balls into a joke that Lucien is the mad scientist who runs the Lesson Laboratory, and this is how we come up with our studios name giving birth to the Lesson Laboratory for Musical Instruction. We offer Guitar Lab, Piano Lab and Bass Lab, and design a hokey logo of a dude holding a guitar in one hand and a beaker in the other.

Decorating this house is like living in an HGTV show and I love, love, love every second of it. I strip the repulsive antique floral wallpaper from the kitchen walls, replacing it with a golden base color sponge painted with a chocolate brown creating our "Nocelli Bistro" look. I make the crappiest curtains you could ever imagine for our bedroom, and pick up a cheap comforter set at Marshalls which helps take the attention off the curtains. Adrian is ready for a toddler bed, so we pick out the Thomas the Tank Engine bed and I hand paint an entire railroad scene all over his bedroom walls complete with a farm, an ocean and a MASSIVE tunnel done in a 3-D technique to make it appear as though his bed is coming right out of it. He loves his new room, and walks around pointing to the various characters I've created, offering a smile.

We officially open our business and it flies on its own immediately. I love every second of sitting at my desk, chatting with our clients all day long – it sure beats all the lonely years I've spent cooped in our various hole-in-the-wall apartments. Lucien's working environment improves 10 fold now that he has all of his teaching tools right at his fingertips, and is able to give proper music lessons to each and every student.

Finally, life feels just right. We spend the summer pushing Adrian around the back yard in his Fisher Price buggy car, watching the boys - Loosh and Justen play on the Slip N Slide for hours on end, playing football in the rain, painting 50 miniature pumpkins for Halloween (one for each student with their names on them) and countless other incredible moments bringing us closer together as a family. It's also these moments that make us realize something is missing, or someone. There's this nagging pit in our stomachs that tells us there's a little girl out there in the universe that's ready to join our family.

March 13 2008 - Thursday

I'm awakened by what looks like a teenager at 6:00 A.M who wheels into my room this massive, black metal contraption, plopping it next to the bed. "I have to weigh you, please step on the scale", she instructs. Still in a daze, I stand up on this strange platform and watch the red display blink my weight in huge block numbers. I sit back on the bed, and the girl places a thermometer in my mouth and a blood pressure gauge around my arm. It squeezes tighter and tighter, finally letting up as the thermometer beeps. The tech glances at the thermometer, jots down something in my chart and heads for the door. "Thanks" she says on her way out. Thanks for what?

I sit back in bed, rubbing my eyes, trying to recall where I am, how I got here, and why on Earth I'm awake at six in the morning. The door swings open, revealing a bright cheerful wide eyed Nurse Cara. "Good morning, Sheri! I hope you slept well! I'm going to be leaving now, but Rosie will be coming in. She'll be your nurse for the day. I'll see you tonight." She erases her name off the dry erase board, and scribbles in her replacement before leaving with a smile.

A minute or so later, the door opens to reveal a short chubby woman with a jet black bob haircut. She hobbles towards me, her heels clicking as she makes her way to my bedside. "Hi Sheri, my name is Genevieve, I'm the case manager for the BMTU. I brought some things for you to look over that might help." She hands me a fancy pocket folder printed with the logo of the hospital and pictures of smiling doctors shaking patient's hands in mock poses. I open it and am a little confused by its contents.

Genevieve reaches for one side, pulls out what looks like a children's book and starts "This is a wonderful book that you can read to your children. It will help explain to them why Mommy is sick and will give them perspective on the situation." I glance at the book. It looks like any other children's book except for the fact that "mommy" on the cover is bald. "And this," Genevieve continues as she points at a piece of Xeroxed paper on the other side of the folder, "is a great resource online where you can chat with other people your age going through the same thing right now, it's a wonderful support system." She smiles, proud of what she has delivered, gives me her card and says goodbye.

When she leaves, I look a little closer at this whole ordeal. This book is about how Mommy needs help to get rid of the weeds in her garden. It says that the weeds are blocking the beautiful flowers from growing, and Mommy needs help to get rid of the weeds so her garden can grow healthy and strong. Cute for some people maybe, but I sure as heck am not going to read this to my emotionally and developmentally delayed son who is in a self-contained class in school because he can barely speak. While this book may be a great tool for some families, it's not for mine.

I take a closer look at the internet print out. It's for a website called Cancer is Dumb. The sheet shows images of kids kicking military style boots at the word "cancer" spelled out in big bubble letters. It clearly states the website's purpose, "A place for pre-teens and teenagers to gather, chat, vent and stay strong in a cool message board environment! Together we can shout at the top of our lungs, we're too young for this!" So while this is a wonderful site for young teenagers to get support... for someone with a 4 year old, an infant, a business, a mortgage, a car payment and an adult life, I don't foresee this being very helpful to me.

I toss this folder into the drawer of the nightstand, where I forget about it completely. I can't believe there are no real resources for a young 23 year old mother. I wish I had my laptop with me so I could get online and dig up some answers. I feel so isolated from the world locked away in this little sterile room. I glance at the clock... all of this excitement and it's only 6:36 a.m.

I maneuver myself out of bed, still trying not to move my neck the slightest bit, grab the back of my hospital gown with my hand, and head for the bathroom. I sit there rubbing my eyes with the balls of my hands, trying to make sense of everything, of anything. I get up, wash my hands with this goopy scientific smelling soap and dare myself to glance into the mirror. My hair is a disheveled mess with brown and auburn streaked tresses lying scattered across my front and down past my shoulders. I move it to the side, exposing the area of the central line – sucking in my breath involuntarily with a shudder of shock as I see what's been done. My skin is stained in a dark rust colored hue, there is a plastic contraption sewn into my flesh with three menacing looking stitches, three clear tubes with plastic colored ends come from the plastic piece – the whole thing is covered in what looks like plastic wrap with white tape edges clinging to my body. This whole thing is the outer shell of some long intrusive tube running through my body, floating in my blood stream, taking me over – like the Leukemia. I feel repulsive, helpless, small and violated. Violated by this creature attacking my neck, by this hospital for holding me captive, by this fucking Cancer for stealing my whole self from right beneath my very own feet!

I crumble into a pile of myself – what's left of me. I hunch over the bathroom sink sobbing, choking and breaking down after being so strong. Glancing into the mirror, I see my reflection – flushed, ugly and beaten down. I hear a pathetic bitty voice in the distance, "… why? …why? …why?".

It takes a minute to realize that the voice is mine.

I'm interrupted by a knock on the door. "Breakfast…" I hear before the door slams shut again. I take a deep breath, look at myself right in the eyes and watch this mess of a girl pull herself together. After a few more deep breaths, I make my way back out into the room and onto the bed. There's a tray on my table with a carton of milk, plastic silverware in a bag and an orange all centered on a blue domed plate. I lift the cover to reveal my meal, which has been chosen for me – a synthetic looking egg pile, a thin piece of toast, and a paper cup containing wallpaper paste looking oatmeal. I wrestle with the cutlery package finally managing to get the fork out and poke a little piece of the egg around on the plate, finally gaining the bravery to put it in my mouth - it's cold, tasteless and has a rubbery consistency. I stick my finger in the paste and put that in my mouth – it *tastes* like wall paper paste too. Finally I take a bite of toast, before tossing it back onto the plate and pushing this whole ordeal off to the side. I have zero appetite anyway.

At 7:15 there's a light knock on the door. Dr. Ayers head pokes around the corner with a half-smile before he walks in. There's two students trailing behind him, who I ignore, giving all of my attention to the doctor who starts, "How are you feeling this morning?" as he heads for the sink under the T.V. and starts to wash his hands.
"Okay." I muster out in a hushed voice.

Dr. Ayers wipes his hands dry and starts approaching my bed, he leans close and fingers around the central line site on my neck. "You got your central line in. It looks good, is it okay, is it causing any discomfort?"

"No..." I reply softly.

"You can move your neck, you don't have to be stiff, it will move with you. I know it's uncomfortable, but you'll start to get used to it and you won't even know it's there. It's going to make things much easier for the nurses and for you. We're going to get you going on an I.V. drip through your line this morning, and then we have a big day planned for you." He sits down on the chair next to the bed. "This morning we're going to run some tests, you're going to have a CAT scan, a chest X Ray, we're going to run some additional blood work as well. We also have to do another bone marrow biopsy before we get started on any treatment so that we can check on the level of the blasts. As of your last biopsy it hadn't started to blast yet, and we have to make sure it didn't start to before we start treatment. Okay?"

I nod, unable to speak – in a state of shock; did I hear bone marrow biopsy again?

"After all of that is done, we'll go over treatment plans. Get some rest, and keep your energy up, okay? Call me if you need anything," He smiles and starts for the door, "I'll see you later on."

The morning is a whirlwind of being transported from one wing of the hospital to another getting a score of tests done. The life of a laboratory rat is what my life has become. It's already almost 11:00 a.m. before I am wheeled back to my room at the end of the BMTU floor. When the transport guy pushes the door open, I see Lucien sitting in the chair next to my bed and I light up!

I can't move fast enough, I can't really move at all actually. I slither off of the gurney, while the transport guy moves the fluid bag to the IV pole. With one hand I clutch the back of my gown closed, and grab the pole with the other hand. By the time I am standing, Lucien is right in front of me and he wraps his arms around me. I let go of everything and embrace him back, tucking my head under his chin where I still fit like a puzzle piece – even if I feel nothing like myself, if I still fit here, I must still be me.

We sit and I interrogate how everything at home is going. One of our student's mothers has Luciana at her house for the morning, and in a few weeks my mother will come down from New Hampshire to help with the kids at home and help to hold down the fort. Lucien pulls the chair close to the bed, holding my hand tight while we talk. I tell him about last night, all the tests this morning and what Dr. Ayers said about coming up with a treatment plan. We conclude that this must be a good sign; if we're looking at treatment plans then they must have an idea of what exactly I have and how long this is going to tie me up in this medical prison.

There's a knock on the door and Dr. Ayers comes strolling in, this time with two other Doctors in tow. He goes over to Lucien, shaking his hand while he greets him, then sits down on the foot of the bed with his thick metal clipboard. "As I was telling you before, today we have to think about a plan of action for your chemotherapy. There are many treatment options we can discuss, but I would recommend that we take the most aggressive course possible. There's a clinical trial you qualify for, it's a pediatric trial which you can take advantage of because you are under 25 years old. Pediatric treatments are more aggressive, because children's bodies are generally able to handle higher doses of chemotherapy better than adult patients. I'll leave this paperwork if you want so you can look over it. If you have any questions, just let me know." He reaches over, and pats my hand – not the bed. "Call me anytime you have a question or concern, okay?" He nods his head again, and starts towards the door. "Hang in there. I'll see you later on."

I look over the paperwork for the clinical trial. The medical dialect and complicated drug names swim around in a murky mess of ink on the page which I can't make left or right of no matter how many times my eyes graze the letters. As I'm staring at the paper, it hits me that he said we need to be aggressive which must mean that this is a pretty bad situation I'm in after all. It all hits me at once – I need to step up, ask questions, do research, listen carefully, stay strong – I need to ramp up my game and survive this shit.

Lucien and I talk about this clinical trial, and within minutes we reach our decision. If we are being offered "the most aggressive treatment plan" then why the hell wouldn't we take advantage of it? We decide to do the pediatric clinical trial and fight this Leukemia with every weapon we can get our hands on.

By the time my blue dome covered lunch plate arrives, Lucien has to leave to head back home to work. As much as we would give up our whole world to stay together through this, it does no good for him to be sitting here with me for hours on end, when he could be working, keeping our business alive – keeping our bills paid and a roof over our heads. Even though I know this is the way it has to be, I cry as he leaves, tells me he loves me, tells me he'll be back tomorrow, I can't handle losing him even just for the day. I have no choice in this matter, and have to say another goodbye – the second of many goodbyes to come.

The door hasn't even shut all the way and Nurse Rosie comes in to take my temperature and blood pressure. She glances at my lunch tray, "You got to eat up sweetie, and you have to keep your energy up. I'll put the menu up here on the table for you, just make sure to call your meal order in an hour before you want to eat, or they'll just send you up anything, so don't forget to order." She scribbles something in my chart at the foot of my bed and smiles on her way out the door.

A ham and cheese sandwich, a bag of Lays chips, a banana and an off shoot brand of ginger ale is what I'm presented with. I pick at the bag of chips, and push the whole tray to the side.

Winter 2005

We've been trying to get pregnant for months. I don't know what the problem could be; I mean I know I'm not in the best health weight wise, and things are super stressful between running the business, keeping up with the rental house, taking care of Adrian who is having major speech and developmental delays, touring with the production and a million other things. Maybe that's the problem. Maybe having no down time is starting to ware on us. Maybe we need medical help to achieve this pregnancy... but how in the world can we afford that?! One afternoon, a client shares her idea with me, "Sheri, maybe you and Lucien can release an album to benefit a fund, so that you can get medical help to have a baby." Brilliant!

Lucien had been writing some acoustic songs during the last year, so we already have a good base to build an album on. He starts recording some of the songs that he's got ready which are mostly instrumental including Sand Walking, Unborn Child, South Georgia Bay, and a few others. He also starts penning some songs specifically for the cause. Light of The Moon is a somber song which was inspired by a story of his oldest son, Lucien, as a child asking the moon to carry him because he was so tired. Teach The Children is a mellow but driven song, "Shape their world, don't leave them behind, make them a big part of your life. And don't forget someday, they'll shape the world the way they were made."

He records every instrument on the album, and we share the vocals. He writes me my very own song all about Adrian being my little boy, which has a bluesy vibe to it. "When he's bouncing off the walls, and I can't take anymore, I run to find the record that settles him down to a dull roar. Mommy's sweet little joy, always into trouble, but he's my little Blues Baby Boy."

The centerpiece of the album is an emotional piece about a father and daughter. It speaks all about his vision of someday being Daddy for a little princess. It's beautiful melody and sentimental lyrics paint an absolute picture of our dreams of a little girl.

Princess Lullaby
Did you ever dream of
Taking walks, daddy's little girl
To castles into the sky
Princess Lullaby

Can we go and wallow
In the sand, wind blows through your hair
Of pigtails, In your dolls eye
Princess Lullaby

Pick out a star, my love
Close one of your eyes
Pinch that star out of the sky
Hold it close, and feel the bright things inside

Can we share a lolly
Take a bite, daddy's little girl
Of sweet things into our life
Princess Lullaby

Are you feeling sleepy
And chilly in the nighttime air
There's one more things you must do
I will do it too

Pick out a star, my love
Close one of your eyes
Pinch that star out of the sky
Hold it close, and feel the bright things inside

Did you ever dream of
Daddy's little Princess Lullaby

At this point with the difficulties getting pregnant, yes, we would be happy with any baby – boy or girl. We are also big believers in putting your hopes, dreams, wishes, desires and intensions out into the universe and you will be rewarded with what you put your mind to. So far in our lives, this method of positive thinking, and dream visualization has gotten us so incredibly far. We've gone from complete poverty, picking up food at the soup kitchen and picking up furniture off the side of the road to starting our own business, renting a nice house, and owning our own bed and couch. These are things we never questioned our ability to have, and with extremely hard work and sacrifice we were able to achieve every goal thus far. Why stop now?

Everything seems to be on the right track until we get a surprise visit from the landlord one afternoon. He asks us how we like the house, if we're comfortable in it, tells us how nice our changes are... then hits us with the million dollar question – do we want to buy the house? Well, we love the house. It's been great to get our feet on the ground and to grow our business, but is it a house I can see us growing into? No. The rooms are small, we share our couch with our clients, the kitchen is tiny, the parking is horrendous, the property is small, and the street is narrow, so unfortunately our ultimate decision to not buy this house has landed us in a new position. The landlord wants to sell the house... so we have to move.

One of our student's mothers is a realtor, so we start looking around with her. We're in a strange market because we have to be specific on several factors that normally don't matter to house hunters. We need certain towns because they allow home businesses, we want a busy street so we don't have neighbors to upset, we need ample parking for our clients, and my number one request – we need a separate living room!

We look at houses throughout Tinton Falls, Red Bank, Shrewsbury, Middletown and Lincroft. There's a property our realtor has been begging us to look at on a major street in Lincroft, but when we drive by the property looks so tiny. After weeks of relentless begging, we finally give in and go to take a look at the house.

When we walk in the front door – we are sold! It immediately opens up to a large narrow room which is the perfect layout for a waiting room. The kitchen is impressively huge with an attached dining room and yes, oh my goodness, there's a separate room for the living room! Upstairs there are two small bedrooms which are perfect for kid's rooms, a slightly larger room which would make a great guest room / playroom and a three piece bathroom with a washer and dryer! Down the hallway when we arrive at the master bedroom, we are in pure and utter shock at its cavernous size – complete with a master bath! The icing on the cake is the finished basement which is separated into one massive room and a smaller room which are the perfect areas for music studios! This house was made for us!

Thanks to the powers above – and the messed up world of mortgages, we are able to get in with a no doc, zero down, and interest only monthly payment. It's preposterous that they let us buy a house, but who are we to argue? We go through with the purchase, and after a few intensive bouts of buyer's remorse it hits us. We have our own house. We also are swamped with a mortgage that I don't know HOW we're ever going to afford – but for this moment, we don't care. We have a legit piece of property, our own little sliver of Lincroft for our family to flourish. Nothing can keep us down now, we can accomplish anything we set our minds to!

March 13 2008 - Thursday

There's a knock of the door, and Dr. Ayers enters soon after. Genevieve, the social worker, and a nurse are with him. He washes his hands, "Have you had a chance to think about the clinical trial?" he asks.

"Let's do it. Whatever is the best chance to kick this is what I want to do. If this is the strongest option we have, then let's go," my voice is steady and sure as I deliver my response with my head held high (and my neck stiff from the central line – I will never get used to this leech on my neck).

Dr. Ayers talks for a few minutes about the clinical trial, the drugs involved and the timing of everything. "First things first; today is prep day for you. We're going to do the bone marrow biopsy right away so that we know exactly what's going on in the marrow and what our starting point is. Tomorrow we start chemotherapy." He hands me a sheet with a calendar and explains, "This is the plan we're starting with. Tomorrow we start aggressively with

Etoposide, Ara C and Daunorubicin, and you can see the rest of the schedule on the sheet. The clinical trial will add in a new drug called Mylotarg which you will get on Day 6." He pauses, letting me soak everything in. "Do you have any questions about anything?"

I look down at my hands which I have rung into a finger pretzel of nerves, then look up at Dr. Ayers. "Yes. Is this hereditary? Do I have to have my children tested; are they at risk of getting this?"

"No, Leukemia is random; you don't have to worry about your children. We don't know what causes it; it's different for different patients. It could be environmental, could be something you individually are predisposed to, we're not quite sure what the cause is." He calmly answers.

"I have one more question," I pause, and fiddle with my hospital bracelet, "am I going to lose my hair?"

Dr. Ayers looks kindly right into my eyes, "Yes, you are going to lose your hair from the Chemotherapy. I don't know when, some patients keep it a little longer than others, but it will be gradual, and you'll have some time to adjust before you decide if you want to get a wig. We can help you with that, but a lot of people end up with hats because they are more comfortable. It's all completely up to you though, but we will help you with your options when we get there. But don't worry about that now, let's just get through today and get your treatments started." He offers a kind smile, and leaves with his entourage.

Now that I'm alone in my room, I think about everything. Thank goodness my babies are not at risk, I can't imagine having to subject them to any kind of torturous testing. Then it hits me. Oh shit, I'm going to lose my hair... I just had it highlighted for the first time since the 5th grade, and now it's going to freakin' fall out anyway, talk about bad timing!

I look at this chart they've given me with my treatment schedule... it makes no sense to me whatsoever. Every day is labeled with drug names and a day number...

DAY 0 - THURSDAY 13th Prep. Bone marrow biopsy, Spinal
DAY 1 - FRIDAY 14th – IT Ara C, Daunorubicin, Etoposide.
DAY 2 - SATURDAY 15th - Ara C, Etoposide
DAY 3 - SUNDAY 16th– Ara C, Daunorubicin, Etoposide
DAY 4 – MONDAY 17th– Ara C, Etoposide
DAY 5 – TUESDAY 18th– Ara C, Daunorubicin, Etoposide
DAY 6 – WEDNESDAY 19th– Ara C, Etoposide, Mylotarg
DAY 7 – THURSDAY 20th– Ara C
DAY 8 – FRIDAY 21st– Ara C
DAY 9 – SATURDAY 22nd– Ara C
DAY 10 – SUNDAY 23rd– Ara C

On the top corner of the paper is printed information describing the patient:
NOCELLI, SHERI
3/12/08 AYERS
5/26/84 23Y F
That's me – just another patient. Twenty three years old and sitting in a secluded hospital room on the bone marrow transplant floor of a hospital while the outside world moves on without skipping a beat. My calendar used to include reading to my son, feeding my daughter her bottle, recording an album, decorating my house, hosting parties – having a life. Now? Every day of my social calendar is booked up with bone marrow biopsies and various versions of chemotherapy. What kind of sick joke is this?

It dawns on me eventually that the word "spinal" is listed on this day, which in medical terms I suppose is called "Day 0" (does that mean this day doesn't exist?). Once I realize that by this they mean "spinal tap" I flip a noodle and buzz the nurses' station. My nurse rushes in, asking me if I am okay – to which I respond – no, not really! I go through great lengths to explain my needle phobia, how I cry through blood work and needles, working myself into a full on crying session.

After trying to calm me, the nurse says that she'll be right back and she leaves the room. Not ten minutes later she returns with an overbearing smile. "I made some phone calls, and Dr. Ayers has arranged that since you need both the bone marrow and the spinal, we can send you through downstairs and have you sleep through the procedures. We can't normally do this for adult patients, but because you are under 25, we can send you through the pediatrics. Since you've had food and drink today, we'll have to do this first thing in the morning."

She is amazing. My doctor is amazing – I don't know how they have pulled this off for me! I release a long sigh of relief, wipe my tears and lean back in the bed. I practice turning my head a little, but quickly cringe at the pulling of the plastic covering sticking to me, grabbing my skin in all unnatural ways. I close my eyes, breathe deep and eventually fall asleep for a long and much overdue nap.

The next morning, transport is knocking on the door at 7:16 a.m. I'm already quasi awake, having been weighed by the gargantuan medieval scale this morning at the crack of dawn, so I've been waiting for transport to go have the bone marrow biopsy and spinal tap. They have me get on the gurney and off I go to procedures. The whole process is easy, and painless – until I wake up of course from the anesthesia.

I wake up in a little curtained off cubicle, all alone. It takes me a minute or two to realize where the hell I am… and it's the throbbing of my hip that reminds me exactly where I am. Just as I'm coming to, a nurse comes into my little cubby with a Juicy Juice box. She asks me how I'm feeling, then asks me to drink some apple juice telling me it will settle my stomach. I take two sips and am nauseated at the thought of drinking anymore. The nurse tells me they're going to monitor me for a little while to make sure I'm stable, and then I'll be transported back upstairs. So I sit there propped up in this bed, and just take in my surroundings. Nurses come and go, doctors look over charts, buzzers go off at the nurses' station, sleeping patients get wheeled past – on their way to wake up to their apple juice boxes I suppose.

After an hour or so, I am brought back up to my room – which still feels foreign and uncomfortable. I look around; taking in all the finite details of the space I've missed before now. At the top of the dry erase board there is a remnant of red Christmas garland taped, probably left over and forgotten from a previous patient's hospital holiday décor. Since this room is an end unit I have an extra window right in front of my bed, letting in a steady stream of sunlight and allowing a pleasant view of the ice blue sky. I stare out into the passing clouds and daydream about all the things I should be doing right now; changing a diaper, calling a guitar student to schedule their lesson, getting my son off the bus, paying the bills... living a life.

At some point before lunchtime, the nurse arrives announcing it's time to start the chemotherapy. She explains the three drugs that I will be receiving today, as well as the Mylotarg (Day 6).

Etoposide – This medicine, like all medicines used to treat cancer, is very strong. It is given via I.V. which is intravenous through an IV line or central line.

Cytarabine – Commonly called Ara-C. This medicine is also very strong and is usually given as a shot under your skin, into a muscle or into a vein and needs to be given on a regular schedule (in my case, every 12 hours).

Daunorubicin – Used with other medicines to treat different forms of leukemia and is given via I.V.

Mylotarg – This medicine is given through a needle placed in a vein, or an I.V. line. It is given slowly, so the needle will need to stay in place for about 2 hours. Drink extra water while you are using this medicine to keep your kidneys working well and help prevent kidney problems.

All mention possible side effects including fever, chills, sore throat, unusual bleeding, uncontrollable nausea, vomiting or diarrhea, painful mouth sores, severe rash or hives or severe itching, trouble standing or walking, yellowing of skin or eyes. The Mylotarg says it can also cause a decrease in how much or how often you urinate. Sounds like a carnival of good times! Nurse Rosanne is taking care of me today, because she is certified to administer Chemotherapy. She starts by putting on a protective gown, hair cover, mask and gloves; all to protect herself from the Chemo chemicals which are about to be injected into my blood stream. She starts doing what she tells me is an I.V. "push" which basically translates to her inserting the needle into the opening on the I.V tubing, and ever so slowly injecting the medicine into my line, flowing up the tube and into my neck, where it goes directly to my blood stream.

Every morning at 5:30 a.m. the nurse comes barreling in, flicking on the light, running the water, making a ruckus as she prepares to draw my blood. I try to sleep through this mania, since they just draw from my central line and I don't feel a thing, except the pulling and tugging of tubes. Every time they draw blood this way, I get a distinctive metal flavor in the back of my throat, which I try to ignore for fear of gagging. They leave and I try to fall back asleep to get some more rest before the scale person comes in at 6:00 and the Doctors come in at 7:00. This is all way too early for me!

The first week feels like I'm waking up as part of the movie Groundhog Day with everything happening exactly the same as the day before without the slightest variation, other than Chemo drugs of course which are changing daily as per the treatment schedule. The nurses all encourage me to "take walks" around the unit to keep myself active – advise I choose to ignore. I am the youngest patient here; everyone else I've seen walking sluggishly past my window are in their late sixties and older – their shoulders slouched with defeat. I honestly feel horrible as I witness them passing by, and I don't feel that being surrounded by them in the hallway is any good for my morale. So, I stay cooped in my room – ignoring all advice from the medical staff to get moving.

Things at home are formulating into some kind of a plan. We've had several people volunteer to babysit the kids for free allowing Lucien to teach his full schedule so that we can maintain our bills. Several families have even brought meals over, diapers for Luciana, groceries and other tokens which help beyond words. The first week, Lucien visits every morning, but by the second week it becomes too much on his plate because he has to get the house in order, relieve the baby sitters and pay bills. I have to start filling my days with something, so I scan T.V most of the day, tuning in especially to All My Children at 1:00 after lunch – this becomes the highlight of my day.

By the time we are finishing up day 10 of chemo – I start to feel it. I'm tired all of the time of course, but trying to hang in there.

The chemo causes all of my blood counts to dip to ultra-low levels, that's the chemo's job after all, to kill off the cells. Ever since my platelets have dropped, I've been getting massive bloody noses that last hours and flow like a friggin' faucet. They're random, but when they hit, they are severe. On the last day of Chemo, Sunday the 23rd, my CBC results are frightening even though they are exactly where the doctors want them to be. Every day after Chemo, my white cell counts continue to fall while the other levels start to creep back up.

LAB RESULTS   NOCELLI, SHERI   5:30 A.M.
CHEM PROFILE   REF RANGE   03/23/08

WBC	4.0-10.0	.8
RBC	3.9-5.2	2.58
HGB	12.3-15.5	8.3
HCT	36-44	22.8
PLATELET CNT	140-440	52 / 1000 UL
K	3.5-5.0	3.7
M	1.8-2.5	2.0

LAB RESULTS   NOCELLI, SHERI   4:45 A.M.
CHEM PROFILE   REF RANGE   03/24/08

WBC	4.0-10.0	.6
RBC	3.9-5.2	2.61
HGB	12.3-15.5	8.3
HCT	36-44	23.1
PLATELET CNT	140-440	39 / 1000 UL
K	3.5-5.0	3.6
M	1.8-2.5	2.0

All If these abbreviations and numbers send my head into a spinning mess, so the next day, at the bottom of the lab results print out, the nurse scribbles some notes so that I can decipher all the numbers.

WBC – White blood cells = immune system.
HGB (Hemoglobin) – Will receive packed red blood cells, usually when lower than 8.0.
Platelets = help blood to clot. Will receive platelet transfusion when count lower than 20 or with bleeding episode.
K = potassium – you will frequently receive potassium

replaced either by mouth or through I.V. Today you had 2 potassium pills (=40meg).
M = Magnesium - another electrolyte frequently replaced.

I would have thought, since I don't really understand this whole chemotherapy process, that once the treatments were done that I would be free to go home. I always think of that Julia Roberts movie, Dying Young, where she is the caregiver for a young cancer patient obsessed with the painter Gustav Klimpt... every day he arrives home and throws up profusely in the bathroom. I guess that made me think that since I'm two days out from finishing the chemo that I would be close to being released...but I am very wrong.

On the second morning after the chemo has finished, with my blood levels all over the map, I start getting blood transfusions. First, I am given a full dose of Benadryl to counter any reactions I may have to the transfusions. They give me a blood transfusion of Platelets and something else, that I am too groggy to take note of. When I finally wake up from the Benadryl nap, I've missed lunch (which truthfully, I have zero appetite for anyway) and I've slept through All My Children (the only highlight of my day). I have to go to the bathroom, so I wobble with my I.V. pole over to the bathroom where I try to relax and go... but nothing happens. That's odd... I feel like I have to go... but nothing's happening. I don't really think anything of it, and head back to bed. The rest of the day goes by at a snail's pace, and I still am not able to pee. No matter how much I try to relax, nothing will happen! Maybe it's just nerves; I'm not really sure what the problem could be.

The next morning Lucien visits early – since it's a Tuesday, he can only stay for a few hours so he can get back to teach for the day. This is the longest stretch we've ever gone without seeing each other and when he wraps his arms around me, I feel so complete. It sits so unnaturally that we are separated, it feels as though the world has stopped turning until we are holding hands and are finally together. My happiness slips away when the nurse arrives with a dose of Benadryl... shit; I need blood transfusions for the third day in a row. This means I'll be sleeping during Lucien's visit – what's left of it.

LAB RESULTS   NOCELLI, SHERI 4:45 A.M.
CHEM PROFILE   REF RANGE   03/25/08

WBC	4.0-10.0	.5
RBC	3.9-5.2	2.70
HGB	12.3-15.5	8.4
HCT	36-44	23.8
PLATELET CNT	140-440	25 / 1000 UL
K	3.5-5.0	3.6
M	1.8-2.5	1.9

I take the pills, and figure I should go to the bathroom while I'm still awake enough to get there. Strangely, I still cannot go. I feel like I have to go... but zilch. Whatever, I'm starting to get tired after sitting in the bathroom for 45 minutes (and the damn Benadryl settling in) so I give up and head back out to my bed where Lucien has been patiently waiting for me. As I'm shuffling back to the bed, grasping the cold metal of the I.V. pole with one hand, and the back of my gown with the other, the nurse arrives with the first of the days blood products I'll be getting.

"Sweetie, you can bring pajamas from home if you'd like," Nurse Tabitha starts to explain, "those hospital gowns sure do get annoying after a while for you." She pauses to hang the bag of opaque blood liquid – which I've come to learn is platelets. "Mr. Nocelli, you can bring her in some nice pajamas from home, as long as they're either button-down or wide around the top, so that they don't bother her central line site." This is the best news I've heard in WEEKS, real clothes, how exciting!

I settle on the bed, and stare over at Lucien as I fight my heavy eyes, fighting the pill induced sleep that is taking me over. Nurse Tabitha lifts my arm to check my hospital bracelet to make sure it matches the numbers on the bag of platelets, then starts the transfusion which drips for hours into my veins.

Summer 2006

I Google "best diet to achieve pregnancy" and scores of results appear in front of me... wow, I didn't realize there was so much information available on the subject! Reading through several pages, it's mostly the typical information of what not to do; don't smoke, don't drink, avoid stress... what about specific foods?

85

One page in particular catches my eye. "Foods to Choose Gender"... Say what?

I click on the link which leads to a message board full of women discussing their mission to not only achieve pregnancy, but also to sway towards a certain gender. I had no idea this even was a possibility! I learn quickly that these special foods and supplements help prepare the body chemically for a pregnancy but also prove very successful in gender selection. My mind is blown by the wealth of information which I expeditiously fill a five-star notebook with in a flash.

Most of the information has to do with your acidity level, claiming that male cells thrive in an alkaline environment but can't survive in an acidic one. The basis of the science here is that you should get your body's chemistry on the acidic level to sway for a female baby. A woman's environment is usually quite acidic with a PH level of around 3 or 4. Levels usually shift at ovulation to more of an alkaline chemistry with the PH reaching between 7 and 14. They suggest avoiding alkaline foods such as fruits, vegetables and nuts because they will lower your PH favoring a boy. Taking a daily high dose of cranberry pills also can contribute to the acidity level staying high throughout ovulation. Heat is another factor in the girl vs. boy equation, since it has been proven that Y (male) carrying sperms don't survive well in a hot environment, but the little X (girl) swimmers will survive.

Immediately we start changing our diet, trying to raise both of our natural acidity levels. We pop cranberry pills, eat the right foods, try to get tons of rest, drink lots of water and anything else we can do to naturally up our chances of conceiving a baby – but swaying also for a girl at the same time! I start charting my cycles, taking my temperature every morning before getting out of bed so that I can track when I'm nearing ovulation. I'd never tracked anything before when we were trying to conceive, I just always assumed the more we tried, the better our chances would be. Tracking temperatures and watching for signs of ovulation is annoying and feels like a huge waste of time, until one morning my temperature finally has a small spike! This means ovulation is super close, and it's time to try! To conceive a girl, you should try to get pregnant before the actual ovulation. We take scorching hot showers to help "heat" things up before things really heat up.

Two weeks later, it's time to think about testing. I have boxes of pregnancy tests shoved under my bathroom sink – we've been trying for a baby for quite a while now. Before bed, I take out a fresh test and lay it on the counter to use first thing in the morning. It's impossible to sleep, knowing that I'll know in the morning the outcome of last month's attempt, but eventually I nod off to sleep.

I wake up to see that Lucien is already downstairs getting Adrian up for school, and as tempting as the scent of Folgers is creeping upstairs, I know I have to take the pregnancy test with the first pee of the day to get a proper result. In the bathroom I practically hit a yoga position to make sure I'm aiming for the narrow stick. I finally wet the thing, then place it carefully on the vanity counter before going to lay on the bed to stare as three minutes ticks away on the clock. Time to check... oh my god... this can't be true! This has to be a mistake, there's no way. I can't believe my eyes, but right there in the little window is a faint plus sign. I'm pregnant?

After retesting on four more pregnancy tests throughout the day, I finally believe it – that we have successfully conceived. All of this time trying, and finally we are pregnant again! Boy or girl – at this moment I could care less, I cannot believe that we are having another baby!

My pregnancy moves along by the book. I love every second of being pregnant; growing rounder and heavier each day, my ankles swelling like water balloons, my cravings of lemonade and burgers taking over my life – it's all heaven on Earth. I absolutely love being pregnant, it just agrees with me so well. There is nothing like feeling the butterfly kicks move inside you to remind you that you've created a miracle.

The curiosity every day regarding the gender is overwhelming. I am dying to start decorating a nursery with my nesting instinct out of control! When I should be working, I spend hours trolling on the internet for old wives tales to predict gender with, which all end up sounding pretty dumb in the end... I mean c'mon, using a piece of string or Drano is irrational. While surfing this on the web, I come across some physic lady on EBay who claims she can tell the gender of your baby if you give her the date of conception, your birthday and the due date of the baby. Yeah right, what a crock... as much as I'm thinking "who in their right mind would believe something like this"... for $3.99... it's kind of worth a shot, even just for the entertainment factor! So I bid on the auction, send her the info and wait for her response.

At three months, it's time for our second ultrasound. The baby's heart looks healthy, its spine is a string of pearls across the screen and it sucks on its thumb as we spy from the outside in. We ask if there's any inkling of an idea as to the gender; our hearts starting to pound so heavy as we await this much anticipated information. The ultrasound tech smiles and responds, "Mr. and Mrs. Nocelli, congratulations, you're going to have a healthy little girl." Lucien and I don't speak a word, but turn to each other and squeeze our excitement into one another. A daughter! We're having a little girl! Whatever we did, must have worked! Cloud nine is an understatement at this point in our lives. We knew this would be our last baby, and topping off with a little girl is just the cherry on top.

That night there is an email from Physic Johanna waiting for me, "The child you are carrying will have a healthy birth after a very healthy pregnancy. There may be a small complication with the Placenta, but it will not hinder the health of the baby. I see this child to be female, she is going to be a very vibrant soul with an artistic tendency and you both will be the best of friends in your future." Wow, this lady does know her stuff, which I leave her a good feedback rating for.

I spend the winter painting the nursery walls a pale pink, hang pink toile curtains and load the room with antique looking white furniture with glass knobs. I buy a whole supply of cloth diapers – which are way better than the old fashioned folded kinds, these days they come in awesome fabrics with fancy ties and covers. I hand sew 50 cloth baby wipes to go with them. All of her clothes are hanging perfectly displayed in her closet, and folded neatly in her little dresser drawers. I spend many mornings sitting in the white rocking chair, staring at all of her little stuffed animals, the dainty crib, the fairy Barbie spinning on her little hook on the ceiling and all of the small details I've prepared for the baby's arrival.

The baby is due in about a week. I have an OBGYN appointment this morning, but man am I tired and wishing I could stay in bed. Lucien gets Adrian out to school on the bus and now heads out to get some groceries. I get in the shower, and let the hot water run down the back of my neck... my stomach feels so funny, I really hope I didn't catch a bug or something with the baby due so soon. All of a sudden, I get the urge to go to the bathroom and before I have a chance to stop myself, I make a complete mess of the shower.

Oh shit! (pun intended I guess?) Lucien is going to freak! His OCD (obsessive compulsive disorder) doesn't deal too well with messes... never mind *this* mess! I get down on all fours and clean the mess with some 409; scrubbing the shower clean the best I can with my belly being so big. Damn, I must really have some messed up stomach bug. Maybe the doctor can give me something to calm it down. I call the office and the sweetheart of a receptionist tells me to come right in, we'll do my appointment early and the doctor can give me something to calm this little virus down.

Lucien gets home, and we head right over to the OBGYN whose office is actually connected to the hospital. Of course when we get there, he has been called over to labor and delivery for an emergency C-Section. The receptionist tells me to just head over to the L&D ward of the hospital, and the doctor will just see me over there for the visit. So Lucien and I loop our arms together and walk outside on this beautiful May morning over to the hospital, laughing and cracking jokes the whole way up to the receptionist of the labor and delivery ward. I explain to her my situation and tell her I'm in no rush. She goes to tell my doctor that I am here.

She returns a few minutes later, "Mrs. Nocelli, the doctor is still in the operating room with a patient, but he requested that one of our nurses here have a quick look at you and then he can prescribe you something so that you can get home and rest." Great, what awesome service, Lucien and I head into a little examination room, still joking like little kids, laughing inappropriately way too loud for a hospital! I get a gown on, lay on the table and the nurse starts feeling around my cervix to check the progress of things. Next thing I know, her face goes pale, and she hurriedly pulls her hand out and excuses herself from the room. "Was is something we said?" we try to joke around, but anxiety has started to show it's ugly face since we're not certain what's triggered her strange behavior. Not two minutes later she reenters the room with another nurse in tow, who suits up in her plastic gloves and shoves her fingers up my cervix again. A look of surprise comes over her face, and as she pulls her glove off she exclaims, "Mrs. Nocelli, you're 9 centimeters dilated. You're having a baby!"

"I'll go to the car and get the camera and the…" Lucien starts to say on his way out the door.

"Not so fast, Mr. Nocelli. There's no time for that. This baby is coming too fast." The nurse stops him. I sit in the middle of this circus wondering what the hell is going on, I mean… I haven't even felt a contraction! How can I walk into the hospital laughing and joking and be told I'm about to have a baby! The nurses swiftly move me into a delivery room, where they get my legs right up into the stirrups. The doctor jogs into the room, asks me how I'm feeling, shoves his fingers up to feel my progress (which I'm pretty sure the nurses must be wrong about!).

"Okay, Sheri, you're fully dilated, you need to push!" He must have lost is mind too like the rest of them!

"There's no way, I can't push, I don't feel the urge, I can't do it!" I counter back.

"Sheri, I'm going to leave the room for 10 minutes. When I come back, if you don't push, I'm going to have to take this baby out with a C section" he threatens before leaving the room.

Clearly in a panic now, I ask the nurses what we can do to help. They suggest a warm shower which I am quick to agree to! I get out of bed, waddle over to the shower and settle into the warm pellets. It takes about 90 seconds of this before I start to feel the pressure! Lucien is standing right there with me and I tell him it's time… he calls for help, gets me out of the shower, dresses me back up in my gown… helps me shimmy shake back to the bed an poof! I push one hard push before the baby slips out into the doctors hands! After 10 minutes of labor, Luciana Virginia Nocelli is welcomed into this crazy world, with her crazy brothers, grandparents and parents – who are all crazy about her!

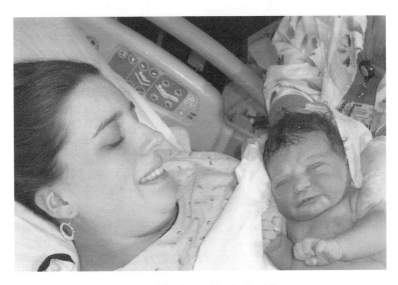

(Above) Luciana at 1 minute old!
(Below) Dressing Luciana to go home for the 1st time

SHERI NOCELLI

March 26, 2008

LAB RESULTS   NOCELLI, SHERI 5:00 A.M.
CHEM PROFILE   REF RANGE   03/26/08

	REF RANGE	03/26/08
WBC	4.0-10.0	.5
RBC	3.9-5.2	2.63
HGB	12.3-15.5	8.4
HCT	36-44	22.9
PLATELET CNT	140-440	40 / 1000 UL
K	3.5-5.0	4.0
M	1.8-2.5	1.8

I'm starting to lose track of the days in this hospital, with days and night flowing endlessly into one another without any significant change. The same nurses come and go on a rotation which I'm starting to know by heart. I'm feeling so out of touch with reality, like just a bunch of numbers on a sheet; just blood counts and percentages. I'm become a petri dish; a source from which to test endlessly the havoc of my disease vs. my body. I have Acute Myeloid Leukemia. I don't really know the severity of this considering I'm so shut off from the world, and I never know the right questions to ask. Because of this, I ask Lucien if he can bring me my laptop from home. Maybe I can find something on the internet to better understand what exactly it is I am at war with.

Unfortunately, he can't come to the hospital today because there's just too much he has to tend to on the home front. He has been more than amazing since he's been thrown into everything; this is just as hard on him as it is on me. He is my very own Superman – although I know he'd much rather be Batman with the cool car.

Every morning he gets Adrian up, fed, dressed and on the bus for preschool all before getting Luciana out of her crib, changing her diaper and feeding her a morning bottle. While he feeds her, we talk on the phone, trying to connect and update on any new developments on either side. At this point he gets any errands done including groceries, banking, pediatrician appointments, post office runs and all that crazy stuff. The rest of the morning he spends on the phone to take care of any scheduling for the students, return new clients calls, log any payments he may

92

have received the day before and everything else on the business front.

By 11:30 it's time to feed Luciana her lunch bottle and put her down for her nap so that he can make lunch for himself. We talk again until his first students arrive for the day at 1:00, so he goes into lessons with the baby monitor cranked so he can hear Luciana's every move. At 3:00 the day's volunteer babysitter arrives. It's someone different every day of the week. I've never even personally met all of the people who are taking care of my children – my children who I haven't seen in weeks – but we trust them with our babies; we have to. Adrian gets off the bus at 3:30; the baby sitter takes care of him and preps dinner for him (which Lucien has prepared ahead of time for them). The sitter spends the rest of the day with the kids in the playroom until putting Adrian to bed at 7:30. They then hang out with the baby until Lucien is done teaching at 9:00. Once the sitter leaves for the day, Lucien has a quick snack then settles on the couch and calls me. We talk about everything and occasionally I get to hear Luciana squeak and coo through the phone line. By 11:00, he prepares her night bottle, and rocks her to sleep in the white rocking chair. Once in bed, we talk one more time, connecting to wish each other sweet dreams.

Without any connection to the outside world, all I can do is tune into the TV. I've developed a complete schedule by now which maps out my entire day like clockwork. First thing every morning I wake up to Good Morning America, order my breakfast from downstairs and eat to Regis and Kelly and The View. When the news comes on, I flip over to the Food Network. I don't cook, and have no appetite, but I sure would rather watch Iron Chef than see who got killed by a subway train in Manhattan today. I order my lunch which I eat at 1:00 when I go back over to ABC for All My Children (my favorite part of the entire TV lineup.) After this, I'm screwed because midafternoon TV sucks, so I flick around hoping to find some random game show or movie. At 4:30 I call in my dinner order, which I eat to whatever I happen to find that's somewhat interesting. Every night of the week I have a set show to watch including So You Think You Can Dance, Wife Swap, Dancing with the Stars, Americas Next Top Model and various other reality shows.

Today I'm having a hard time watching anything. I haven't been able to go to the bathroom in days and am frequently spending long periods of time sitting on the toilet just pushing with all my might to get something – ANYTHING out! Maybe if I get creative I can help the process along… I reach over and turn the faucet on, letting it trickle as I try to relax. Nothing happens. I shut the light off in the little bathroom, leaving me in complete darkness hoping this will calm me into a blissful pee. Nothing happens. Angry at the whole situation, I bear down and push, what the hell, why can't I freakin' pee?!?!

After an hour, I give up and head back to bed. Joy and Elizabeth are arguing about some politician on The View, but I can't concentrate because something in my rear end is throbbing with pain, forcing me to lie on my side trying to alleviate it. When the nurse comes in, she can see I am grimacing and inspects the area – how dignifying. Turns out, I have developed a hemorrhoid from all the pressure when I try to go to the bathroom, something she apparently has to notify Dr. Ayers of immediately for some reason unknown to me.

When Dr. Ayers arrives, he has me turn on my side so that he can also have a look at my backside. With a gloved hand, he pokes at the area which causes a sharp pain echoing through me. "You have a hemorrhoid; we'll have to keep an eye on it to make sure it doesn't bleed. You're at a high risk of infection right now with your blood counts so low, and your platelets are too low for us to be able to operate. We'll have to treat it topically with ointment and Tucks to keep the area from getting too enflamed and to keep you comfortable. I'll also get you a donut seat cushion so you can sit up to eat. Try not to strain when you go to the bathroom so it doesn't get worse."

Seriously? So now, not only can I NOT go to the bathroom, I also cannot sit up right. Throughout the day I try different chairs in the room, angles on the bed, anything to stop the pain from this thing, but nothing is working. Sitting on the toilet has gone from bad to worse in the course of the day, and still by the evening, I haven't been able to do anything in the bathroom. When Lucien calls at 9:00, I can barely hold the phone and balance my body in a way that is somewhat comfortable. He tries to reassure me, tells me to hang in there and that everything will be okay. They are simple words, but mean the world to me to hear in his comforting tone. Eventually it's time to say our goodnights and get some sleep. Easier said than done.

All night I toss and turn. Even the nightly Ambien doesn't help me sleep since the throbbing of this hemorrhoid has something against me catching any sleep tonight. The nurses see my struggle, and try to be extra careful when they come in late the next morning (by their standards) to draw my blood at 5:45, trying not to wake me up. The throbbing is unbearable, which is blaringly obvious to the nurse who is surprised to see me to awake at this hour of the morning. She helps me to reposition myself on my side and readjusts the call button near my hand before leaving with the blood sample.

LAB RESULTS **NOCELLI, SHERI 5:45 A.M.**

CHEM PROFILE	REF RANGE	03/27/08
WBC	4.0-10.0	.6
RBC	3.9-5.2	2.43
HGB	12.3-15.5	7.6
HCT	36-44	21.3
PLATELET CNT	140-440	26 / 1000 UL
K	3.5-5.0	3.6
M	1.8-2.5	2.0

Dr. Ayers comes in at 7:00 and is also surprised to see me so awake at this hour. "Good morning, how are you feeling today?"

"Okay, the hemorrhoid really hurts; it kept me up most of the night. I still haven't been able to go to the bathroom either." I hate giving negative reports since it always means more treatments and more time wasting away in this room.

"Yeah, these are side effects of the treatments. What we're going to do is to treat you to help with these side effects because everything works hand in hand. This morning we're going to give you a red blood cell transfusion and we're also going to get you going with patient controlled IV Morphine to help with the pain of the hemorrhoid. That should help you relax to be able to go to the bathroom as well." He starts towards the door, "We'll get you comfortable. In the meantime, call me if you need anything at all." He offers a caring smile as he leaves my room.

Sometime later, the nurse comes in with a cup of Benadryl and a massive block of machines which they add onto my IV pole. She flushes out a tube on my central line, then hooks up a tube which leads to this new machine leading up to a what looks like a glass bottle. She hangs the bottle upside down from the IV pole and flicks the tube a few times with her finger to get the fluid moving. She hands me a little wire with a black button. "This is your Morphine drip. When you feel the pain getting worse, just give the button a click and more medicine will be released. If you don't need it, just don't do anything, but if you feel pain, click for more." She explains as she pushes a bunch of buttons on the screen of the machine. "I'll be back in a few minutes with the blood transfusion bag."

I test out this new button, clicking a few times until the pain in my rear starts to subside. As I'm experimenting with this new toy, Lucien arrives! He washes his hands and comes right over with a big smile, "My love," he kisses my forehead "My sweetie, I missed you." We find a way to hug around all of my tubing. "I brought you something," he reaches into his bag, "your laptop! Now you can get back in touch with the world! Do you want me to hook up the wires for you?" He runs the mouse; power chord pulls my wheelie table over and fires up the computer for me. This is awesome, now I won't be so shut off from the rest of the world, can do research on things and educate myself.

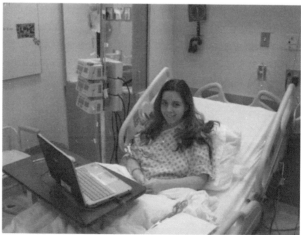

(Above) Getting my laptop set up during my first inpatient stay at Guardian Medical Center for Chemotherapy

We're interrupted by Nurse Carolina who makes a huge ruckus as she enters the room. She has a large metal thing with a blue center; it looks like a chair or something. "I brought you a commode to put next to your bed, so if you get the urge to go to the bathroom, it might be easier for you to get to this since you have the morphine." She places the potty chair next to my bed. "I'll be back in with the transfusion."

"Do you want to try to go to the bathroom? I can help you while I'm here." Lucien offers. He helps me to stand up. My legs are shaking, presumably from the morphine intake (maybe I had too much?). It takes me forever to get to the bathroom, and by the time I finally get there, I'm exhausted from the journey. I sit, but refuse to close the door and waste away this precious time for us, so Lucien pulls a chair over outside the bathroom door, and we continue to talk while I attempt to pee. Nothing happens, and I'm starting to get really upset. As tears flood my eyes, he comes right over with a tissue wiping them away. "Never mind, if you can't go right now, that's okay, my love. When you're ready, it will happen. How about I help you clean up, maybe you'll feel better?" I fight this idea, as it just seems like so much work, but eventually give in when he won't give up.

He goes out to the nurses' station and gets a fresh bar of soap. When he returns, I'm still sitting slumped on the toilet hopeless. "Okay, c'mon." he starts as he helps me up. Holding me with one hand, he reaches over and starts the shower with the other. He reaches around back to untie my hospital gown, and I use him to balance as I kick off my hospital grade netted underwear. He helps me into the shower, positioned so that my central line is out of the water. "Okay, hang on to the bar here, and I'll clean you." He soaps me all over with a gentle touch while I concentrate on my strength to not fall. "Now let's wash your hair. Lean back a little bit, yes, perfect. We're almost done my love." He shampoos and rinses my hair – something I can't imagine I would have been able to do on my own. When we're done, he towels me off, and dresses me in a new gown. By now I am exhausted between the Benadryl and all of the excitement, so he helps me back to bed where I nod off within minutes. I fall asleep as he kisses me on my forehead, "sleep well, my love. I love you." He squeezes me a long embrace as I fall asleep as soon as he leaves for the day.

The next morning I notice strands of hair scattered all over my pillow and it hits me; I'm losing my hair. I reach up, combing my fingers gently through the length of my hair, and inspect the resulting clump in the palm of my hand. I knew this was coming, but I wasn't prepared at all for the moment. When the nurse comes in, she catches me in the act of trying to clean up my pillow. She tilts her head to the side, sits on the edge of my bed and puts her hand on my leg for comfort, "Sweetie, I'll get you a fresh pillow, don't worry about cleaning up. You know, some patients choose to beat the system, and trim their hair before it starts to really come out. It can make the process a little easier to go through. If you'd like, I can send Michael in later on, he a social worker here and gives great cuts to everyone. Would you like that?" She continues to rub my leg.

I toss this around for a minute, and realize that maybe she's right, that maybe I should take a little control over this. "I would love that actually." I finally respond.

After lunch, Michael arrives with a little black case filled with professional looking shears and clippers. He washes his hands, "Darling, are you ready to be fabulous?" He comes over to the bed, plays with my honey tone tresses and starts to get an excited look on his face, "Oh darling, I know what we're gonna do! We're going to give you Barbra Streisand! So chic..." He helps me up and over to the visitors chair which he has placed in the middle of the room. I toss my donut pillow on the chair and try to find a comfortable position which proves impossible. My bottom is throbbing, so I click my morphine button twice.

Michael takes an elastic and pulls a tight, low pony tail a few inches above my neck. "Here we go Darling," he preps me as I hear the cutting of my thick hair in progress. My head jolts forward as the final strands are cut, releasing the tension of the pony tail. He hands me a mirror, "You are absolutely fabulous, hunny. Go ahead, check yourself out!" I have to admit, I kind of like this short cut. I've never had hair this short before, but this is pretty cool. I can rock this look! Until it all falls out of course.

When he leaves, I go to the bathroom and try my hardest to go, but I still cannot get anything out. I turn off the bathroom lights, run the water, and visualize faraway lands - nothing works. I haven't been able to pee in a week, I'm so frustrated, all I want to do is fucking pee! I take the bath towels I'm supposed to use for showering and fold them on floor into two knee pads. I struggle down onto all fours, and push a little pink container that's meant for vomit underneath me. I rock myself back and forth, hoping that this position will relax me enough to pee, but after an hour I still have no luck. Throughout the day, I attempt this position a few more times in the pitch dark of the bathroom – but have no luck.

Since I have my laptop now, the nurse gives me the wireless code for the hospitals internet connection. I'm swamped by at least 500 e-mails including lots of junk advertisements as well as a boat load of messages from family, friends and clients wishing me well, asking if I need anything and telling me they are praying for us. Finally, I sweep through the pile of e-mails and pull up Google. I take a deep breathe… preparing myself for the masses of information I'm about to take in as I research. "Acute Myeloid Leukemia" … search.

Acute Myeloid Leukemia: AML is common in male adults but rare under the age of 40. This type of Leukemia creates abnormal cells inside the bone marrow which grow very quickly replacing healthy blood cells causing the bone marrow to stop working correctly. This causes an increases risk of infection and bleeding as healthy blood cells decrease. AML can be caused by blood disorders, radiation, exposure to harmful chemicals, weakened immune system due to an organ transplant or problems with your genes. Once you are diagnosed with Leukemia, your doctor will determine the specific subtype of AML which are based on genetic changes or mutations.

Subtypes? I decide to look further into this, seeing that there are different types of AML, I start to wonder what that could mean as far as my diagnosis. I Google "AML Subtypes" and find charts explaining the types.

M0 (Undifferentiated AML) Average prognosis

M1 (Myeloblastic Leukemia with minimal maturation) Average prognosis

M2 (Myeloblastic Leukemia with maturation) Prognosis is better than for most other types of AML

M3 (Promyelocytic Leukemia) The best prognosis of all AML subtypes

M4 (Myelomonocytic Leukemia) Average prognosis

M4eo (Myelomonocytic Leukemia with eosinophilia) Prognosis is better than average

M5 (Monocytic Leukemia) Prognosis is worse than average

M6 (Erythriod Leukemia) Prognosis is worse than average

M7 (Megakaryoblastic Leukemia) Prognosis is worse than average

I wonder which one I have. I mean, it looks like it makes a huge difference between the different types of AML... I had no idea! I really thought it was a done deal with the title of Acute Myeloid, but there's more to this. When the nurse comes in, I ask her if she knows the answer to my burning question, but this is something apparently only a doctor can discuss with me. Dr. Ayers is not in this week however, and when I question the doctor who is doing rounds, he is unable to find any information on a subtype in my file, and tells me to wait to speak to Dr. Ayers when he returns. He does suggest that perhaps they haven't been able to identify the subtype as of yet, but admits that after this many weeks, it should be in the file.

The next morning, since I finally am given the okay that I can see my children after not seeing my babies in almost a month, Lucien keeps Adrian out of school and brings them in early to see me. I am shocked at how much they have grown in such a short time! Adrian's little face lights up, "Mommy!"

"Come here and give me a hug you monkey boy!" I call out to him, he comes over and I squeeze his little body.

"Mommy, bunny!" he hands me a little stuffed pink bunny before sliding off of me and reaching for the remote control for the TV. I help him to put on some kids shows and he is occupied to his heart's content watching TV and playing with the remote.

I turn my attention to Luciana who is snuggled in her carrier. She has gotten so big! I can't believe my baby is 10 months old already! Her hair is swept to the side with a purple poodle barrette, and she is sucking on her entire hand; poor baby is teething. I pull her seat in front of me and tickle her little toes, she scrunches up her nose and closes her eyes as she giggles a laugh of pure joy, the laugh of an angel. My babies have grown without me, their little lives containing so many daily activities that I will never know about. In this moment though, I can't think about this, I can only absorb as much of them as possible while I have the chance. I'm able to visit with Lucien and the kids for a few hours, before they have to head home to start the work day. I kiss my babies, hug them, stare them in the eyes and tell them Mommy loves them, and wave goodbye with a smile on my face – until the door closes. Then I lay on the bed with the pink bunny they brought me, and release my tears that I will not let them see.

Adrian and Luciana visiting me during my first inpatient admission at
Guardian Medical Center

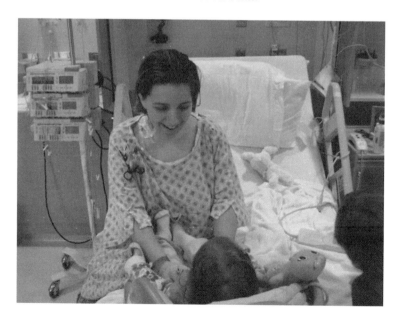

LAB RESULTS   NOCELLI, SHERI   6:40 A.M.
CHEM PROFILE   REF RANGE   03/31/08

WBC	4.0-10.0	.5
RBC	3.9-5.2	2.70
HGB	12.3-15.5	8.0
HCT	36-44	22.9
PLATELET CNT	140-440	45 / 1000 UL
K	3.5-5.0	3.6
M	1.8-2.5	1.9

Saturday morning I wake up extra early, excited for the day ahead. I position my donut pillow on the recliner so I can nibble at a piece of toast, sip some coffee and wait patiently for the morning to drag on. Eventually, there's a knock on the door... and I sit straight up in anticipation... I burst out in an overbearing smile when my father pokes his head around the corner; my mom comes in just behind him and my brother, Scott, picks up the end of the caravan. I sit up, leaving a blanket of hair on my pillow, which I can tell my parents see, but they smile and act like they don't. They each pull up a chair and we just sit and talk about anything and everything for hours. They stay all day, visiting for hours until it's time to say goodbye. They tell me they'll see me in the morning and they blow me kisses goodbye.

Since my family is in town and can watch the babies, Lucien stays with me overnight at the hospital. He arrives around my dinner time, which I can't stomach to eat anyway. I show him my new hair style and he updates me on all of the happenings of the day at home. As much as I would give the world to breathe in every second of him, I feel like I have to go to the bathroom, so I have to go in and try. I can't believe I'm wasting all this precious time staring at the bathroom floor when I should be spending time with Lucien. After an hour, I emerge from the bathroom, lugging my IV pole with me and am clearly upset. I try to lay in bed so we can watch a movie, but I'm in pain and feel like my bladder is going to explode.

After the nurse comes in for final rounds of the night, I want to try to pee one more time. I get down on my knees leaning on the bed with my elbows and place the pink bucket on the floor under me. I close my eyes and try to relax while Lucien rubs my back. In the background Julie Andrews is crooning about her favorite things to the Von Trapp kids... I tune in, trying to listen to every trill of her voice, trying to take my mind off of the task at hand, but still to no avail, I cannot get anything out.

The next morning is a circus with Lucien heading back home for the babies so that my parents and brother can visit for a few more hours before heading home to New Hampshire. They arrive to my room early and have hands full of gift bags to give me from everyone up north. My Aunts, Uncles, friends and my mother's co-workers have sent various care packages for me including jammies, body creams, lip balms, pens and notebooks, and a multitude of hard candies.

I'm going through all of my wonderful and much needed gifts when Dr. Ayers enters the room. He introduces himself to my parents with a hand shake, then washes his hands before addressing me. "Everything looks good with your blood counts this morning; everything is right where we want it to be. You'll need a transfusion to replace what's too low later on in the day. Also, I'm exceedingly concerned about your situation concerning going to the bathroom. I've been trying to let you naturally go, but it's reached the point now where without urinating or having any bowel movements, you're at a high risk of internal infection. I'm going to have the nurse set you up with a catheter right away."

My eyes bulge out of my head, "No, please give me the rest of the day to try. Please, I really don't want that!" I'm in a mini panic at this point.

"I'm sorry, we really have to. It's been too long, and we have to do something. The nurse will be right in." he waves to my parents and leaves the room.

I waste no time, looking over at my mother, "Mom, fill that jug over there." I point to a large plastic water jug on the counter the nurses had given me during my first night (which I never used.) She fills the jug with tap water and I guzzle the whole thing down. 15 minutes later I go into the bathroom, place the urine sample seat cover thing on the toilet and take the longest pee of my life. Yes! Victory! No way is anyone giving me a catheter!

When the nurse arrives a short time later with an arm full of tubing, bag looking things and a multitude of supplies for the catheter I am quick to inform her, "We won't be needing that." From this point on, I think to myself – I can do anything, beat anything, and accomplish anything I put my mind to. I got this.

The rest of the day I spend enjoying my families company laughing, telling stories and just bonding as a family. Scott and I swap quotes from our favorite movie The Cable Guy, "Hey, Scott... Nice jump Spiderman!" "Oh yeah, sis', red knights goin' down! Down, down, down!" We laugh until it hurts to laugh anymore.

LAB RESULTS   NOCELLI, SHERI   6:54 A.M.
CHEM PROFILE   REF RANGE   04/02/08

	REF RANGE	
WBC	4.0-10.0	.7
RBC	3.9-5.2	2.99
HGB	12.3-15.5	9.1
HCT	36-44	25.0
PLATELET CNT	140-440	23 / 1000 UL
K	3.5-5.0	3.6
M	1.8-2.5	1.9

LAB RESULTS   NOCELLI, SHERI   5:35 A.M.
CHEM PROFILE   REF RANGE   04/03/08

	REF RANGE	
WBC	4.0-10.0	.7
RBC	3.9-5.2	3.02
HGB	12.3-15.5	9.3
HCT	36-44	25.1
PLATELET CNT	140-440	19 / 1000 UL
K	3.5-5.0	4.0
M	1.8-2.5	1.9

The hours roll into days which roll in weeks. I'm in a comfortable rhythm as I get more and more accustomed to living at the hospital. My platelets are finally going up at a slow but steady pace some days, occasionally taking a dip down before climbing again. My red cells are finally starting to climb as well as the other numbers on the blood result printout the nurse hands me daily. I spend most of my days laying on my right side to avoid laying on the tubes leading to the central line, taking pressure off my rear which hasn't shown any improvement. I'm a lot more comfortable now that I can wear real jammies and not those hideous hospital gowns, and feel like I am starting to build back the pieces of myself, reforming some kind of an identity beyond numbers and test results.

Last night before bed I noticed that my hair is really thin in the back, and the amount of strands on my pillow, shoulders and clothing is out-of-hand heavy. As I was talking on the phone with Lucien last night and mentioning this, he offered to bring his buzzer in over the weekend. I'm embarrassed, but agree that it would be easier to deal with if we just take it off.

Finally it's Saturday, and time for Lucien to visit. He enters my little room, and my heart just flies as he comes right over to the bed and kisses me on the forehead. He caresses the back of my head, "Oh sweetie, I missed you." He whispers in my ear as we hug for an eternity.

After dinner, we decide it's time to take care of my hair. Lucien pulls the visitor chair to the center of the room, just like the social worker Michael did for my first makeover. I gradually get out of bed, grab my pole and make my way over to the chair. Even with my donut pillow, I hurt when I sit, so I tilt my body to one side trying to take the pressure off of the hemorrhoid. Lucien starts up the buzzer, leans forward to kiss my head, and starts shaving away what's left of my hair. As much as I am struggling with this as he's stripping away my locks, part of me feels like we are taking control – I'm not losing my hair, I'm choosing to take it off.

My nurse enters while we are in the middle of our salon moment and shares a big smile across her face. Lucien finishes up the last of the cutting, shuts down the buzzer and leans over my shoulders to embrace me; not noticing the nurse as she creeps back out of the doorway. We embrace for some time, until Lucien suggests a shower, which he assists me through the whole way. It's an extraordinary feeling as the shower rains over my smooth head and down my back – a refreshing cleanse.

By the end of this eventful evening, I am spent. Cutting my hair was emotionally draining and the shower physically exhausting.

We settle in with some lame made-for-TV movie for the night, poor Lucien all sprawled out on the recliner with a flat hospital pillow and a bed sheet. He stretches his hand over across the arm of the chair to my bed, where I cuddle him. The nurse comes in and hands me a cup with my sleeping pill, "You know," she softly starts, "I just have to tell you two, that I see a lot of moments that stand out, but when I walked in and saw you cutting her hair for her, that really struck me. Watching the two of you share such a beautiful moment filled with so much love and devotion; I just want you to know, that I will cherish and never forget that image."

When she leaves the room, Lucien gets out of the recliner and crawls into bed with me. We lay inches apart, staring into each other's eyes; eventually falling asleep wrapped in our love.

Summer 2007

Life could not be any better. Having Luciana as part of our family feels so complete; like we were always meant to be a family unit of four. We take this time to slow down a little in our lives, really trying to soak in every magical moment our children create with us. I drown Luciana in every hue and shade of pink I can get my hands on, enjoying every girly second.
In the spring we decide to put an above ground pool in the backyard, so that during the summer months we will have plenty to do with Loosh, Justen and Adrian without having to leave home with the baby. We have an eventful summer celebrating birthdays, baptisms, and just throwing massive summer parties with tons of food and margaritas flowing.

Luciana rocks for hours in a tabletop infant swing which fits right on my desk, so she is able to sleep right next to me throughout the day while we are working. She is an angel, sleeps through the night, laughs at every silly face we present, loves to model her baby fashion and just lights up our hearts more and more every day. The summer passes us by, turning to fall, and I can't believe how fast time is passing. By Halloween, I'm thrilled to dress Luciana as a little pink fairy – something I've been planning ever since we knew we were having a daughter. Adrian dresses as a big green dragon, and we trick or treat for hours, flaunting our beautiful children down the sidewalks of Lincroft. At

Thanksgiving we dress in our Dallas Cowboys football jerseys, and deck out the baby in a DC Cheerleader uniform for the big Turkey day game. Soon enough, we're decorating the house for Christmas and I can't believe the year is coming to an end.

All throughout the whole year, Lucien and I spend hundreds of hours in the recording studio, finishing up his new Rock album, "Deal With It". It's been an incredible amount of work writing, recording and producing this album, but we are so proud of the way it has been turning out. The music is real with meaningful lyrics, insane guitar riffs and solos and a unique blend of Jazz Fusion, Rock and Singer Songwriter feel. Lucien performs almost every instrument on the album, but shines on the guitar work which is his virtuosity. I'm thrilled to have been given such a large portion of the vocals which we share throughout the album. We're so proud of the entire album; it's a labor of love and we can't wait for the release date in February of 2008. Just before Christmas, we send the album off for its final mastering. The next time we hold it in our hands, it will be a finished product ready for resale.

Christmastime rolls around and as completely excited as I am (I must have been one of Santa's Elves in a past life), I sure am exhausted. I mean, I can see why, we had a baby, finished an album, have been working like mad on the house and a million other things. I do have a couple random episodes of getting faint while showering, passing out mid shower and falling into Lucien's arms – but we don't think too much of it. We figure I'm exhausted and still recovering from giving birth, so we move on with our lives.

We have so many things lined up this January; I honestly wonder how in the world we'll keep up with everything. We have photo shoots, radio interviews, TV interviews, band rehearsals, meetings with the record company regarding the upcoming "Deal With It Tour" and a million other tiny details as we prepare for the February 11th launch of the album. Time flies by, and before we know it – Deal With It is released with flying colors. Sales go through the roof, the radio plays it non-stop and the fans bombard Lucien with their praises of the album. Everything is perfect, just the way it should be in the world – lasting for two weeks, until I start getting this pain in my side. I otherwise feel like a healthy 23 year old wife and mother of two, rock n roller... but there's more here than meets the eye.

Look at me. Really look at me. Do I look like someone about to face a battle for my life? Do I look like someone who's body is secretly turning on me with cancer cells quietly sabotaging me from the very factory of my body, taking over my marrow, slowly taking over my body and my life? I don't see it... I don't see how it's possible, but sometimes it's what we can't see that can hurt us the most.

(Above: January 21, 2008) – About three weeks before first ER visit

Deal With It

Yeah, yeah.
Make the decision and face the day
There's no one to be by your side
Take it really slow
Cause your thoughts of tomorrow won't fade away

When times are looking bad
And they're hard to swallow
Now, think about all good times and leave the rest behind

Take one day at a time and the things that are so far become so near

And don't you feel like there's no one to believe in
You don't need an angel by your side

You have to wake up from the dream and face your days now
When it comes crashin down
You really have to deal with all the things you bring into your life
Deal with it
You really have to deal with all the things that fall into your life

Get up, get up, get up when it's time to get up
There is no time to be a stride behind
Catch up to yourself
Don't let the minds around you get in your way

And when you take another hit you have to deal with it
Get right out there and take no fears friend
You don't need an angel by your side

You have to wake up from the dream and face your days now
When it comes crashin down
You really have to deal with all the things you bring into your life
Deal with it
You really have to deal with all the things that fall into your life

Just one more thing before we go
This one dude by now you already now
Play with all the hands that your life deals you along the way
Take those chances and have no fears friend
You don't need an angel by your side

You have to wake up from the dream and face your days now
When it comes crashin down
You really have to deal with all the things you bring into your life
Deal with it
You really have to deal with all the things that fall into your life

PART II
. . .*Leukemia*

You work all your life

To play in this game work it overtime

Put on those shoes you need to

Brace them up, lace them up, can't sing the blues

Raise the sword - Give them a stare you know they can't ignore

Show your face - Let them see your scars

Back 'em down, turn 'em round, they won't get too far

Give 'em a fight, the fight of their life

Give 'em a fight now, Give 'em a fight now

You planned for this fight

And battered through, now kick it in overdrive

Annihilate, it's time to terminate culminate and liquidate

- Lucien Nocelli "Give Em A Fight" (Lyrics)

Note: Within this part of my journey, I have included the original online blog entries which I published during my hospitalizations, beginning with my second inpatient stay. At the time, I tried to update the blog daily, or as often as I could through the draining treatments. Many times, I would blog in a much more positive light about things going on, to project an upbeat mood, while in reality, I was struggling with the events of the day, which I chose to keep to myself. I have left these entries as-is to reflect my state of being at the time they were written.

SHERI NOCELLI

April 8 2008

Today I'm leaving the hospital for the first time since being first admitted 28 days ago. I exit my ivory tower, emerge from the revolving doors and breathe in this picture perfect Tuesday afternoon. The brisk air tickles my skin, daring me to smile – a dare I cannot resist. Perching on the cement wall surrounding the circular driveway of the hospital, I close my eyes and soak in the freedom. My Father-in-Law pulls into the driveway and enthusiastically comes around to open the car door for me before putting my bag in the trunk. Since it is a weekday, Lucien is teaching, but thankfully my Father-in-Law was able to move his schedule around to bring me home.

I arrange my donut seat on the passenger side, and slide myself into the car, trying to avoid putting any pressure on my rear. My movements are lethargic and labored as I stretch to close the door; I'm exhausted from this simple task. Finally, I find a comfortable position just as my Father-in-Law is getting into the driver's seat. "Alright kiddo, we did it. Here we go", he announces as he starts the car. As we start driving away from the hospital, my stomach rolls with a sudden anxiety. I'm so freaking eager to go home, to <u>my</u> home, to my family, my children... my bed, even! At the same time, I'm permeated with a sensation of fear; what if something goes wrong... will we be quick enough to catch it without daily blood draws and doctor visits? I feel like a baby bird being pushed helplessly from the nest by my caretaker, hoping that my wings will soar through the air and I can fly on my own. Can I? I know I'll be back in for a visit in two days, but leaving my protective haven is frightening all the same.

Cruising down the parkway, I get my first taste of my new found liberty. My Father-in-Law asks every three and a half minutes if I'm hot, if I'm cold, if I'm comfortable; adjusting the knob on the air conditioner before I even answer. This is my first inkling that while I'm released as a hospital patient, I am still a cancer patient. Life is not as I left it. I realize that this is my new reality; I will be babied and treated with kid gloves by everyone I come in contact with. Through my eyes, peering out at the world, nothing has changed, but through their eyes looking at me, I am a different version of myself. I am weak, vulnerable, needy and broken down. I am gaunt, bald, and dreary; I am a burden. I am a dismantled version of the person I used to be. This truly is my new reality.

I feel myself light up as we pull into the driveway. The burst of energy I feel internally, however, does not translate to my body; when I rush to get out of the car attempting to leap up the front stairs, I feel like I have run face first into an imaginary brick wall. I can't physically keep up with myself; I am out of breath and my legs literately shake underneath me. I am rescued by my Father-in-Law who instantly appears at my side, steadying my weary body in his arms. He assists me as I gradually climb the three stairs to the front door. I go to turn the knob, but hesitate as I remember there are too many germs lurking there for my low immune system; I lower my hand down in defeat. He reaches around me, opening the door for me, and I am able to enter my home.

Immediately, I am greeted by the mother of a student in the waiting room, who jolts to her feet, so excited to see me. She smiles, but I peer into her eyes. I witness the look on her face change as she takes in this new version of me, I watch as the happiness in her smile turns to pity. I don't really care though. I am here, I am alive, I am HOME and I want to see my children. After trekking to the second story, which feels like a slow motion climb up Mount Everest, I approach the playroom door. The sounds of cartoons fill the air as I crack open the door. "Mommy!," Adrian exclaims in his little voice, "Mommy you're back!" he runs over and hugs my legs. Luciana bounces in her pink saucer, sending all of the attached rattles into action. The babysitter, who I have never met before this moment, gets up from the couch with a grin from ear to ear, "welcome home!" Sigh... I'm home.

I'm drained after the drive, taking on a flight of stairs, seeing the kids and all of the emotion of the day, and head right to my room for a rest. I lay in my bed, snuggling with my blankets as I inhale their familiar scent, and drift into a blissful sleep to the sounds of my babies playing in the background. When Lucien gets out of lessons, and I am still in a deep sleep, he sits Luciana on the bed inches in front of my face. I stir awake to her little feet, her little hands waving around and her amazing little smile. Reaching forward, I grab my baby close to me, as Lucien leans in and we embrace together, the three of us.

After sitting together for a while, Lucien feeds the baby her night bottle and puts her to bed as I listen on the baby monitor. He then comes back into our room, and without a word he lays on his side of the bed. "Welcome home, Sweetie. I can't tell you how much I've missed you here. We have to enjoy every second together," he's staring into my eyes, cradling my face in his hand, "we've always worked so hard to be together, from the very beginning. We'll get through this together, just like we always have." We lay in a blissful silence for an eternity before we finally fall asleep in each other's arms, like we always have - like nothing has changed.

Waking up the next morning in my own bed actually has the power to make everything disappear like it never happened. For a split second, as I blink the sleep out of my eyes, I feel like I've been here at home all along. It's not until I feel the cool pillow on my bald head, that I realize this has not all been a bad dream – it's real. Lucien has already gotten out of bed; I can hear him downstairs taking care of Adrian for school. Over the baby monitor I can hear Luciana cooing in her crib and singing a song of oohs and aahs. Gradually I sit up and stand. The carpet feels foreign between my toes, and I almost feel lost without a pole to grab onto and no wires to maneuver. Creeping down the hallway, I get to Luciana's door; it's adorned with a little white quilted pillow with an appliqued tutu and reads in pink cursive letters "Shh... Princess Sleeping." From behind the door I hear her coos, which evolve into a giggle as she sees my head pop in the door.

"Well, good morning my little mama girl," I lean on the side of her crib for stability, "you've got so much to say today!" By now she is standing in her crib, gripping the railing. How ironic, both of our hands are holding onto this railing to assist our balance. I let go and reach for her around the waist to pick her up, but she wiggles in my hands and breaks into a jumping motion, which is too much for me to handle. I keep trying to pick up my baby, but my arms have become spaghetti and she is too heavy for me to lift. I can't pick up my own baby. "I'm sorry, mama," I apologize, staring into her big brown eyes, "I'll be better soon, and we can cuddle, and play, and dress up and dance and do all kinds of fun things my little mama." She reaches for my nose and blows raspberries from her lips – we both laugh at this, the best medicine in the world.

After a tiny breakfast of coffee and a piece of toast (about all I can stomach these days), I delve into my regimen of pills.

- Acyclovir – 400 mg, by mouth, two times a day (an antiviral medication)
- Fluconazole – 400 mg, by mouth, daily (an antifungal medication)
- Levaquin – 500 mg, by mouth daily for 7 days (used to treat fungal infections)
- Restoril – 7.5 mg, by mouth, nightly for insomnia
- Nexium – O.T.C – Twice daily before meals (to prevent acid reflux)

After this wholesome breakfast, Lucien suggests a shower. Just the thought of it exhausts me, but I know he is right – he always knows best! I make my way to the bathroom to get ready, and pause in front of the mirror. Last time I saw myself in this mirror – I looked nothing like this person staring back at me now. I have no hair on my head, dark cumbersome circles under my eyes and I am just about 30 pounds lighter than I was. I still have my eyebrows and eye lashes, which only adds to the strange image staring back at me.

Lucien walks in as I'm standing there which snaps me back to reality and the task at hand. I finish undressing as he turns the shower on, and we get into our tiny corner shower. I try to relax and enjoy the invigorating flow of warm water down my back – but I start to wobble – and have to reach out and hold onto Lucien's hips for stability. Finding my balance, I shake my head in defeat.

"It's okay, Sweetie, don't rush yourself," he assures me, "I'm here, I'll help you." He softy takes the bar of soap and cleanses me all over. Little by little, he gradually washes away the scent of my despondency. I lift my feet one by one into the palm of his hands, as he continues to cleanse me of my desolation. I raise my arms, and he soaps away my uneasiness. By the time he massages baby shampoo into my smooth scalp, I am refreshed, optimistic and ready to face the new day. Of all the drugs and medications I'm on right now, nothing makes me feel as well as his gallant love.

As much as it's wonderful to finally be home, my body cannot physically keep up with my mind. I spend the day resting in bed, dozing off, catching some cable T.V (which is like GOLD after the 24 channels I got at the hospital) and listening to all of the regular day to day activities unfolding all around me. At 1:30 the first student of the day is here... I find myself peeking out the window to see who it is, but I don't recognize this woman, she must be a new student. Every half hour when the next client arrives, I find myself curiously peering behind the curtain to see who it is. Familiar faces come and go while I sit alone in my little shell. Around 3:00, the baby sitter arrives; I listen in as she goes into the nursery, picks up Luciana (something I'm too weak to do) and feeds her a bottle. At 3:30 the sitter goes outside to meet Adrian when he gets off the bus. He gives her a big hug and they come inside.

At 5:00, Lucien runs me up a plate of dinner in between students. I fork around the piece of chicken, green beans and the mashed potatoes have a few bites of the mashed and take my pills. The stench of the chicken is revolting so I lock it in the bathroom and close the door. After a few minutes, I think maybe I can muster some energy to go see Adrian and Luciana. Opening the playroom door, I take in the scene in front of me; Adrian is watching Little Bill and playing with his Magnadoodle, while the babysitter gently bumps Luciana around on her knee. I stay for fifteen minutes or so, making small talk with the teenage babysitter, draw letters with Adrian and tickle Luciana's feet – after this I am zonked. I spend the rest of the night in bed napping until Lucien is done teaching. We sneak in a little cuddle time on the couch before my sleeping pill kicks in and it's back to bed for the night.

The next morning, it's time to go for blood work and an appointment back at the hospital. I get dressed in a comfortable sweat suit and put on my wig – there is no way I'm going out in public with no hair. Once Adrian is on the bus, Lucien, Luciana and I pile into the van and hit the road for the forty minute drive.

Dr. Ayers' office is part of a large Cancer center which is attached to the hospital where I'm being treated. It takes us a while to find the right wing of the Cancer center, where I sign in and we wait. There are a fair amount of people waiting for their appointments as well. They are mostly older - much older than me. Everyone has their own entourage with them of at least one person to be with them for their appointment. After a while I am called to enter, and am led to a small room with a massive scale, and two terrifying torture chairs – aka: blood drawing chairs.

"Please step on the scale," the male nurse instructs. He fiddles around with the metal sliding part until he settles on the groove indicating my weight of 129 pounds. I hadn't realized I've lost so much weight, last time I checked around Christmas time I was hovering around 155. "Please have a seat Mrs. Nocelli," the nurse guides me.

I start to freak at this point, "Um, I can't have blood done in this chair... I really need to lay down..." my eyes start welling with tears, "I really can't."

"It's okay, Mrs. Nocelli, we're just going to take your blood pressure and temperature, and we'll do your blood draw in the exam room." He calms and assures me as he wraps the blood pressure cuff tightly around my frail arm and sticks the thermometer under my tongue.

When we've finished, the nurse leads us past a bustling nurses' station and into an exam room at the back of the cluster. Before he leaves, he hands me a cup and points me in the direction of the bathroom. Ugh. Lucien and Luciana take a seat in the exam room and I make my way to the bathroom, shaking my head and shrugging as I lock the door behind me. Damn it! I guess I shouldn't have gone while we were waiting before, now I got nothing! I sit and try to relax, trying to release some kind of a sample. Ten minutes later I finally get something into the cup, but I start to worry at the color... why is it red??

Back in the exam room, Lucien is rocking Luciana's carriage back and form, calming her into a blissful sleep. I sit next to them, grab Lucien's hand and lean on his shoulder. He cracks a joke about the company name "Ritter" on the side of the exam table, which just happens to be my maiden name, "Hey look, maybe someone in your family invented this table."

"Yeah, my brother is a famous inventor and we didn't even know it!" I answer with a grin. We both giggle. There's a hard knock on the door, and the nurse enters with the inevitable collection of blood taking tools. I take my position on the examination table, laying back and immediately turn my head towards the wall – away from the line of sight of the needle – and the tears start to flow.

"I didn't even do anything yet! C'mon now, sweetie, don't make *me* nervous now!" the nurse has a southern twang, and laughs a hearty belly laugh at herself. Ignoring this, I just keep crying myself into a black hole of turmoil. Lucien comes to my side, taking my hand, "Just look at me, and try to relax. It's okay, it'll be over before you know it, and we'll be on our way back home."

Nonetheless, I cry hysterically through the entire blood drawing process, calming down only once the nurse has left the room shaking her head at my drama. Taking a seat back on the chair next to Lucien, I try to calm myself down knowing the worst part of this visit is over.

There is a gentle knock on the door and Dr. Ayers comes in, and heads right over to the sink to wash his hands. "Wow! You look so different; I didn't recognize you with your wig! You look great, how has it been to be home?" He takes a seat on his stool, wheels closer to us and waits for my answer. I respond that it's great; I've just been so tired. "That's to be expected, but the best thing you can do is rest. Okay, come up and have a seat on the table for a minute." I make my way on the examination table, trying to avoid the crinkling paper as best I can to no avail.

Dr. Ayers shines his otoscope in my eyes and mouth, asking me to say Ahhh. He prods my neck checking my Lymph Nodes, then listens to my heart with the stethoscope. "Great, everything looks really good, Sheri. Now, I'm going to listen to your lungs, so I'm just going to lift the back of your shirt a little, okay?" I nod, and he proceeds to place the cold metal of the stethoscope on my back, directing me to take a deep breath, and exhale, deep breath, and exhale. We do several rounds of this, which takes the wind right out of me. "Great, your lungs are clear," he takes the ear pieces out as he walks around towards the front of the table, leaning on the counter behind him. He proceeds to ask me a multitude of questions from a preprinted sheet; have you had any fevers, night sweats, diarrhea? Have you had any dizziness, fainting, vomiting, lethargy, pain or fatigue? I shake my head at everything – I mean sure, I've been tired, but I don't think beyond a reasonable amount for someone who just went through Chemo and weeks in the hospital. There are a multitude of questions which he continues to rattle off, while I shake my head at everything.

"I did notice you had some blood in your urine sample," Dr. Ayers continues with, "but, it appears that you have started to menstruate. Since your platelets are on the lower side, and we can't risk you going through your menstrual cycle right now, I'm going to put you on birth control to stop your cycle during the course of treatments. This should stop your current cycle that is starting, so we'll just have to keep an eye on that. The only other thing today is I'd like to check the hemorrhoid to make sure it's healing."

I tell him okay, I mean, I can't say "no", can I? So he pulls the curtain across the room to separate the table from the chair area where Lucien is sitting... for privacy from my husband I guess? I don't get it, but I pull down my sweatpants and the Doctor pokes at the area with his gloved hand, "Looks good, it's healing well." He announces. How dignifying. When I'm situated, I sit back in the chair next to Lucien and the two of us wait for the next move.

"So, your type of Leukemia is Acute Myeloid, which you know, but your type doesn't fall within the parameters of AML subtypes which we normally categorize with. When we got the results back from your first bone marrow biopsy, we were perplexed at the resulting Leukemic cells in your sample. I've been treating and specializing in Leukemia for many years here, and I have never seen a case like yours, nor has anyone here seen any cases of this type in the Cancer center. I got together with the other top specialists here and held meetings with our affiliate hospitals nationwide until one of the top oncologists recognized your specific type; she had seen it in one past case. Your Leukemia is very rare, and is a malformation with what we call translocation between chromosomes 16 and 21. Technically, it is considered AML with Maturation (FAB M-2), but has the additional chromosome abnormalities. There is only record of about fifty known cases of this type of Leukemia. Usually, any Cancer that has five hundred cases or less it is considered rare, so this type of AML, we are considering extremely rare. We feel we need to be aggressive with your treatments, you are young and otherwise healthy, and we feel that you can handle the strongest treatments available." Dr. Ayers takes a breath as he sees that I've started to cry. He hands me a box of medical grade tissues – but no amount of tissues can clean up the sorrow pooling out of me.

"The best course of action for you is a bone marrow transplant. There's not a lot of statistical or treatment information available for your type of AML, so we want to be aggressive and get you out of here and back to your family and your children," he continues in a steady, composed, reassuring tone, "the bone marrow transplant will give us the best chance at getting you out of here for good." He pauses, nods his head looking for a response from me to signal that I hear and comprehend what I'm being told.

I take a deep breath, "Okay. So how does this work? What do we do next?"

"Okay, so we're going to let your body recoup for a few weeks before we start your second round of Chemotherapy treatments. We're going to keep giving you strong chemo while we start the process of the transplant. In the meantime, do you have any siblings?" Dr. Ayers asks.

"Yes, I have one brother," I hesitantly respond.

"Great, if you think he'd be willing, we'd like to test him to see if he matches your marrow type. When we look for a bone marrow match, we test HLA, or Human Leukocyte antigens. These are hereditary proteins found on most cells in the body and are markers signifying which cells belong to the body and which don't. Being that the HLA antigens are hereditary, every person has two sets including one from each biological parent. When we look for a match, we test 8 to 10 antigens to ensure a successful marrow match. This confirmatory typing process ensures we find the very best match for each patient. Now, since the HLA tissue is genetic, siblings give the best chance of being a match with a thirty percent match rate. So, we'd like to test him first. If he is not a match, we will look into the National Bone Marrow Registry for the best match for you. But, let's take this one step at a time. If you could have your brother contact us, we'll set him up with a testing kit as soon as possible. It only involves swabbing his cheek, and we can test from that sample," he leans forward in his stool and asks me if there's anything I want to ask him.

"Well, I guess, of the other fifty people who had this type… how did they do?" my quiet, insecure voice feels barely audible.

Dr. Ayers looks down at the floor for a second, then lifts his chin and looks right into my eyes, "Being that this type of Leukemia is so rare, and there are not a great amount of studies on it as there are for more common types, it makes the statistics difficult to work out. Given the results of previous patients with this particular AML, we would have to group your case into the lower percentage of survival rates where we would place the more severe cases. However, we really can't go on the previous patients' results as a base, because there are so many other factors involved. For example, they could have been much older than you, had other chronic issues like diabetes, high blood pressure or previous Cancers. There are too many variables to really use their cases to gauge yours."

He pauses and softens his voice as he continues, "I once treated a young man who had just turned eighteen years old. He was diagnosed with a very severe case of Leukemia, and was given a very low chance of survival. He had chemotherapy and a bone marrow transplant, and achieved remission. He was driven, always with a positive attitude and determined to get out of the hospital. Now, he's celebrating his five years since the transplant, is married and is expecting his first child," he pauses, "We're going to get you better, and in five years, I'll be telling people about your story of beating this. We're going to do this together, okay?"

He offers a kind smile, and I can't help but smile back. I see the big picture. While this may be a hard ruthless battle, I will be victorious. I will prevail over this disgusting disease; it cannot stop me from living my life. Screw you Cancer, you are nothing to me. With my team assembled I am ready to battle. I stand at the front of my army, but I do not stand alone in this combat. My family, my friends, my husband, my children and my doctor will not let me falter – we are an unstoppable force, and Cancer doesn't realize who it's fucked with this time.

BONE MARROW BIOPSY EXAM RESULTS & DIAGNOSIS:

NOCELLI, SHERI
23 YR   F
PERIPHEAL BLOOD RESULTS   .
CHEM PROFILE   REF RANGE

WBC	4.0-10.0	1.6
RBC	3.9-5.2	2.8
HGB	12.3-15.5	9.0
HCT	36-44	25
PLATELET CNT	140-440	91

LYMPHS: 18   MONOS: 5   EOS: 1   BASOS: 3   BLASTS: 23

PERIPHERAL BLOOD COMMENTS:
Pancytopenia. White cells: 23% blasts
MARROW DIFFERENTIAL (%):
Erythroblasts: 21
Blasts: 37
Neutrophilis/precursors: 21
Eosinophils: 3
Basophils: 6
Lymphocytes: 6
Monocytes: 5
Plasma Cells: 1
ERYTHROPOIESIS: Decreased
GRANULOPOIESIS: Occasional dyspoietic hypogranulated forms – many forms with abnormally purple granules (possibly basophil lineage)
MEGAKARYOCYTES: Present
PLASMA CELLS: Medium sized to large cells with moderate amounts of cytoplasm. Fine nuclear chromatin. Conspicuous nucleoli. Cytoplasmic azurophilic granules present in a few blasts.
CELLULARITY: 70% cellular – Markedly hyper cellular for age

BONE MARROW COMMENTS: Decreased trilinear, maturing hematopoiesis. Much of the marrow is occupied by an interstitial infiltrate of blasts.
SPECIAL PROCEDURES: Immunophenotyping by flow cytometry shows 43% blasts positive for CD34, CD117, CD7, CD13, CD33 and in a subset CD56. Peripheral blood shows that the blasts are positive for myeloperoxidase and negative for TdT.

FINAL PATHOLOGIC DIAGNOSIS:

PERIPHERAL BLOOD: Pancytopenia with 23% Blasts

BONE MARROW: Acute Myeloid Leukemia with Maturation (FAB M-2) (addendum diagnosis includes note as follows)

NOTE: A Karyotyping study shows a translocation between chromosome 16 and 21, which is a recurrent translocation in de novo AML. The genes involved are FUS on 16p and ERG on 21q.

FINAL DIAGNOSIS: AML FAB (M-2) t(16;21) (p16;q21)

The prognosis of patients with this translocation appears to be unfavorable.

The next two weeks are heaven on Earth and I don't let a minute slip by without soaking in every ounce of it. I slowly regain my strength allowing me to spend more and more time with my babies during the day. By the second week, I am strong enough to be downstairs in our music studio waiting room. I sit at my desk, greeting clients, answering phones and scheduling. Things feel somewhat normal; the perfect soul medicine. I take my pills like a champ, try to eat as much as I can and rest to build my strength.

Every other day I go back up to the Cancer Center for blood work and a physical. Most mornings my blood counts are off, and I have to stay in the clinic of the Center for most of the day for treatments. The nurses are sweethearts; each taking their turn learning how to deal with my childish outburst when it's time to get an I.V. line put in. On these mornings, I am given Benadryl

124

usually by 9:00 a.m. and can barely keep my eyes open for the duration of my blood transfusions. Some days I need red cell transfusions, but usually I need platelets. The lunch cart lady rolls around offering me a sandwich, a bag of Lays and a bottle of water at noon; a poor selection for someone who is neutropenic. So I pick at the bread and the chips while I watch T.V. and gauge the rate of the dripping infusion into the tube... can't it drip any faster?

The nurses usually end up feeling bad for me since I hound on them to please, please, please make the transfusion go faster. They are sticklers with protocol however, and only up the drip rate when they're allowed to; once I've passed the tests of course. Temperature – check. Blood pressure – check. How are you feeling? (Great! I want to get out of here!) – check. Okay, we can up the drip rate slightly. It takes FOREVER and a day to get a little tiny bag of blood cells into me, but it's all for good reasons; to avoid a reaction. I understand, but am impatient all the same!

My doctor also schedules a bone marrow biopsy the week before I am getting readmitted to give us a base line for the next round of treatments. We need to see how much Leukemia – if any – is present in my marrow. The morning of the procedure, I take a HEAVY dose of Ativan to calm my nerves... which does zilch! In the car on the way to the Cancer center, I am a royal mess. Lucien spends the drive trying to calm me down, talking about the fun weekend we have planned and attempting wholeheartedly to get my mind off of the biopsy. By the time we arrive at the clinic, I am a mess, crying well before we even get into the room. The nurses all try to make light of the situation, cracking corny jokes and telling me the famous line, "it'll be over before you know it." Yeah? Really? I'd like to know how many of YOU have had your pelvis drilled into before... then, and only then, do you have the right to tell me it's no big deal.

I am completely awake and aware throughout the entire process. My body quivers as they instruct me to turn on my stomach on the examination table, I sob as the nurse swabs an area of my hip with alcohol and am in a complete melt down by the time they start administering shot after shot after shot of local anesthetic. The nurses and doctor are all talking to me, which I am completely oblivious too through my hysterical state. All the while, Lucien is gripping my hand, talking to me, trying his hardest to get me to focus – but even he can't get through to me. I am suddenly struck by a sharp piercing pain shooting from my hip all the way down my leg; I let out a blood curdling scream and shift my body away from the drilling needle. The doctors and nurses yell for me to stop moving, stay still, but it is beyond my control. They hold me down, and suck the marrow sample from my hip to finish the biopsy. No sooner do they announce they are finished, do they file out of the room, leaving me broken down, shaking and crying on the table. Lucien scoops me into his arms, squeezes me tight against his body, tucking my head under his chin and rocks me as he calms me down. He tells me is over, but the tears and shaking take an eternity to subside.

Eventually I calm down, and take the limping walk of shame out of the room, past the nurses' station and through the waiting room. The look of horror on the other patients' faces fire in my direction, vivid through their stares – and I limp out of the building completely embarrassed. By the time I'm in the car, I fall into a deep sleep induced by the heavy dose of Ativan I took this morning to calm my nerves – complete bull. The rest of the day I spend in a coma in bed from the supposed anti-anxiety medicine.

My time home starts to wind down, and readmission to the hospital is closing in on me. I find myself mentally starting to prepare for the chemical and mental hammering I'm about to endure. All the while, I try to maintain a level of normalcy for the kids. I feed Luciana all of her meals of green beans and rice, and cuddle with her on the couch for nap times. I read Dr. Seuss books to Adrian, complete with comical character voices before I tuck him into his Thomas the Tank Engine bed every night.

I find it an incredible gift when Luciana shocks us one evening with the sweet sound of her angelic voice as she exclaims her first word! "Ma ma ma ma ma," she looks right into my eyes as she calls my name! Her first word – and she waited for me to be here to witness this first of many firsts to come. My baby, she is such a joy in my life, and one of my shining stars to hold onto through my battle.

We celebrate Luciana's first birthday while I am home, since I will be in the midst of chemotherapy on her actual birthday May 1st. My baby is a year old. I wish I could throw her a big extravagant princess ball for this milestone year, but we settle with a small cake for four from the grocery store. We huddle around the lit candle, just the four of us and sing her the birthday song. I help her open her present of a Fisher Price set called "My First Purse" and her first tea set, all made of cloth pieces. The rest of the afternoon I play tea with her and Adrian. It's the perfect birthday celebration.

I sit one Saturday morning with my coffee, taking in the montage of pictures hanging in our living room, and realize that we haven't done a family portrait since Luciana was born. Since I'm not sure how downhill my appearance will go with the upcoming chemo, I decide I should schedule a photo shoot before I go back to the hospital. I dress the kids in their finest spring outfits, Lucien picks out a seasonally pink button down shirt and I head to my closet to find just the right ensemble. I start trying on different pieces to find the right match for what the rest of the family is wearing – and it hits me... everything in the closet actually fits! I try out jeans that I haven't worn since high school – and they all fit! Damn, this is pretty awesome! I laugh out loud to myself, "Wow! Thanks Chemo for giving me a whole new wardrobe!"

Feeling great about myself, I pick out a floral flowing skirt and a white halter tank top; I put on my wig and do up my make-up. The icing on the cake? I still have my eyebrows (for now). So, all primped up, we head out for our first family photo shoot to capture memories of our blissful little family unit. I want the kids to have an image of us all "American pie joyful" to look at now, and in the future. Maybe if they have these happy-go-lucky pictures when they're older, then the year Mommy wasn't home, didn't have energy and was sick all the time will be a distant, close-to-forgotten memory... or maybe just a bad dream.

Our family photo shoot taken right after my first round of intensive Inpatient Chemotherapy... I may be wearing a wig, but still had my real eyebrows! - April 2008

(This Page) Our family photo shoot April 2008, taken right after my first inpatient chemotherapy

Journal - April 22, 2008 (Tuesday)

Hi everyone! Well, today I was readmitted into the hospital to begin round two of chemotherapy. This one will not be as intense as the first time; there is one less drug this round (Mylotarg) and this course will run 7 days instead of 10. It's still an intense regimen, just a little less than last month. Since I've been in today, the only excitement was going down to small procedures and getting a triple line put in on my neck (always fun). It's a little less painful than last time though, so that's a positive.

I did see my doctor today, and he had the results back from last Fridays Bone Marrow Biopsy, he said there were no traces of Leukemia found, so *technically* we have achieved remission. In his words, the goal is to stay there now for "60 to 70 years". As encouraging as that news is, we have to remember though that Leukemia hides, and will come out again, so we are continuing with the chemo treatments, and the Bone Marrow Transplant. My brother, as willing as he was to be my donor, was not a match. Of my matches in the national registry the doctor said that they will be contacting 4 of the 7 good matches, and that they were all young which works in my favor. The overall feel of the day was optimistic, which is a really nice way to head into this second round.

I do want to say really quickly what a wonderful week home I had with my family. We were able to celebrate a proper Easter with the kids complete with baskets and an egg hunt. They had so much fun, it was precious.

We also got to celebrate Luciana's first birthday even though it was a week early. She looked like a little angel in her little Gymboree Ice Cream Party Dress. We had some portraits done, then came home had cake and gifts. All I can say is that girls got a sweet tooth!

At home after my first round of Chemotherapy... experimenting with
My wig and my little hats – the hats are WAY more comfortable! April 2008

April 22 2008 (Tuesday)

As much as I try to be a warrior as I return to the hospital for the first time in exactly two weeks as an inpatient, my heart is sinking. This morning I had to say goodbye to my kids and I have no idea when the next time is that I'll see them. I tried to explain to Adrian that Mommy will be away for a little while again, and he just continued drawing on his Magnadoodle until it was time to get on the bus for preschool. Sometimes I'm thankful for his learning and comprehension delays; especially in times like this where he doesn't understand that Mommy is sick. Luciana made the trip with us back to the hospital, all the way up to the Bone Marrow Transplant Unit.

This time around, I completely understand that I will be here for the better part of a month, making it a no brainer when it comes to packing my bag. I toss some notepads, pens, lip balms, body butters, jammies, Crocs, my laptop, camera and some pop tarts into my suitcase. These are the survival tools I'll need stocked in my bunker for this war. Entering the hospital lobby, we head straight for the elevator for the 4th floor – my new home away from home for the next 4 weeks. We get buzzed through the double locked air-tight doors of the unit and get led to my new room like royalty. This time around, they've moved me a little closer to the nurses' station... I guess I'm no longer considered the least "at risk" patient on the unit - an unsettling promotion.

Lucien places Luciana's carrier on my bed and I waste no time tickling her little feet and getting my peek-a-boo on. I want her to see every second of Mommy that she can – and while I am able. After an hour or so, it's time for them to head home to get ready for the work day, and with a crushing blow, I am alone in my solitude once again. As soon as the door closes behind them, I am a tearful mess, turning myself into a tight ball on the bed. As much as I thought I'd prepared myself for this – I realize now I'm nowhere near ready.

By mid-morning, I've calmed down and am gliding along with an even calmness – the only way to stay sane for the long term. Nurse Mary Ann is on today, she's a really hip younger nurse who I get along with terrifically, and I'm happy that she's on for my first day back. Dr. Ayers is away this week, but he has given instructions to another doctor who will be in doing rounds and will be in charge this week. Wow, is Dr. Stein *old*. He is the slowest speaking person I think I've ever met with his drawn out sentences; by the time he finishes one, I don't even remember what the beginning was about. He cracks abysmal jokes so ancient in wit that I don't have a clue what I'm supposed to be laughing at. He's not at all what I'm used to! Most of the doctors here are amusing and clever, and light up the room with their presence – not make you strain to understand them!

So Dr. Stein hands me a printout listing the treatments to expect on this round. After he leaves and spares me of his humor, I read it over – trying to understand the medical jargon scribbled in typical "doctor handwriting".

CHEMOTHERAPY ORDER FORM
NOCELLI, SHERI   4/22/08
5/26/1984   023YRS   F
DIAGNOSIS: AML
HEIGHT: 5'2" **WEIGHT**: 137 lbs
BODY SURFACE AREA: 1.65 m2
IS PATIENT ON STUDY PROTOCOL: Yes, AAML0531
THERAPY TO START: 4/23/08   **CYCLE OF DAYS:** 8
PRECHEMOTHERAPY MEDICATION ORDERS:
Zofran 16mg IV – 30 min prior to chemo (for nausea)
Ativan 1 mg PO – 30 min prior to chemo (for nausea)

CHEMOTHERAPY BELOW IN SEQUENCE IT SHOULD BE ADMINISTERED

DRUG (GENERIC)	DOSE PER UNIT	PATIENTS DOSE	ROUTE	TOTAL VOLUME	DATE TO BE GIVEN	24 HR DOSE	TOTAL # OF DOSES
Cytarabine	100 ms/m2	165 mg	IVP (a.m.)	Q12H -	Days 1-8	330 ms	16
Daunorubicin	50 ms/m2	83 mg	IVPB	In 250 m2 IVS over 6 Hours	Day 1, 3, 5	83 ms	3
Etoposide	100 ms/m2	165 mg	IVPB	500 ML over 4 hours	Daily Day 1-5	165 mg	5

TABLE KEY: m2 = meter squared   Kg = Kilogram   IVP = Intravenous push   IVPB = Intravenous piggyback   Mg = Milligrams

POST TREATMENT MEDICATION ORDERS
PRN N/V - Zofran – 8 mg PO/IV Q8n
      Ativan – 1 mg PO 28n
Neupogen – 6 mg subcutaneous injection x 7 dose 24hrs after
      chemo is completed

Having no clue what the majority of this stuff means, I tend to hone in on the negative words popping off the page at me like IV, INJECTION and INTRAVENOUS. I try not to get myself all worked up, and trade this paper for the remote to tune into my normal hospital TV regimen. Just as I'm settling in with The View, Nurse Mary Ann comes in with a little Dixie cup in hand.

"Hey Sheri," she gently greets me, "I brought you some Ativan, we're going to be sending you down to special procedures to get your central line put in pretty soon. Just let me know if this isn't enough, and I'll get you some more before you go down." She hands me the cup, a bottle of water, watches me take the pills and heads for the door. "I'll come back in and check on you in a half hour, and we'll go from there." She smiles and leaves me.

Ugh. Two Ativan are no match for my nerves. Immediately, the horrific memories of my last central line procedure flood vividly into my mind, and I am a mess. When Nurse Mary Ann returns a half hour later, I am clearly wide awake and in the beginnings of a mini breakdown. She swiftly administers another Ativan before calling for transport to come and fetch their next victim.

This experience is just as traumatic as the first time around. I've come to the conclusion that I am immune to Ativan – the only effect it has on me is making me extremely nauseous (ironic considering it is also used as an anti-nausea medicine). By the time I'm being pushed away from special procedures, with my new central line inserted, I am wiped out, literately falling asleep during my ride back to the fourth floor. Okay, Sheri, time to gear up for round two. Ding, ding.

Journal - April 23, 2008 (Wednesday)

Hello! Well, today I started my second round of chemo. I got three different drugs today (I don't have the names in front of me though). Other than that, it was a pretty calm day with not too much else happening. Here's a picture of me getting the chemo today.

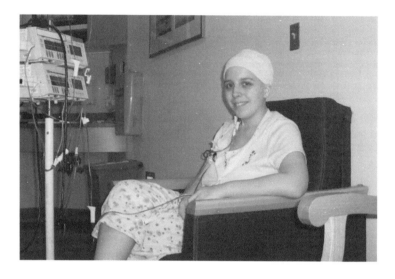

It's nothing eventful, just different bags hung up on the IV. The orange tube you see is one of the Chemos, it's actually a light sensitive one that had to be hung on the IV pole in the dark before they gave it to me, if it gets any light it goes bad. (I don't know, I guess I find that interesting).

So, that's it for today. I feel good, optimistic and am looking forward to watching America's Next Top Model tonight... hey gotta have fun! :)

Journal - April 24, 2008 (Thursday)

Hi everyone, day two of Chemo went well. I'm starting to get tired again, and I really miss being home with Lucien and the kids. I did get a print out about the drugs I'm getting during this round of Chemo. I'll be getting Cytarabine IV pushes every 12 hours for 8 days, Daunorubicin (Ara-C) on Days 1, 3, 5, and Etoposide daily for the first 5 days. The doctor today told me that for me to qualify for the Bone Marrow Transplant, I have to have an echocardiogram, some kind of deep breathing test, and meet with the social worker and have a psycho analysis to make sure I don't have a screw loose.. haha, I laughed and told them, "Okay, I'll have to act normal that day." So that's all no big deal and I'll probably do most of those things tomorrow and maybe over the weekend. My father in law visited today for a while, so that was really nice. I also spent some time shopping for a travel sized guitar online, that's what I want for my birthday so that I can play while I'm in here. Otherwise, spirits are good, and everything looks good today!

Journal - April 25, 2008 (Friday)

Hi everyone, day three of Chemo has arrived. Today I'm exhausted. They woke me up at 7:30 this morning and brought me downstairs to have the Echo Cardiogram done. It was kind of interesting actually; it was just an ultrasound of the heart. Everything there looked good. Then they whisked me away to do the pulmonary test. I had to breathe into this huge machine taking deep breaths on command and all this wacky stuff. I did fine with that too. So at least those two tests are out of the way so we can try to get this transplant moving along.

I got a ton of emails today, it was so nice to hear from everyone. And before I forget, Happy Birthday Uncle Skyp!! I wish we could have made it to your surprise party, it sounded like a lot of fun. And also to let everyone know, I'm mad at Lucien because while he was running errands today he christened the new Johnny Rockets burger place at the mall without me! My burger partner tried the Rocket without me, I'm astonished! Well, I hope that was the best, juiciest, scrumchiest burger you've ever had! Just kidding hunny, I love you :) I'll update everyone tomorrow, bye for now!

April 25 2008 (Friday)

I'm not a morning person in normal day to day life, so this waking up early business is for the birds. I'm starting to get used to the early morning blood draws again, and am almost able to sleep through them. Today the tinny taste in my mouth as they draw blood from my central line in my neck is so potent though, that I can't help but get up for some water. Just as well, since I know I have a whole schedule of tests lined up for today, which I'm sure we'll be starting bright and early.

Sure enough, 7:30 on the nose, transport is here to whisk me away to the magical land of unicorns, rainbows and Echocardiograms! This test is a graphic outline of the heart's movement. It uses ultrasound to get pictures of the heart's chambers and valves, allowing the sonographer to evaluate the pumping action. This basically assesses the overall function of the heart, while also checking for heart disease or other complications. I get wheeled into a tiny curtained off cubical, one of ten or so, and wait for my turn. Eventually, a nurse comes into my area pushing a machine with her in one hand and closing the curtain with the other. She blankly asks me to raise my pajama top, which I do without hesitation; after all, do I have a choice? That's the one thing you quickly learn when you're inpatient; they tell - you do.

Now the nurse places three sticky electrodes on my chest; one of my pet peeves, these little pieces of disgustingness never fail to make my skin crawl. She attaches the electrodes to the ECG monitor to chart my heart's electrical activity. She asks me to lie on my left side – easier said than done now that I'm all wired up, but I shimmy around eventually landing in the right position. She waves the wand around my chest until she finds what she's looking for.

"See this right here?" she points to the screen at a fuzzy incoherent mess of black and white static, "This is your heart. The movement you see is your heart beating." She continues to look at the screen, occasionally repositioning the wand to get different views of my heart. I lay still, with my chest exposed, wires all around and watch as my heart pumps in a steady rhythm on the screen putting me into a hypnotic trance.

When the test is done, I cover myself up and wait to be brought back to my room. It comes as a surprise when the transport guy arrives and tells me I'm going to get a pulmonary function test. I should have known; I have so many tests to do today that I'll probably be ping-ponged around the hospital until they're all complete. When we arrive to the area of the test, I am moved to a wheel chair and pushed into a hallway to wait. A few minutes later an older technician in a stark white coat comes out of one of the rooms.

"Hi there, are your Sheri?" he asks, which I answer with a nod. "Alright then, let's go." He steps behind the wheelchair and brings me into the little room he just came from. Taped on the door is a computer printout reading "Shhh. Pulmonary Function Test in Progress" which looks like it's been hanging here for quite some time judging from the dust bunnies dangling from the corners. He silently closes the door behind us before turning right to business.

"Have you had a Pulmonary Function Test before?" he asks, and I shake my head – my second silent answer in two minutes. "Okay, so basically we're going to be measuring the function of your lungs using assessments of lung volume, capacities, rates of flow and gas exchange. So just follow my instructions and we'll be finished before you know it." Great explanation Doctor Personality. He wheels me closer to the massive machine in the center of the room. It looks like some kind of U.F.O. apparatus, with tubes, pumps and buttons all over.

"This is the mouth piece, place this in your mouth and close your lips around it, please," he instructs. I lean forward a little, positioning this awkward white pipe into my mouth as best I can. He then takes out this clip thing and puts it on my nose. "The nose clip will make sure that your air is coming from your lungs and not your nostrils." Gee, maybe you could have told me what you were doing *before* you clipped my nose closed? I can tell I'm not going to like this test already.

The test starts out by breathing normally into this machine for about a minute, until you're instructed to take a very deep breath in, then release the breath as long as you can until every bit of air has left your lungs. Doctor Personality instructs every step in a total un-encouraging droning tone, "Breath normal... okay, now deep breath in. Now deep breathe out... push, push, push, push, push, push, deep breath in. Good." I breathe normal into the machine for a few seconds, but my next instructions are already being given. "Now, same thing, breathe normal then deep breathe in, breathe out, then I'm going to have you do short little pants, heh, heh, heh, heh, heh, heh, until I instruct you to stop." As we run this drill, my nose starts dripping, which I have to ignore till the end. After he tells me to stop, I remove the clip, grab a tissue and wipe my nose. This must happen to everyone considering the strategic placement of the tissue box *right* next to the machine.

The technician doesn't seem to notice, or care, about my running nose and keeps rattling off instructions. "Now, I'm going to calibrate the machine, and then we're going to do the next test. Breathe normal, then I'll instruct you to take a deep breath, let it alllllllll the way out, repeat this, then take a deep breath in and hold it. You're going to hold it for 10 seconds until I tell you to let it out." He flicks a switch and the machine goes into a high pitch hissy fit, sounding like it's going to take flight. "Okay, breathe normal," he abruptly starts, "deep breath in, now out... blow, blow, blow, blow, blow, blow, blow... deep breath in.. now hold it. Hold it, hold it, hold it, hold it, half way there... hold it, hold it, hold it... and breathe out."

I'm exhausted! I look like a hot mess with my nose running, cheeks flushed, eyes watering and ugh... my lungs feel like they are about to implode. The doctor is staring at rows of multicolored graphs on the computer which are images created from my forced breathing. He gruffly stands up, starts wheeling me back into the hallway and heads back to the room. "Thank you." He mutters as he disappears into the room. No Doctor Personality, thank you! Thanks for the lack of support through this; it sure would have been nice to have a little cheering section, or maybe just a "Good job" or two. Oh well... I sit in my little wheel chair, look down, pick at a thread on my little blanket Nurse Mary Ann had given me for my morning adventures, and enjoy the chance to breathe normally again.

The rest of the day sways towards the uneventful side of the spectrum. In the afternoon, my mom calls to check in and to fill me in on all the excitement going on in New Hampshire. Tonight they are throwing a huge surprise birthday party for my Uncle Skyp. I can picture all of my aunts, uncles and cousins, having a great time, eating, laughing, dancing and being their regular crazy selves. I wish I could be there; I miss my family so much. It's such a wacky group of people and when you fling us all together in one room, things get foolishly amusing. In the evening, Lucien calls, and I explain all the tests I had, what I watched on T.V. and all the riveting details of my day. He tells me about his day teaching, Adrian's school shenanigans, Luciana's new milestones and other little tidbits of family life I might like to hear about.

Journal - April 26, 2008 (Saturday)

Hi everyone! Things are going okay here, I'm starting to feel really tired now from the Chemo, and this sinus infection I'm dealing with too. The cough is driving me insane! I am happy though because it is finally the weekend, and Lucien is here visiting me. I wait all week for his visit. We'll probably watch a movie tonight, snack and cuddle as much as we can. Not too much else went on today, I pretty much slept all day until he got here. So other than being tired, it's been an uneventful day. I'm just looking forward to a nice date night with my sweetie.

April 26 2008 (Saturday)

It's an odd feeling to wake up after a full night of sleeping, and still be heavy with exhaustion. The chemo is starting to wear me down again, stealing away what little energy I have in one clean sweep. Usually, during the week I try to force myself to stay awake in the morning, so I don't miss my afternoon shows. Later today Lucien is coming to visit though, so I try to squeeze in every second of sleep I can fit before he gets here. I dose off and on as nurses come and go, the cleaning lady does her business and the food delivery girl drops off my blue domed meals. My eyes drift open, survey the person in the room, and heavily close again sending me back into my long nap.

Its 3:30 and I hear the door, open my eyes, and am jarred awake! Lucien is finally here! He puts his bags down on the recliner, and comes right over, hugging and embracing me. It's forever until we break our hold, but we remain sitting as close as we can while we take in each other's presence, like opposite ends of a magnet, holding onto our connection as long as we can.

He starts to unpack some presents from home; a frame with the kids' picture in it, a new notebook and a gigantic purple pen – this thing is literately a foot long! "I figured, this way, you can't lose it! I mean, how can you lose a giant purple pen?" he explains with a big goofy grin. I love it. I love that we can be so ridiculous and immature with each other; it's such a foundation in our relationship. During the course of a normal day, 90% of our conversations are wisecracks, celebrity impression voices and sarcastic remarks – it's freaking hilarious. We laugh so much, I swear if we die in our house, our ghosts will be the kinds that you hear laughing in the night – humor is at the core of our relationship.

When I put my order in for dinner, Lucien heads downstairs to the cafeteria to grab himself something so we can have our meal together. As my appetite and taste is starting to decline, my choices of acceptable foods are swiftly diminishing. I have learned which items on the menu sway towards the bland side – and I stick to those few choices. Lucien, however, has loaded up his tray with all kinds of goodies. He has a medium rare burger, a salad, French fries, soda and a piece of chocolate fudge cake. While all of this looks incredible, I'm limited in what I can have now that my white cell count has started to drop, landing me on the Neutropenic diet. This diet helps protect my body from bacteria and other harmful organisms lurking in certain food and drinks. I'm not allowed to have any salads, deli meat, and certain soft cheeses like Brie, Bleu and Gorgonzola. I can't have any rare or uncooked meats, fish or eggs – only meat cooked well and no runny eggs. I also have to avoid any uncooked vegetables or uncooked fruits unless they have a thick skin I can peel off like oranges and bananas. The hardest part of this diet for me is no salad... it's actually one of the few foods I'm craving, and it's off limits; go figure!

After dinner, and a bite of fudge cake, I'm exhausted again. We flick around the T.V. until we land upon some random Jennifer Aniston movie to settle in with for the night. As we're watching, my hands start to bother me with a burning sensation, causing me to continuously take my hand out of Lucien's hand to scratch. It's at this time that I realize the palms of both hands are covered in a red blotchy rash. Upon further inspection, I notice that the bottoms of both feet are also covered.

When the night nurse comes in to give me my sleeping pill, she knows right away what I'm showing her. "This is very common; it's called an Ara-C rash referred to as hand-foot syndrome. Many patients get this rash after being administered Cytarabine. It can be very uncomfortable, but as soon as you're done with the Ara-C the rash will go away quickly. In the meantime, I'll get you some topical moisturizing cream and some Ibuprofen to help with the discomfort." She then leaves the room to get the cream and pain meds for me.

Lucien and I continue to watch the movie, and I try my best to hide my discomfort from the rash. Before bed, he helps me cream my feet and hands and kisses me goodnight on my forehead. He makes his little pull out bed next to me, and tries to find a comfortable position, squishing the horrible hospital pillow around into a ball and pulls up the thin bleach white sheet to his chin. We wish each other goodnight. He's right next to me, but I feel so far away.

I lay in the bed, with my feet poking out the bottom of the sheets to allow the cream to stay in place. My hands lay flat at my side, palms facing up, again so the cream can work its magic. Tubes lay strewn across me, attaching me to my IV pole. I turn my head towards Lucien; I can see him clearly even though all the lights are out – hospitals are never completely dark between all the little lights shining off of IV equipment and the glow from the hallway halogens seeping under the door. I watch him as he falls asleep, despite the uncomfortable circumstances he's dealing with. I find myself mimicking his breathing until I am inhaling and exhaling in rhythm with him which sends me into a peaceful sleep.

Journal - April 27, 2008 (Sunday)

Hey everyone. Today was a nice relaxing day with Lucien. I love when he stays on the weekends; it's what I look forward to all week. I'm feeling okay, other than a really bad rash. I had this same rash on my first round of Chemo, so I know it's going to get worse. It's caused by the drug Ara-C. It's pretty bad and very itchy, and will keep spreading until the day I stop getting the Ara-C. So that will be Wednesday – I can't wait! It's the worst rash you could ever imagine. Anyway, Lucien just went home to the kids and its back to just me, hanging out in my little hospital room. Sunday nights get lonely after having Lucien here with me for the weekend. So I'll probably just lay low and watch some TV.

Journal - April 28, 2008 (Monday)

Hello! Today was yet another uneventful day. I'm starting to get really tired, and just feeling a little sick, but that's to be expected. I'm just feeling everything a little sooner than I did on the first round of Chemo.

Anyway, I revamped the website today which took most of the day. I had some time to try out the new pen Lucien brought me over the weekend (that's the large purple thing I'm holding in the picture). The thing is like the size of a hotdog. He's right, it's big enough that I certainly won't lose it. And it matches my jammies!

So that's it for today, I still haven't met with the lady who has to make sure I'm not a nut case with the psycho analysis thing (for the bone marrow transplant approval), so hopefully that will happen tomorrow.

Journal - April 29, 2008 (Tuesday)

Hey everybody! Again, nothing much went on today. I have a sinus infection that I've had since before I came back into the hospital for this round, and it got a little worse today, so they took a chest x-ray to make sure it doesn't turn into anything else. That took all of 5 minutes of my day. Other than that, nothing new on my end really. Tomorrow Lucien is bringing the kids to visit, so I'm really looking forward to seeing them. I talk to them every night on the phone, and it's amazing all the new things they're saying and doing even since I saw them a week ago. So I'm just going to hang out tonight, maybe watch some Dancing With The Stars (go Kristi!) and of course talk to the munchkins before they go to bed. I can't wait to see them tomorrow though!

April 29 2008 (Tuesday)

Things are starting to fall into more of a routine and life living in the Bone Marrow Transplant Unit is starting to build somewhat of a normalcy. I know all the nurses, doctors, technicians and cleaning staff by first name. It's awkward to admit, but I feel at home here now – no longer a visitor to a foreign and unknown land, I'm learning to thrive with the locals. I don't know how much of this new level of comfort is real, and how much is my subconscious kicking into survival mode. It doesn't matter, because I feel that if I can get through this without being miserable, then I will be a stronger competitor in this whole game. If endorphins are the key to winning then I got this in the bag.

I'm not used to actually feeling sick while in the hospital – other than Chemotherapy sickness of course. Having a sinus infection while battling the Chemo symptoms simultaneously is cruel and unusual punishment if you ask me. I've been suffering with a runny, stuffy nose and a little cough since just before I was admitted. Once the Chemo started and my white blood cells dropped, I've only gotten worse with the cold.

Doctor Ayers is getting progressively more concerned about the sinus infection, especially because today it took a slight turn for the worse, so he orders a chest X-Ray to see what's going on. A technician comes to my room with a portable machine in tow. The thing is huge and barely fits through the door; I'm truly amazed that they can bring the X-Ray to you and not have to cart you down to radiology. The technician adjusts my bed so I'm sitting in a perfectly upright position and places a big metal sheet wrapped in rubber on my chest, asking me to hold it in place. It's difficult to hold still since I am having a hard time breathing from the infection, but the whole test is done in a matter of a minute anyway.

This whole X-Ray takes up just about five minutes of my day. After it's over, I flip right back over to my normal routine of T.V, napping and blogging. The nurses come in and chat occasionally, asking me how the kids are doing. With great delight, I share with everyone that my babies will be visiting in the morning. I feel myself glowing with excitement every time I talk about their visit. It's been way too long since I've seen their little faces. I do talk to them on the phone every night, but it's just not the same. I love hearing their little voices, which sound even slighter through the phone.

The next morning finally rolls around; I can't wait to see the kids! Finally, I hear the faint pint-sized sounds of Adrian's voice coming from down the hallway and I sit up straight in bed awaiting their arrival! The door opens, and Adrian comes running right over to me! "Mommy!" he jumps on my bed and I maneuver around so that he doesn't hit any of my tubes or wires. He starts poking around the plastic clamp which dangles from my shirt, "Mommy, why do you have scissors?" he questions. I'm impressed by his inquiry, or more in the way he has asked since this is such a complete sentence coming from him.

"They're not scissors, they're a clip to hold my wires up so they don't pull on me," I start to explain, but he is already reaching for the remote control to the T.V. I switch gears, "Do you want to watch T.V?" I ask as I put on some cartoons for him. He jumps into the recliner and tunes into the show I've put on for him; this is Adrian at his happiest. Lucien takes Luciana out of her carriage and hands her to me on the bed. He's styled her hair into a spout, and dressed her in the cutest little sweat suit! "Ma, ma, ma, ma!" she exclaims, and I can't help myself from grinning ear to ear! As she speaks, I can see she's sprouted a few new teeth since last week, which I can't believe! Both of my babies have grown up so much in a week, it's shocking actually. They stay for a few hours, which flies by way too fast and it's time to say goodbye before I know it.

Later on, right as my hemoglobin transfusion is finishing up, I get a surprise rare afternoon visit from Dr. Ayers. He explains to me that things are moving along very smoothly as far as the Bone Marrow Transplant goes. They've been testing several of the best matches from the registry, and are in the process of scheduling more extensive blood work and HLA testing with the best candidates. He expresses with promise in his voice that the goal is to go ahead with the transplant on my next inpatient stay, amazing news, as this is the planned to be the final blow to the Leukemia.

This gives me a timeline to hope by.

Journal - April 30, 2008 (Wednesday)

Hello! This morning I got to see the kids. It's so amazing how much they can actually change in a week. Luciana has so many teeth coming in, she looks like such a big girl. Adrian had so many questions, about the tubes and everything which is new, he never used to ask about things like that.

I did see my doctor today, and he said that he is hoping for the Bone Marrow Transplant on the next round. That was really encouraging to hear, because the sooner we get going with that, the sooner we can start working on recovery. They did have to give me blood today, because my hemoglobin levels were low. All the other numbers look good and haven't dropped yet. That's all for today, it was so nice to see Lucien and the kids, that totally made my day.

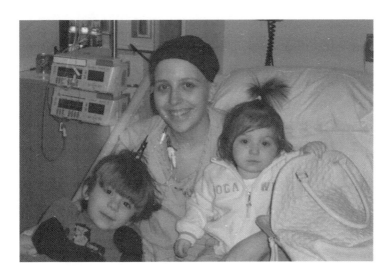

Journal - May 2, 2008 (Friday)

Well it's been a crazy two days! First though, May 1st was the baby's birthday, Happy 1st Birthday Luciana!!

As far as me, I have a sinus infection that is getting worse by the day (at least I think it's a sinus infection), so I've been feeling pretty sick. Yesterday we got a false "You can go home today" alarm. So I started packing my stuff, and five minutes later the doctor came back in the room and said that I had to stay because I had an appointment in the morning. It all worked out in the end, because last night I got a high fever and got a lot sicker and had a rough night.

So this morning I had my appointment, and the doctor came in with the same line, "Okay, you're going home today". But once I told him about the fever last night, he changed his mind and said I have to stay. I'm perfectly fine with that, because the last thing I want to do is to go home for a few hours only to come back to the ER with a fever. It's crazy, all the back and forth, but this is the best place for me to be, especially if I'm not feeling well to begin with.

That's it for now, thanks for all the e-mails! I love hearing from everyone!

Journal - May 3, 2008 (Saturday)

Hey everyone. Today was a lot of fun because my Mom and brother came down from New Hampshire to visit. We had a really good time. I was going to go home this afternoon, but because of the sinus thing I have they did a catscan which does show inflammation and infection. So that, and the fact that my blood counts are starting to go down now from the chemo made the doctors and myself agree that staying here is the best thing for me to do.

So things continue here, kinda slow and boring compared to the normally crazy lifestyle we lead. I really miss Lucien, he usually comes and stays with me on Saturday nights, but he has a show tonight. I'll see him all day tomorrow though, so I'm really looking forward to that.

Journal - May 5, 2008 (Monday)

Hey everyone. Today my blood counts went down a lot more, which is good, that's to be expected after

Chemo. I had to get red cells and platelets through the IV since the numbers were low. This is the part of treatment when I get really tired, and it gets hard sometimes to get on the computer every day. I really miss the kids, and Lucien, and just being home and working... I miss everything and want to get back to the normal routine.

Things are good overall, I'm just exhausted. I'll try to update every day, but it might run into every other day for a little while until the blood counts start to go up again.

Journal - May 7, 2008 (Wednesday)

Hey everyone. I tried to update yesterday, but the Internet wasn't working here. Yesterday was a little crazy.. Lucien brought the kids up to visit me, but the whole time they were here I was having a pretty bad nose bleed. It lasted two hours, and the doctor's weren't able to stop it. It eventually did on its own, but I was pretty upset that I really didn't get to enjoy the kids. The doctor also mentioned that he would like for me to meet with a psychologist to work on my "needle" phobia. He told me they would work on getting over the fear with me by doing exercises like injecting an orange. My response — why? So then I can have a fear of oranges? Just let me cry, that is my coping mechanism. It shouldn't bother anyone if I want to cry, let me cry through the needles — it's how I deal with it.

Today's been pretty good; I'm still just really tired. If things stay stable for the next couple days, then I could get to go home for Mothers Day. I hope it works out.

I also want to let everyone know about a bone marrow drive that my friend Mya has organized in my honor. All of the information on the drive is on the website. Please become a donor if you are able, and you could help to save the life of someone like myself who needs a transplant. I also want to say a big Thank You to Mya for all of her time and work she's doing to set up this drive, you're the best!

May 7 (Wednesday)

I finally feel my strength starting to creep back gradually but steadily. This past week has been crazy all because of this awful sinus infection which has been haunting me for weeks. Wednesdays Lucien keeps Adrian out of school and brings the kids up to visit me, which I can't wait for this week especially. Just before they're due to arrive, my nose springs a leak.

The blood starts to pour out suddenly and swiftly without warning, without reason. I try like hell to keep it under control myself without asking for help; I hate bothering the nurses. With one hand holding a pile of tissues to my face, and the other hand guiding the I.V. pole; I make my way as fast as I can over to the sink where I snatch as many paper towels as I can from the dispenser. By now, the tissues are drenched, so I lean over the sink to quickly swap hands, covering my nose with the paper towels. As I make the switch, blood drains into the sink at such speed, that I realize no amount of paper towels are going to do the job. I go back to bed, and place a towel on my lap to avoid messing the sheets. With one hand I'm holding the paper towels, and with the other I pinch at the bridge of my nose trying to get the vessels to clot (a trick I learned from my Elementary School nurse).

It doesn't slow down at all. Just as I'm attempting to swap out for another paper towel wad, Lucien and the kids come in. He takes one look at me, and beckons for help from the nurses who rush in and scold me for not calling for help. They fuss around me trying to see how bad the bleed is, and how they're going to take care of it. Peeking above the towel they have handed me to use, I watch helplessly as Lucien puts something on the T.V for Adrian, and rattles a cloth baby book around for Luciana. This nose *has* to stop! I am *not* going to miss spending this little bit of time with them!

A half hour later, nothing has changed. My nose is still bleeding with such force that the nurses have set up a bucket at the foot of the bed. They have me lying on my stomach, leaning over this bucket, letting my nose drain a disgusting, revolting river of red. They tell me my platelets are very low (as per my morning blood work), so my nose is just not able to clot. For two hours my nose bleeds at this rate, eventually letting up – just as it's time for Lucien and the kids to leave. My whole visit with my family I just spent hunched over a bucket, bleeding.

I am a very positive person. I try to always see the bright side of everything no matter what, but this is a tough pill to swallow. I don't get to see my children or my husband often at all, and to lose this precious two hours with them is enough to send me into moping mode for the rest of the afternoon. At least I have Benadryl in me to make me sleep off my misery today. I watch my platelet transfusion drip sluggishly into my tubing. Where were you when I needed you this morning you damn platelets? This thought makes me laugh out loud, and with this I fall asleep for the rest of the afternoon. The rest of the night I take really slow; I'm just feeling so run down and extra exhausted tonight. Every time I go to the bathroom or get up to stretch, I just feel so dizzy. I just about make it through some T.V. before shutting the light and calling it a night.

I wake up at some point in the night with the urge to pee, so I slowly sit up, fighting off the lightheadedness as I fiddle around with my feet to find my Crocs. Yawning, I stand up, grab my I.V. pole and head to the bathroom. I finish peeing, clean up, stand up, and feel a little dizzy again. Usually, when I get this feeling, I know if I'm going down or not, and this time feels like a minor dizzy spell so I just brush it off. As I continue to pull up my pajama pants, I suddenly feel super flush – and that's when I black out.

I open my eyes, and I'm lying on the bathroom floor with my head pounding like a wicked migraine. After taking a few deep breaths, I manage to use the sink to pull myself up. My wires and tubes are all hanging directly from my central line, having been pulled from their clip which usually holds most of the slack. As I stand there hooking them back into the clip, I glance at myself in the mirror and am shocked at how pale I look. I figure I better get back to sleep to rest, so I get myself back to bed, cover up and fall right to sleep.

Of course, this morning as I tell my nurse what happened in the night, she freaks out on me! "What do you mean, you passed out?? Why didn't you call a nurse?" She exclaims in a worried tone.

"I hate to bother anyone. I was fine, so I just figured I'd go back to bed." I answer honestly. It's the truth; I really never, ever, ever call the nurses' station unless my I.V. pump is beeping with a tube occlusion or air in the line.

"You need to call us if this happens again. You could have gotten really hurt, and we never would have known you were injured. Your platelets are very, very low right now, and you could have had an internal injury." She hands me a cup with my morning meds and watches me take them. "The rest of the day, you have to call the nurses' station to notify us anytime you need to get out of bed. We need to keep a close eye on you today to ensure you don't pass out again. We're also going to get you a transfusion of platelets right away to help boost your levels." The ultimate punishment – now I have to call them every single time I get out of bed. Of course... I don't. I'm not about to call them every time I lift a pinky, c'mon! I'm a rocker, an artist, a musician; I go against the grain. That's right, I'm a rebel patient!

There's something to say for a rebel patient though; I beat all odds, and get shit done! By Saturday morning my blood counts are high enough that I get the official word that I can go home! My goal was to be home for Mother's Day and I've done it. As soon as the on call doctor gives the word to let me go, the big push to make it happen begins. The nurses all scurry around like rabbits to gather the paperwork, medicines from the pharmacy and medical supplies. Lucien arrives just as I am getting my blood transfusion hooked up. We know we have to wait a majority of the day for the transfusion to finish, but our excitement knowing I'm going home is so great, that we make the best of the day. We have lunch and watch random Saturday afternoon made for T.V. movies to pass the time.

Everything moves along smooth until we hit a snag with the insurance. Lucien and I sit in a state of waiting all day in my room for this discharge business to be worked out. For hours on end, the nurses and doctors try to get me an injection of Neupogen, but the insurance won't allow it unless I am first discharged. Apparently, I can only get this shot if I return as an outpatient. Finally, the doctor green lights a discharge, as long as I come back first thing in the morning to the unit to receive the shot. Done deal, you got it Doc! It's a long day, and we don't get home till ten, but I could care less. I'm so thankful to be officially out and to be sleeping in my own bed.

First thing in the morning, we trek off for an early appointment right back up to the hospital and right up to the outpatient clinic. I sign in, and the nurse tells me she'll be right back with my shot. It really isn't until this point that I realize what's going on here... a needle. I had been so focused on going home, that I had brushed off the whole idea that I had to get a shot today. After some freaking out to pass the time, the nurse is back, but I don't see the needle anywhere.
"Sheri, let's do your blood draw first. I have the Neupogen in the pocket of my lab coat, because it's cold right now. If it warms up a little bit, it won't hurt as much. So let's go ahead and do a blood draw first." She explains. So we struggle through blood work with the tears and tantrums of a child and it's inevitably time for the shot.

"Before I give this to you, I want you to know what you're getting this for. Neupogen is prescribed to help stimulate white cell growth to help fight infection." She puts her hand in her pocket, cupping the dose of Neupogen in her hands. "I'm trying to warm it up as much as I can. Where do you think you'd like me to inject it? It needs to be in a fatty area, like an arm, rear or stomach." I'm flabbergasted by this question. I can't answer this. How about we don't do it at all and call it a day? When I don't have an answer, she suggests the stomach, because it will be the least painful – so she claims.

She brings me into an adjacent room lined with gurneys and a wall of cabinets and sinks, and instructs me to lay down on one. I lie down flat, and Lucien comes to my side, holding my hand as I start to cry profusely. The nurse lifts my shirt up, and swabs a cold alcohol on an area of my stomach. She takes the shot out of her pocket, holds it to the light and checks the dose for any imperfections. Through my amped up crying fit, she remains calm as she pinches a large portion of my belly fat. As soon as she stabs me, I bellow out a loud sob; the stinging is severe, and in my stomach no less?! Once I calm down, we are free to go home.

Just as we arrive home, Lucien's parents pull in with the kids soon behind us. Adrian runs into his room, and then returns with his arms behind his back. "Happy Mother's Day, Mommy!" he shouts eagerly as he reaches forward handing me a paper plate with strings hanging every which way. "It's a hat, just for you!" he explains proudly. I give him a big hug and thank him for the beautiful present; my little man.

The rest of the afternoon I make sure to spend every second soaking in my children on the most meaningful and perfect Mother's Day I've ever celebrated. I lay on the floor, the only position that I'm comfortable in for long periods of time due to the never healing hemorrhoid saga, and play Little People with the kids for a majority of the time. We set up a whole village of Little People; Adrian runs the farm, I take care of the main living house and Luciana puts Noah and his Arc animals in her mouth (a slobbery flood indeed).

Lucien and his parents make an incredible feast for dinner featuring an overabundance of food for just the six of us. "You got really skinny, Sheri, you need to eat," my Mother-In-Law tells me throughout the meal. Everyone takes their turn telling me I need to eat to gain energy – and weight. I just don't have much of an appetite, and have recently developed mouth sores making it painful to eat certain foods. After dinner, Lucien, Adrian, Luciana and I snuggle on the couch for a family movie night. This is what Mother's Day is about, and this is why I fought my way like a rock n' roller to get back home to my family.

Journal - May 8, 2008 (Thursday)

Hey everyone. What a day! I had a little bit of a rough night. When I got up to go to the bathroom I passed out. I get dizzy a lot, but this time I just didn't see it coming and went down! I was okay though and went back to bed. In the morning when I told the nurses everyone freaked out! Turns out it is a big deal because my platelet levels are so low that if I hit my head it could be really dangerous. So now I have to tell the nurse every time I get up (yay). On the other hand, looks like I could still go home on the weekend, I really hope so!

LAB RESULTS   NOCELLI, SHERI   8:35 A.M.
CHEM PROFILE   REF RANGE   05/12/08

	REF RANGE	
WBC	4.0-10.0	26.5 (H)
RBC	3.9-5.2	3.62 (L)
HGB	12.3-15.5	11.2 (L)
HCT	36-44	31.6 (L)
PLATELET CNT	140-440	47 / 1000 (L)

KEY: H = High L = Low

Journal - May 12, 2008 (Monday)

It's been a couple days since I've been able to update on here, but everything is really good. It got crazy because the big push went on to get me home for Mother's Day, so I didn't have time to get the computer out. I got home really late Saturday night, it took a while to get discharged because I needed a blood transfusion that day and it was taking forever. Finally Lucien and I got home around 10 pm Saturday. Sunday morning we had to get back in the car at 9 am to drive all the way back to the hospital because I had to get a shot of a drug called Neupogen that will help my white cell count to get higher. There was a silly insurance issue that I had to be discharged first and go back the next day to get that drug for some reason.

Finally we got home again on Sunday and the kids were home soon from their Grandparents and we had a wonderful Mother's Day. We had a nice dinner, and I got to play with the kids all day (to the best of my ability). I'm still really tired and due to some little issues that come along with Chemo, I have to really be laying on my side to be comfortable most of the time, but by the end of this week I think I should be back to Mommying. I'm pretty much in bed, and I can't really be in contact with anyone so I have to stay upstairs all day as much as I would love to be downstairs and see everyone! But my immune system is ultra-low and I don't want to end up sick and back in the hospital before I really have to go back. Lucien and his parents were telling me how skinny I got from this round, so everyone's trying to pork me up before the next hospital stay. (I love that ALL my clothes fit though!) Anyway, I will keep updating while I'm home to keep everyone in the loop.

Receiving my Mother's Day gifts from Adrian and Luciana

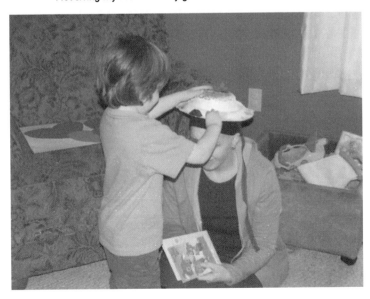

LAB RESULTS CHEM PROFILE	NOCELLI, SHERI 8:45 A.M. REF RANGE	05/15/08
WBC	4.0-10.0	32.9 (H)
RBC	3.9-5.2	3.64 (L)
HGB	12.3-15.5	11.1 (L)
HCT	36-44	31.6 (L)
PLATELET CNT	140-440	139 /1000 (L)

KEY: H = High L = Low

Journal - May 16, 2008 (Friday)

This has been a great week so far being home. Every day I feel a little stronger and slowly I am able to do more. I had a doctor appointment on Thursday. All the blood work came back looking good and I didn't need any transfusions which is great. I don't go back to the doctor now until Monday, and it's really nice to know I have a couple days off from going. I probably get to stay home another week as long as I don't get a fever or infection. The hope is that the next time I am admitted to the hospital it will be Transplant time. They have contacted 4 of the 7 matches to see if they are still willing to be donors. Hopefully one of them is willing and able to do it quickly and we can start the process. Otherwise, if it is getting to be too long then I will get one more month of Chemo while we wait for the donor to be ready.

It's just so nice to be home, and spending so much time with the kids. I still needed the babysitters this week to help me because I can't physically handle the kids yet - mostly the baby! I swear I think she weighs more than Adrian now! I think my favorite part about this week is picking out outfits for Luciana to wear. We even played with her tea set for the first time the other night, and I'm starting to teach her how to play with her baby dolls. I got to play with Adrian on his video game learning system a lot too, and it was great that he was telling me how to play. I can't believe how big he is either, it's so amazing.

Journal - May 22, 2008 (Thursday)

Hey Everyone! This has been a really great week home; I've been able to visit in the waiting room with most of our students and their parents which has been a lot of fun. I'm able to do a lot more around the house too, like get my summer curtains up! I'm really obsessive about changing curtains with the seasons, what can I say. I'm also able to take care of the kids this week on my own, which is wonderful.

I did have a doctor appointment on Monday, and everything looked good as far as blood work. We also know that I will be admitted to the hospital again next Wednesday the 28th for another round of Chemo. We don't have the donor ready to go ahead with transplant just yet, so the plan is about 2 - 3 weeks in the hospital, then 2 weeks home. Hopefully we'll be ready by July to go ahead with the Bone Marrow Transplant. I also will be going into the hospital on this Friday to get a Bone Marrow Biopsy done, as well as a spinal tap (they keep checking to make sure the Leukemia hasn't spread to the brain and spinal fluid). Luckily, I get put to sleep for that so I don't mind and I'm not nervous at all.

Anyway, it's wonderful to be home, I'm feeling great and everyone keeps telling me that I look good. I joke with them that it's my "radioactive glow"... I think that's a funny joke, but not everyone laughs with me. Oh well!

One more note – My birthday is on Memorial Day and I have received such wonderful early gifts from people. I don't have room to thank everyone here, but I really need to say thank you to Jean for such an amazingly generous gift card, that yes I promise I will spend on myself! Thank you so much. Also, thank you for an incredible early birthday present from two of our students and their family, a gorgeous travel size Taylor Acoustic guitar for me to bring with me to the hospital. Thank you so much, I'm still shocked, and I can't tell you how much your gift means to me. I'm actually looking forward to having so much time to playing it, and not dreading going back to the hospital quite so much. Thank you a million times, you're the best, and you truly blew me away with such a thoughtful and incredible gift.

May 23 (Friday)

Getting up at 7:30 stinks like a garbage can on a summer day – it's not pleasant. I fumble around the bed room, finding my "trip to the doctor" go-to outfit of sweat pants, t-shirt and hoodie and get dressed as quickly as I can. Running downstairs to get my coffee, I'm greeted by my Father-in-Law who is already here to get me. He's bringing me up to the hospital today, where I'm having my bone marrow biopsy and spinal. As I reach for the Folgers, I realize that I can't have any since they'll be putting me to sleep. This is *not* cool. I am not a pleasant person in the morning – never mind without a coffee! I give Adrian a hug, kiss Luciana on her chubby cheek and share a long hug with Lucien before taking off.

I'm so thankful that my Father-in-Law was able to rearrange his schedule to help me get to and from the hospital today. He pulls into the circular driveway of the Children's Center of the hospital. There are statues of children playing ball, running and laughing at the center of a beautiful water fountain. The building is painted with bright primary colors; all in an attempt to make this a cheerful place for children to visit for their treatments.

The way insurance and hospital policy works is that adults cannot get put to sleep for "simple" procedures such as bone marrow biopsies and spinal taps. Due to my undeniable phobia when it comes to these procedures and my age (which groups me technically into pediatrics), Dr. Ayers is able to pull some strings to help me through this. He submits his orders through the pediatric wing of the hospital, therefore allowing me to be put to sleep. I could not be more thankful!

When we enter the lobby of the Pediatric Hospital, we are greeted by colorful wall murals, stuffed animals clad in scrubs, and a multitude of toys. After signing in, we take a seat in the waiting area where there's a T.V. playing Yo Gabba Gabba and a coffee table made of one of those multi colored wire toy contraptions. I scan the room like a game of I Spy… I spy a dollhouse, I spy a rocking horse, I spy a bucket of Legos. I spy a room full of things that my children would flip a noodle over; an uncomfortable feeling.

"Sheri, you can come out back, Hun," a young bubbly nurse decked out in Elmo scrubs calls me over. We follow, dodging scooters and tricycles, down a corridor of mini hospital rooms as she leads the way. I glance into the rooms as we pass; many have rocking chairs and cribs for babies, the rest have regular hospital beds for tweens, teenagers… and the random 23 year old mother of 2 I suppose. The nurse leads us to the room all the way at the end of the hallway; we pass several patients on the way. There's a mother rocking her toddler who's wearing an oxygen mask, a 6 year old girl playing with Barbie in between her tubes and wires and a teenage boy playing X-Box in his bed.

My room is a good size; there's the bed, a few chairs and an area of cabinets. On the counter is a package of Pampers diapers, which the nurse is quick to shove into the cabinet away from my view. I don't know how, but the subject of wine comes up in the room, and before I know it, there is a group of several nurses talking wine with my Father-in-Law. Once he tells them he is a wine salesman, they have a million questions. They go on and on about regions, wine types, scents and flavors. I sit on the bed and take out my phone to keep busy. Finally, a doctor comes in and introduces himself. He explains the procedures I'm about to have done, and tells me that before they put me to sleep, they need to start an I.V. as a precautionary measure. Say what?

I put up a big ass stink about this... why can't we just put it in as soon as I am sleeping? Why do I need to go through the mental trauma of getting one awake when in a matter of a minute I'll be yours to torment all you want? I beg, I plead, I bargain... and I win! I actually get the doctor to agree to wait until I am asleep to do the I.V. A small victory, but still a win! Ten minutes later, I'm being wheeled into the operating room. The ceiling is decorated with images of Tweety Bird and Bugs Bunny painted directly on the ceiling tiles. The anesthesiologists smiley face banana comes into view as he leans over me, placing the mask on my face and directing me to count backwards from 10 slowly.

"Ten... nine... eight..." I start counting as the nurses bustle around in their various cartoon character attire. "Seven... six... five...four..." I try to squeak out the rest, but my eyes are getting super heavy, "three..." and I'm down for the count. I wake up back in the room at the end of the hallway. A nurse is in the room looking over the clipboard at the end of the bed. "Good morning sunshine!" she greets with a smile – the way she wakes up all us kids in here I suppose. "How are you feeling? How about some juice?" she hands me a Juicy Juice box and I can't help but wonder if it's the same kind in Adrian's lunch box today. I take a few sips before she heads for the hallway, "I'll let your Father-in-Law know you're awake. He's a real trip! He's been keeping all of us laughing and talking about wine this whole time; he's a real pleasure! I'll send him in."

My head feels fuzzy, like I'm in the clouds, my hip throbs with the distinct biopsy prompted pain and my hand is aching. I look down at my hand; it's wrapped in hot pink gauze where the I.V. must have been put in; I feel like I'm being sucked into this cartoon land of the children's hospital. My Father-in-Law pokes his head in the door, "Hey kiddo, how you feeling?" He comes over and sits on the chair next to my bed. "The nurses said as soon as you drink a little and get moving around then we can go. Take your time, make sure you're ready."

I drink my Juicy Juice like an honest obedient little girl, start to sit up and try to move around a little. My hip is super sore and throbs a constant beat through my muscles and bones. By the time the nurse comes in to check on me, I have manipulated myself to sit on the bed – complete with a wide smile... whatever it takes to convince them I'm ready to be released! She checks my vitals, and announces I'm free to go as soon as I sign my discharge papers. My Father-in-Law pulls up the car, so that by the time the nurse is pushing my wheel chair down the hallway, past the children's hospital rooms, through the playroom lobby and into the sunlight, he is waiting for me with the door open. It takes some slow measured movements, but eventually I am able to lift myself out of the wheel chair and into the passenger seat of the car. My backside aches, but I just try to position my body in a way that it bothers me less.

Back at home, everything is suddenly ten times more difficult than it was yesterday. My strength has grown so much since I've been home, that most daily activates feel almost normal again. Now that I've had this biopsy however, I feel like I've been thrown back at the brick wall. The only thing I want to do is lie down; it seems like the only way to take the pressure off of my hip. The stairs to the second floor however are absolutely impossible. I go to lift my leg up the first step and pain shoots up my back. Okay, take it slow. You can do this, it's only stairs. I grip the railings, and using my arms for leverage, lift my first leg up to the first step. I breathe deep. One down, fourteen to go. I slowly make my way up the stairs taking what feels like a complete eternity. By the time I get to the top, I am out of breath and in so much pain. I sleep the rest of the day, once again unable to play with my children. At least I know this pain is temporary, and in no time I'll be able to get back to life once again.

Journal - May 26, 2008 (Monday)

Hey Everyone! Today is my birthday! That's right, the big 24. Whew, gettin' old! Saturday we had a little birthday celebration at Lucien's parents' house, and we were able to see my step-sons Lucien and Justen. We had such a great time! We brought the kids to the park and played football for a while, which was more fun than I can even say. We were all taking turns Quarterbacking, receiving, playing defense and just running routes. It was great, every muscle hurts but it was so worth it. The tackling was a bonus too! Then we had a barbeque and some birthday cherry pie and ice cream. It was beautiful outside and was just the perfect day.

Sunday we ran out and got some errands done, which I am probably not supposed to be out doing but, oh well! We needed silly things like pot holders and seat covers for the car under the kids' car seats. It was kind of a day to catch up on the little things we let go over the past three months due to the craziness.

And wouldn't you guess, this morning we spent my birthday organizing the bedroom closets and re-vamping the filing system! That actually was all very important to me before I go back to the hospital on Wednesday, so I am totally excited that it got done.

The rest of "my day" I'm going to hang out with Adrian and Luciana and finish up some photo albums we're working on. And of course before I wrap up, thanks Mom and Auntie Carole for the lovely 'Happy Birthday' renditions, they were great! :) I'll update on here once I am settled in the hospital, probably sometime on Thursday. See ya later!

Celebrating my 24th Birthday with the whole family – 2008

May 28 (Wednesday)

Bring it on round three! Coming back into the hospital today felt like visiting friends – something I never thought I'd say! This morning Nurse Cara, Mary Ann and several more of the nurses popped in my room to say hello. I have a different outlook heading into this round, which I assume is because I finally know what to expect. This morning I'm heading down to special procedures to have my central line put in which I am dreading with a capital D. After that though, I got this. Chemo this time is going to be a little shorter running only for five days. The nurses are telling me that if I do well, I may be able to go home super quick once I finish the chemo, to recover at home – unless I get in infection of course. I'm hopeful that Karma will throw me a bone and let this one slide... I think I deserve it this time around.

Transport comes to get me for special procedures around lunch time. I hop on my chariot and we're off. I'm doped up on Ativan, even though I know it's not going to do a damn thing but make me nauseous. Arriving downstairs, I'm shocked to see that there's no one waiting in front of me; crap, I'm next! My typical anxiety kicks in and I'm once again a blubbering fool. As they bring me into the operating room, I mentally try to gear up for this, trying to tell myself it'll be over soon, telling myself I can do this. I'm in the middle of my internal pep talk, when I realize something isn't right here... something is different. The doctor has taken my right arm and tied it to a plank which they have attached to my gurney. They take my pillow from under my head and place it at my side. I feel like I'm tied into some medieval contraption.

In a panic, I speak up, "I get my line put in my neck." My voice is a quivery slight sound, barely audible in this cavernous operating room.

The doctor leans over me, "We're going to be inserting a PICC line today, which is a little different. It's a peripherally inserted central catheter, which is very similar to a central line except that it will be inserted in a vein in your upper arm. It still has the slender tub which will run through your veins to a larger vein near your heart for intravenous access."

Cue panic mode... now! What the hell, I can't have this thing in my arm? What if it hurts even more? I *just* got used to the central line, why are we changing to this PICC thing? My head is spinning in an unstoppable tornado of chaos as the doctor and nurses start doing their work around me. Someone opens my right hand and places a cylinder rubber weight in my palm, closing my fingers around the weight, instructing me to hold on to it. Another nurse starts draping sterile blue cloth, revealing only a small rectangle visible at the crook of my arm. They wheel over a mammoth machine and start poking around my arm with a wand, explaining that they're using ultrasound to find the vein. They locate the spot and the table starts too look like a game of Twister.

Right foot blue – one nurse holds the ultrasound wand steadily in place, so they don't lose their spot. Left foot green – the second nurse swabs alcohol around the spot. Left hand yellow - a nurse wraps a tourniquet forcefully around my arm. Right hand red – the doctor starts administering the local anesthetic, stinging, stinging, stinging my arm. I yelp in agony, with tears in full force. A nurse hands him a hypodermic needle which he inserts into the vein. They now start to insert the guide wire several centimeters into the needle, before removing the needle. The sound of my sobbing is deafening inside my own head; I don't even feel like it's me who's crying. I feel a peculiar disconnect from myself, like I'm witnessing this happen to someone else, but feeling the pain all the same.

Through my distress, I realize that the game of Twister has come to a halt. The doctor is asking the nurse to adjust the ultrasound wand, and he grunts in clear disgust. "Okay everyone, we have to start again, we've missed the vein we were aiming for." He announces in a pissed off tone. *He's* pissed off? How the hell does he think *I* feel about this whole menagerie?! With this, the whole horrifying process starts again. More ultrasound, more needles harassing me with every cruel pinch and more of this hurricane of emotions. Once the new spot has been established, and the new guide tube has been run through the needle, into my vein up to my shoulder. A nurse hands the doctor a scalpel; I feel immense pressure as the ultrasound wand pushes into my arm and the doctor pushes down as he cuts into me. "Don't move!" they holler at me in a chorus of voices. They place an introducer sheath with a dilator is over the guide wire then remove the dilator and guide wire. They catheter is now advanced through the introducer sheath, through my veins, past my shoulder and stopping just before my heart. They remove the introducer sheath. I have tumbled psychologically in a burrow of despair. It's not till this point that I realize I've been mangling my pillow with my left hand; I've been gripping it, releasing my angst the one physical way I could.

One of the nurses pushes over a massive machine over me. "We're going to take an X-Ray to make sure the PICC line is placed properly," she explains as she arranges it over me. She snaps the X-Ray – the entire medical staff stands around scrutinizing the image, and finally announces the placement is perfect. This whole time, I lie on the table in a puddle of tears, with my arm splayed straight out to my right like some kind of tied up, strapped down criminal. I'm mortified as my body is being corrupted and there's nothing I can do about it.

The swarm of nurses hovers around me once again, sideswiping me with another round of local anesthetic injections – my crying tantrum amps up a few notches at this unannounced attack. Once the needles have stopped, a nurse sutures the catheter line into place with three ugly stitches. She places a clear sterile circular bandage over the whole thing and then takes the weight out of my hand – I never did hold it tight like they told me to, my arm has been a limp dead weight at my side this entire time. She unstraps my arm, lifts it and lays it at my side. I'm a shattered ball of nerves at this point, but I know this is no state of mind to remain in for too long. There's no time to remain negative and broken down when there is a battle on the horizon.

The rest of the day I do everything with my left hand, leaving my right hand dangling at my side like it doesn't belong to me. I don't know how to cope with this shit coming out of my arm. Quite frankly, I'm afraid if I move my arm, I might pull the line out from where it's floating in my bloodstream. When I had the central line in my neck, I didn't have to see it, so I could forget it was there... but this... this thing stares at me with a ghoulish stare all day long. I hate it.

After dinner, I try to play a little on the Nintendo DS I got for my birthday, but I just haven't learned how to use this arm yet, so I give up. There's absolutely nothing on T.V either... so I just decide to chill with some Food Network, even though I don't know how to cook. Maybe I'll learn by osmosis by watching Bobby Flay and Giada.

Everything is just better in the mornings. I love the fresh optimism I feel just by seeing the daybreak sunshine. Once Nurse Fantasia has done my blood draw, the massive scale has come to weigh me, the on call doctor has done his rounds and I've poked at some toast and eggs with a plastic fork, I'm bored of the scenery in here. Pushing my I.V. pole with my left hand, I make my way over to the window. The way the room is set up, when you close the bathroom door, you can see the window to outside. In front of the window is a countertop where I usually store my suitcase and other random items. It's impossible to really see out the window by standing there. After deciding this just isn't acceptable, I shift all my stuff to the side, and with my one good arm, I hoist myself up onto the counter. Perfect! I can see everything! The city is bustling with people coming and going, doing their regular business. I sit on my perch for hours taking it all in. College age couples walk down the alley, stopping for a smooch when they think no one is looking. Adult men compete in a sweaty basketball game at the public court. Cars circle around generally about seven and a half times before they find a metered parking spot. Birds swoop past me – flying free through the air with no boundaries – making me feel even more closed off behind this industrial grade glass window.

There's a knock on the door. It opens to reveal a young woman in a brown suit. She is my lawyer. When I first found out how serious my condition was, I realized I needed to make up a Last Will and Testament. There is a chance that I will not survive this – statistically, I probably shouldn't. It would be foolish to head forward without a will due to the severity of my diagnosis. I asked the unit social worker, Michael, for guidance on where I could find a lawyer for a situation like this, and he had given me the name of a local lawyer in town. She often comes to the hospital to work pro bono writing up Last Will and Testaments for patients.

"Come in, you must be Laura?" I greet her as I gingerly dismount my window perch.

"Yes and you must be Sheri. It's a pleasure to meet you! You know, you can probably see my office building from where you were sitting up there. And, I have to say, I've visited a lot of patients here over the years, and you're the first one I've seen use the countertop as a window seat! Very clever!" Laura pulls up a chair next to the bed where I've returned to. "So, I have everything drawn up here that we talked about on the phone. I'll go over everything with you again, just to make sure we got everything right, okay sweetie?" She starts rustling through her briefcase, pulling out a bunch of papers. She hands me a grouping of cream papers with scroll work lettering on the coversheet reading "Last Will and Testament of Sheri Lynn Nocelli".

"Okay, so I'm going to read through this with you," she starts pointing with the backside of a pen as she reads out loud from the sheet. "I, Sheri Lynn Nocelli, being of sound and disposing mind, memory and understanding do herby make, publish, and declare this to be my last will and testament, hereby revoking all wills and codicils thereto made by me at any time heretofore made." She pauses, glances at me to make sure I'm comprehending, and continues, "First, I direct that my just debts and funeral expenses be paid as soon as practicable after my death, except that any debt secured by a mortgage owned by me after my death shall not be paid by my estate, but such property shall pass subject to such encumbrance. I direct that my body be buried at Holy Cross Cemetery in North Arlington, New Jersey, in the Nocelli family plot." She leans back, "Did you have a chance to verify that this plot space is available?"

I swallow the lump in my throat and respond, "Yes. When my Father-in-Law visited, I asked him if there was room for me there, and he said of course there is." I can tell I made him a little uncomfortable when I asked him this; but on the other hand, he is the most practical person I know. As much as he told me that it won't matter anyway, that I'll be fine, I know he was proud of me for thinking ahead and covering all bases.

"Great. Sounds good," Laura leans in, pointing the pen tip again, "Second, I give all of my property, both real and personal, to my beloved husband Lucien Nocelli Jr. If my husband predeceases me, I give all of my property to my beloved children Adrian Robert Nocelli and Luciana Virginia Nocelli to be divided equally. Third, I hereby appoint my husband Lucien Nocelli Jr. as the executer and I direct that no bond shall be required of him as executor of my estate in this or any other jurisdiction. If my beloved husband, Lucien Nocelli Jr. predeceases me, I hereby appoint my beloved Father-in-Law, Lucien Nocelli Sr. as the executor and I direct that no bond shall be required of him as executor of my estate in this or any other jurisdiction." She goes on to read the rest of the document as I try to follow along the best I can to the unfamiliar legal lingo. Once we wrap up, she goes out in the hall to find two nurses who would be willing to be witness to me signing my will. Nurse Cara and Nurse Rosalie (who I'm not as familiar with) come in and sign their names. Done deal, my will is done. Laura folds up the document and places it in a fancy envelope adorned with matching decorative lettering reading "Last Will and Testament". She wishes me the best, hands me her business card and tells me to contact her if I ever need anything.

I hold the ornate envelope in my hand, staring at it. When I first mentioned that I was going to work on a will, everyone shrugged it off and had the same reaction. They all said the same thing, "What are you talking about? You don't need that. You're going to be just fine." Can you guarantee that? Can anyone? Isn't it better that I plan everything out in writing just in case? I made the appointment with the lawyer and worked out all the details completely on my own. I'm proud of myself. I'm proud that I have the head, in the middle of this cancer whirlwind, to think about the future – either way that it might wide up. There can only be one of two outcomes at the end of this journey; life or death. While I'm planning on life, death has a chance too, and if I can be prepared either way, it can only help the situation. Writing the will is the only preparation I make for the chance of dying... because in all reality, there's not a chance in hell that this is going to kill me. I have way too much fight for that.

Journal - May 29, 2008 (Thursday)

Hey Everyone! Well I've been back in the hospital for two days now, and everything is going to plan. I came back in Wednesday to the same day operating room where I was put to sleep for a bone marrow biopsy and spinal tap. When I woke up from that, I was in the pediatric recovery area (since I'm under 25, I sometimes get treated by the pediatric doctor). I ended up hanging out there for a few hours while we waited for a bed to open up for me. Finally one did and over I went.

A was in my room for about an hour then I went to special procedures to have a line put in. Usually I get the triple line in my neck, which I'd rather have, but this time they did a PIC line in my arm. I don't like this one at all, it's harder to type, I can't sleep on my side and I would just rather have use of both arms.

Today has been much better. This morning my attorney, Laura, stopped by to have me sign my Will. She was so nice, we ended up chatting for about an hour, she was awesome. So that was that, we had two nurses be witnesses and it was done.

A little while later, Lucien and the kids got here to visit. They brought me the rest of my things that I didn't bring yesterday like the computer, guitar and coffee from home. I was so happy to see the kids again.

So the general word so far on this Chemo round, is that the Chemo runs for 5 days, then I could be sent home at that point! That would be nice to give me a nice chunk of time home again before the transplant. And I just want to say another birthday 'Thank You' to

Josephine for the gorgeous jewelry and the games (Cooking Mama and My French Coach) for my Nintendo DS.. I promise I'll cook you a "gourmet French dinner"!

Journal - June 2, 2008 (Monday)

Hey Everyone! Things are moving right along here, today is actually my last day of Chemo, it was only a 5 day course. What's crazy is that on Friday I did start to get chills and fever. So I'm on antibiotics since then and still feeling really tired and under the weather.

Lucien came up to visit and I was just so happy to see him. We played guitar for a little while, then we tried out the new Nintendo DS I got for my birthday. Lucien wanted to play Cooking Mama and he did really good at it! We had a wonderful weekend together, watching TV and just spending time enjoying each other. It was perfect.

Today's been okay, I'm exhausted and I'm starting to get a rash all over my neck and upper body.. it's awful! But I know it will go away as soon as the Chemo ends. I just can't wait to be home with my kids and with Lucien. That last three weeks home was such a gift, I can't wait to get back.

Journal - June 5, 2008 (Thursday)

There's not too much going on here, we're just waiting around now for when my blood counts go back up, and to make sure I don't get an infection. So, I should be back home by mid-next week if everything goes smooth. My only complaint is this awful rash I have... I'm just so itchy everywhere! Hopefully that goes away soon though.

Other than that, I've just been playing guitar and Nintendo DS most of the time. I miss this kids a lot, I won't see them this week because I didn't want Adrian to miss any school since it's almost over and they're doing all of their end of the year activities. But I'll see them next week when I get home; I'm just looking forward to that.

June 5 (Thursday)

This round of Chemo is hitting me hard. Treatment has been over for a few days, I'm so knocked out exhausted. I try to watch as much T.V. and play as much Nintendo DS as possible to keep busy, but it's hard to fill your days with mindless activities when you're so used to life in the fast lane. Besides feeling like crud, I have developed the worst rash you could ever imagine. It started on my neck, spread to my upper body and now covers every part of me. I look like a blotchy mess and feel like I was left under the oven broiler. It's itchy and it burns like red coal. Anything touching me sets my skin on fire; jammies, socks, the sheets, even my own hands. The nurses keep trying different ointments and lotions, hoping that one of them will calm down this nasty chemo reaction. My body is on mutiny, however, and is not interested in bargaining. One of the lotions we try actually sends me into an allergic reaction on top of the rash... causing my legs to transform into two large blisters; I literately cry in pain. Eventually, with the chemo over and boat loads of Benadryl, the rash subsides but it takes the better part of a week.

Even though I'm weak and tired, I remain positive, always offering a smile to every nurse, doctor, visitor, worker and fellow patient I come across. There's no time to be negative or dwell on the pain. I decide to make it my mission to be a constant ray of sunshine, optimism and affection; spreading encouraging vibes to everyone around me in hopes they will ricochet back my way.

All of this positive energy comes back to reward me when the doctor comes in Friday morning announcing that I can go home! I'm under strict instructions to be ultra-careful with germy situations since my blood counts are still super low from the Chemo. As an added bonus, the doctor is also letting me go home with my PICC line still in! Amazing news! This means on my every other day return visits to the hospital for blood draws, the nurses can draw right from my line – no needles necessary! If for some reason I need to be readmitted, the line is already in... so NO trip to Special Procedures either! What a score – I kind of dig this whole Karma thing!

DISCHARGE SUMMERY REPORT:

ADMITTING DIAGNOSIS: Intensification chemotherapy for acute myelogenous leukemia.
FINAL DISCHARGE: Acute myelogenous leukemia
HISTORY OF PRESENT ILLNESS: The patient is a 24-year-old female who had been admitted with a history of AML admitted on 5/28/08 for intensification chemotherapy after undergoing a lumbar puncture and a bone marrow biopsy.

PHYSICAL EXAMINATION: The patient really had no complaints. Mental status: Alert and oriented x3. Pupils equal, round, reactive to light. Cardiac: Regular rate and rhythm, no murmurs, rubs or gallops. Lungs: Clear to auscultation bilaterally. Abdomen: Soft, nontender, non-distended. Extremities: No adema.

LABORATORY AND DIAGNOSTIC STUDIES:
(Day of admission)
CHEM PROFILE   REF RANGE   06/06/08

	REF RANGE	06/06/08
WBC	4.0-10.0	5.2
HGB	12.3-15.5	10
PLATELET CNT	140-440	119

Sodium: 136, Potassium 3.7, Chloride 104, Bi carb 27.3, BUN 3, Blood glucose 92, Mag 1.8, Cal 8.6

(On day of discharge)

CHEM PROFILE   REF RANGE   06/06/08

	REF RANGE	06/06/08
WBC	4.0-10.0	1.6
HGB	12.3-15.5	7.5
PLATELET CNT	140-440	24

Sodium: 135, Potassium 3.6, Chloride 103, Bi carb 27.3, BUN 6, Blood glucose 94, Mag 2.1, Cal 8.4

HOSPITAL COURSE: Nothing major happened. The patient had no complaints. Was started on chemotherapy. Bone marrow aspirate showed less than 17% blasts. She was admitted for intensification chemotherapy. At the time of discharge patient was in stable condition, tolerating diet, having no difficulty of bladder or bowel, ambulating without difficulty.

DISCHARGE INSTRUCTION/PLAN: The patient is to follow up with Dr. Ayers on Monday 6/9 at 1:30 p.m. and in addition to that she is supposed to come to treatment center on 6/8 for complete blood count and possible transfusion.

DISCHARGE MEDICATIONS: Levofloxacin 500 mg daily, loratadine 10 mg daily, Zolpidem 10 my orally nightly at bedtime as need for insomnia, acyclovir 400 mg orally two times a day, fluconazole 400 mg daily.

I heed the germ warning with my full attention, spending most of my time at home in bed avoiding the student waiting room downstairs, door handles, bathrooms, etc. Every other day I travel back up to the hospital for blood work, crossing my fingers each and every time that I won't need to stay for a lengthy transfusion. I luck out most days and bolt out the revolving hospital door as soon as they give me word I'm free to go. The weather is gorgeous; as I wait for my ride home, I sit on the stone wall overlooking the water fountain. I don't read, text, surf the internet during this time. Instead, I take in every breath of fresh air with pure content; I watch the birds playing in the fountain water; I close my eyes listening to the gentle wind. I witness all the other patients coming and going through the revolving doors – so few of them walk with promise in their step. Most are slouched, defeated, worn down and drenched with a negative sorrow emitting from their energy. It's so miserable to

179

observe; I feel bad for them. I completely understand that everybody deals with any situation differently... never mind a Cancer diagnosis and battle. But fighting this war with a frown and a negative outlook can only bring more negative your way.

I'm not some physic, Tarot card reader, physiatrist or doctor – but I'm a human, just like these people, fighting for my life, which I feel gives me a tad bit of opinion. I'm not saying they're wrong in the way they are feeling, acting or surviving... but I'm saying, why be miserable? Maybe they just don't want to be happy through this disgusting disease – or maybe they don't know how.

Maybe this is my purpose. Maybe I'm supposed to be a little beacon of light in this dark tunnel. I remember the first time I came to the clinic for my appointment with Dr. Ayers after the first round of inpatient treatments. I was miserable, withdrawn and mopey as I sat in the waiting area waiting to be called. Everyone in that waiting area was absolutely depressed with me; we were one puddle of sorrow. A bald man walked in, maybe in his early forties. He was alone, dressed nicely in a black bowling style button down shirt, but most notably was the way he carried himself. He held his head high, back straight, shoulders back; he walked into the room like he owned it. He was smiling. After greeting the front desk staff with a cheerful tone he came over to the waiting area, sat down next to an elderly man with an I.V. pole, and introduced himself. They didn't talk about Cancer, but instead about fishing, the Pocono Mountains and dogs. They shared life stories with pure interest. I remember watching as the slouched saddened elderly patient sat up straighter, smiled, laughed and got back the twinkle in his eyes. It was amazing to see the energy transfer from one person to another. By the time my name was called, I found myself with a little smile on my face. The positive energy was as contagious as malaria in a swamp.

This is my goal. I want to spread my energy with as many people as I possibly can – even if I only get them to smile. Maybe though, just maybe, I can light up their day and make them forget about their battle if only for a few minutes.

Journal - June 9, 2008 (Monday)

Finally we have lots of updates to talk about! Much to my surprise, I got to come on Friday. They worked it out so that I can keep the central line hooked up, which is in my arm this time. It's really nice to be able to leave it in, because if I have to be re-admitted if I get sick, then I won't have to have the surgery done again to put the line back in. It's nice too because when I go in for blood work, they can take it through the line and I don't have to think about needles! That's a nice perk.

So I got home and went right upstairs away from the teaching area because my immune system is ultra-low now. I stayed up there all Saturday morning too until Lucien was done teaching. On Saturday evening, a nurse from the visiting nurse association came to teach Lucien how to clean and flush the two little tubes that come out of my central line. It's nothing hard, but it's very sterile. He just has to take these syringes of saline, and put it through the line. This just makes sure that the tubes don't clog up. After the nurse left, we decided to hit the town! Luciana and Adrian were still at their Grandparents house, so we were able to get some much needed 'us' time. We went to the beach at Pier Village. It was a nice safe place that we could walk without being close to any people (for germs), and we just got to take in the air and watch the waves, it was wonderful. We really needed a nice date night like that.

On Sunday I had a follow up appointment at the hospital to check the blood work. Although the counts were all very low (lower than I thought they were), they let me go and I didn't need any transfusions. So we headed home where the kids were waiting for us already! We celebrated Father's Day this weekend with a big barbeque dinner. We even stopped on the way home and picked up a little kiddie pool for the kids to go in. They had so much fun. It was a shame because we have an actual pool, but we aren't opening it this year with everything going on.

Anyway, it's great to be home. I have to go back for follow ups every other day, but at least I get to sleep in my own bed at night. I am not really supposed to touch the kids too much for germs, so I'm trying not to. I can't pick them up because of the central line in my arm, so I still will need babysitting help the time that I'm home. I'm just concentrating on not getting sick so I don't have to get re-admitted, that's the goal!

June 13 (Friday)

Passing out equals zero fun. This morning I have a regular appointment at the Cancer center to get my blood levels tested, but while I'm here they want to take care of the blood tests required for the transplant. I don't mind at all, since I still have the PICC line in my arm, bring on the blood work! As long as there are no needles involved, I'm game! The nurse comes over with a literal tray of vials, telling me she has to take 16 for the numerous tests for the transplant. Holy guacamole Batman!

No sweat, I got this. I give her my arm and she starts filling vial after vial of blood. I keep watching the little TV, trying to avoid watching the blood as she takes it out. She finishes up after what seems like an eternity, and wishes me well as she walks away. That was pleasantly easy! As soon as we get the results back for today's levels, I should be good to go home!

My head starts to get heavy, bobbing down a few times. My muscles relax suddenly. My eyes start to glaze over and my breathing slows way down. At this point, I realize I'm about to pass out. There are no nurses in sight. There is another patient on the other side of the curtain to my right, but we can't see each other. Across the room, there is an older lady patient in a recliner watching T.V. I try to raise my hand to get her attention, but I can't lift it. I open my mouth to call for help, "I'm...going. ... to... pa...." my mumbled, slurred words are inaudible, and as they're leaving my lips, my head falls limp and I go out cold.

I wake up to a million people fussing around me. They've reclined my chair putting me all the way in a laying position, someone is putting a blood pressure cuff around my arm, and another nurse is in my face calling my name. All this commotion is embarrassing; I try to sit up and they lay me back down telling me not to move. "I'm fine!" I try to convince them but it's a lost cause.

Two men in uniforms come in the room pushing a gurney and announcing they're here to bring me to the E.R. What? I get defensive now, "Oh come on! I'm fine! I only passed out because I had so much blood taken. *Any* person would after that much! I'm fine, I can go home, really!" I plead, I beg, I try to reason with them and in the end I fail. They insist that I'm going to the emergency room. Not only am I going, but I'm riding the gurney to get there. The EMTs reach out to help me out of the chair and onto the gurney, but I tell them I'm okay and get on by myself. I can see in their faces they agree with me that this whole thing is a little overkill – but its protocol. They strap me on the bed and start wheeling me towards the front door.

Outside, there's an ambulance. "Are you for real? Do we really have to take an ambulance? I literally can see the entrance to the ER over there." I point behind me where the driveway to the ER is about 200 feet away. Again, I'm told this is protocol. They lift me into the back of the ambulance and pile around me. Because of the street we're on, we have to actually circle the whole hospital, driving practically back to where we started so that they can park in the ambulance dock. We chat the whole way around the building, "Well, at least I got to ride in an ambulance for the first time." I joke.

I get put right into an air tight little room in the ER and hooked up to an IV right away through my PICC line. (Thank goodness for this thing today!). No one really knows what to do with me... I don't need treatment, just monitoring. They leave the blood pressure cuff around my arm, setting it to go off automatically every fifteen minutes. They check in, asking me if I'm in any discomfort, to which I answer, "Yeah, from this cuff squeezing me so much."

I'm sitting up Indian style on the bed munching on a strawberry pop-tart when Doctor Ricci comes in. I love Doctor Ricci; he is the complete comedian of the staff and always has a wisecrack up his sleeve. He's who arranged getting me released with the PICC line still in. I'm happy he's the doctor on call today, maybe he can bust me outta here!

"What are you doing back in here, couldn't stay away?" he asks.

"They took so much blood for the transplant tests, so I passed out. No big deal, anyone would have passed out after losing that insane amount of blood." I take a bite of my pop tart.

"Wow, pop tarts, I haven't seen those things in ages! What flavor is that, strawberry with frosting and sprinkles?" he asks.

"Mmhmm," I nod, then with my mouth full, "it's the best flavor next to s'more pop-tarts, but you need a toaster for those, it's the only way to eat them."

Doctor Ricci laughs and leans back on the wall. "I hate to tell you, but we have to admit you again. Because you passed out, but coupled with your low platelet count and the bloody noses you've been having, it's probably best. You're going to need some transfusions, so we might as well keep you over the weekend while your counts build, instead of coming back and forth every day." He explains to me. I tell him I understand, say goodbye and finish my pop tart.

Thankfully, by Sunday morning my counts have improved enough that Doctor Ricci tells me I can go home again after three days of observation. I get sent home with multiple prescriptions;

Acyclovir – 400 mg, by mouth, two times a day (an antiviral
    medication)
Ciprofloxacin – 250 mg, by mouth, every 12 hours (a bacteria
    fighting antibiotic)
Fluconazole – 400 mg, by mouth daily (an antifungal medication)
Amoxicillin – 125 mg, by mouth, every 12 hours (treats infections
    caused by bacteria)

Lucien picks me up, and we plan a Father's Day feast with the kids and Lucien's parents. The whole day is amazing; it just feels so right to be home again. The next few days are great and I start feeling so much better with more energy and stamina with every passing minute.

By the time Tuesday rolls around, I'm back at the Cancer Center for blood work, which of course shows I need platelets. It's not a bad transfusion though, and I'm outta there by 1:30 back on my way home. I'm extra zonked today, so I lay down for a nap when I get home. Everything is all fine and dandy until I get the chills. My whole body shivers, trembling like I'm sleeping in an igloo. Uh-oh... this is not good. I take my temperature and wouldn't you know I have a fever of 102.2. A call into Doctor Ayers confirms what I was afraid of... it's back to the hospital for me.

Wednesday morning Doctor Ayers comes to my room on rounds and explains the plan of action. I'm getting round the clock IV antibiotics to get whatever infection I have under control. He says as soon as I finish the round of antibiotics and the fever is gone for a twenty four hour period, I'll be free to go. This is discouraging news, given that the average course of antibiotics is five to seven days. He does suspect the PICC line might have something to do with the infection and wants to have it removed. Since he's planning on this being a shorter hospital stay for me, he does not want me to have another central line put in. Instead, he puts in orders for the nurse to give me an IV for my antibiotics to be administered. The drawback, this means every single blood draw will be via needle. My absolute worst needle nightmare is about to come true with early morning panic attacks imamate when they come in at 5:00 for their daily sample.

My heart sinks, but I try to remain positive. It's a little easier to swallow this pill, when Doctor Ayers tells me he has some good news for me. They have picked my bone marrow donor. He can't tell me anything about the person, but he can tell me that they're working on coordinating a date for the transplant in July. This is phenomenal news which manages to lift my spirits to the heavens!

This hospital stay is frustrating, to say the least, since I feel fine, have tons of energy and have no inkling of feelings sick (other than the nightly fevers from the infection). Still, if I'm getting fevers, I need the antibiotic treatments – this is the place to be I suppose. At least for this stay, I'm not in the BMT unit (there were no available beds), and I was lucky enough to get a corner room with five huge windows! All day long I can kneel on a chair and watch the world turn five floors down. It helps pass the time and is way more unpredictable than TV! My mother and my Aunt Carole have been planning on coming down from New Hampshire to visit me while I was home in between treatments, so it's super upsetting that I'm in the hospital instead. They brighten my days while they're here so much! We chat about family happenings in New England, shopping, food and a million random ridiculous topics; it's awesome. Aunt Carole is a trip...

when the nurse comes in for a mid-morning blood draw, and I start plummeting into a hysterical crying fit, Aunt Carole knows just what I need. As the nurse is preparing to start the draw, Auntie stands up at the foot of my bed, lifts her shirt and says, "Sheri, look at my boobies!" I swiftly change from tears of despair to tears of laughter, joining Mom, Auntie and the nurse as we roll into a jovial group giggle.

I finally get discharged from this impromptu inpatient stay. The fevers have subsided and my counts are climbing at a nice rate.

Journal - June 18, 2008 (Wednesday)

It's been a long time since I have been able to get on here to update. Things have been a little wacky! Last Friday (the 13th go figure) I went in to have routine blood work testing. I also had been having awful nose bleeds all week that lasted between 45 minutes to an hour each time. So I go in for the blood work, with a nose bleed, and then they take close to 16 vials of blood for testing for the transplant. Like any living creature – I passed out! I was depleted of my blood supply. Of course this caused a huge uproar, and they had to call the EMT to bring me *by ambulance* across the street to the hospital. I was totally fine once I came to, but ended up having to stay in the hospital all day Friday, Saturday and most of Sunday morning. So the weekend was wasted.

So I finally got to go back home, for Father's Day. We stopped at the store to pick up some steak for dinner. And wouldn't you know, while in the store Lucien ran into Debra Harry (Blondie!). The timing on that was perfect, we never would have ran into her if I had still been in the hospital. So anyway, we had a great Father's

Day. Luciana was walking all over the place! And Adrian was so happy to have me home.

So, on Tuesday I had another appointment to get blood work checked at the Cancer Center clinic. Everything looked fine, I just needed platelets and was able to get home by 1:30. Had a little lunch, did some paperwork for the show this Friday coming up, and then decided to lay down for a little while. That's when I started to get the chills. No matter what I did, I could not warm up. I did fall asleep, and when I woke up I could just feel how hot I was... I had 102.2 fever. So I called my doctor right away and he told me to get right to the emergency room. Great. So, here I am now back in the hospital – the total last place I want to be. I was really enjoying the time home with the kids, because the transplant is coming up, and I know I'll be a lot weaker after that.

That is the good news out of everything. They picked a bone marrow donor, and have requested dates to schedule the transplant for July. That is awesome news. So now I am trying to lay low, not get a fever again, so I can try to get out of here by Friday. I really want to make it to the Beatlemania show Friday night, I really want to see the kids dance around and have fun.

Journal - June 26, 2008 (Thursday)

And another huge update, I can't believe I haven't posted anything in a week, things have just been that crazy! So I was kept in the hospital a week. Ugh! Of course it was really that much more boring this time because I really did feel fine, but I was getting antibiotics through IV. So I really did need to be in there, as much as I was trying to get out. There were some highlights though!

My mom and Aunt Carole came down to visit me from New Hampshire over the weekend. That was so much fun! There's really nothing like having your family visit. Talking on the phone with everyone and emails are great, but it's so nice to see them actually there. I really wanted to be home for their visit, but it just didn't happen. We had a good time though, telling stories and catching up.

Lucien had a Beatlemania show over the weekend which we always look forward to annually because it's right near our house (usually they are always so far away). It's nice because everyone we know comes every year. I was very upset that I couldn't make it – not for the fact of the show, I really don't watch it when I am there because I am working the whole time, but I really wanted to bring the kids and see them dance and everything. So I was stuck in the hospital watching bad TV instead, but it was a great night at the concert.

I finally got discharged this Monday and got to come home! I'm exhausted of course, because the blood counts are very low right now, but are going up pretty well. I did have to get a shot once a day Tuesday and Wednesday – at home! (which for me is a very traumatic experience). But, my friend Mya (who had organized the bone marrow drive last month) was so amazing and came over on her lunch break Tuesday to give it to me, and she was here anyway on Wednesday too (because she babysits for us on Wednesdays). She is amazing, always there to help (especially give shots, she had a little too much fun doing that! :)

So now things are nice and calm, it's great to be home with the kids. Adrian is so happy to have me home, and is afraid for me to leave his sight, I think he's afraid that if he loses track of me I might end up back in the hospital. And Luciana is a little demanding princess! As she gets older she is dethroning me as the royalty of the house, because instead of me, it's her who is getting everything she wants all the time! (I taught her well how to get what she wants I guess!!)

Journal - July 3, 2008 (Thursday)

Well, I seem to be on more of a 'weekly update' right now. It's hard to log on here when I am home, when I'm back in the hospital I'll have more regular updates again.

We have been doing so much since I have been home, things feel almost normal sometimes. I'm trying to maintain some sense of normally for the kids, so maybe they won't realize what's going on, especially before the transplant comes. Sunday we took the kids to the Philadelphia Zoo. They had so much fun. Adrian loved seeing all the animals, and wouldn't you know, his favorite one there was the duck that tried to steal his sandwich at lunch time. Luciana's favorite part was the duck pond, I think because she could easily see them swimming around. (And in case you're keeping track, my favorite part was the Zebras!)

Okay and now the big news that I've been holding off on, but been reaalllly wanting to say – *We have a date set for the bone marrow transplant!!!* They found a matching donor and I will be admitted to the hospital on Monday July 14th to begin the Chemotherapy. I will get Chemo for about a week, and then I will receive my new bone marrow! This will be about a month stay in the hospital and if all goes well I should be home before September. I won't be able to work for a few months still, but at least by September I will be sleeping in my own bed and hopefully everything goes smoothly. We are excited and of course very nervous that it's transplant time, but we are ecstatic that we are being given this chance and we just keep praying that this is my cure!

July 3 (Thursday)

Life is amazing. Living is everything. I wouldn't change a thing in this moment. My optimism has hit an all-time high, which is amazing considering what I'm days away from enduring - a bone marrow transplant. I could not feel better about myself right now; I hold my head high, embrace the baldness and forge forward with remarkable confidence. Every day I pick a vibrant scarf and big obnoxious earrings to rock out. I don't care that I'm bald, I have no eye brows or how pale I appear to the general public like I did in the beginning. I choose not to care. I choose to embrace this, and be a shining beacon of positivity for all to see. There's no time in the world to be hopeless; life is short as it is, so *live* it – own it – enjoy it! It is a gift. Life is truly a gift from the universe to each and every one of us. You're fortunate, I'm fortunate; every human we encounter on this planet during our lifetime has the gift of *life* – so LIVE it!

I want my children to have every second with me I can possible give them. I also want to create as many wonderful memories with them – just in case this is it. There is no guarantee I will survive this transplant, and I would be an idiot to forget that fact. I don't plan on dying, but it's always in the back of my mind given the severity of the procedure. While I'm here, I want to give my children every family experience I can. We have movie nights, go on day trips and a few longer trips. We even bring them to the Philadelphia zoo for their first zoo visit. There's nothing like witnessing the expression on your child's face as they see magnificent sights for the first time. Adrian and Luciana eat up this experience with so much excitement and wonder; it's beautiful to experience. We trek all through the zoo, up and down hills, in and out of exhibits, seeing all kinds of amazing animals and creatures. It is the middle of the summer though, and by 1:00 with the sun at its peak, I'm spent. I get super weak and dizzy from the heat of the day. It's with a sense of quitting that I tell Lucien I can't walk anymore, I need to go home and rest. He pulls me out of my funk, reassuring me that the kids had a wonderful time and are probably tired themselves. This gets proven when on the hour and a half car ride home on the New Jersey Turnpike both kids fall asleep along with me for a much needed nap.

Right now, I'm all about laughter, devouring experience like it's going out of style and living this life to my absolute fullest capacity. Mall walking, boardwalk people watching, road trips, restaurants, movie nights, kiddie pool soaking, princess dress up, barbeques and concerts – these are the squares that make up my quilt. My time home before my transplant is winding down, and preparations have begun. I have many tests lined up which are mandatory before the transplant, including another Pulmonary Function Test, a MUGA scan of my heart and another bone marrow biopsy – awake this time. I can't worry about them until they happen; I don't want to waste a second more than I have to in panic about needles or anything else medical related – there's plenty of that to come.

Journal - July 7, 2008 (Monday)

Hey Everyone! Everything is going pretty good for the most part, there's just a lot of preparation for the transplant and the recovery period at this time. On the 4th of July we got done teaching a little early so we had a quickie burger on the grill (so that we would feel festive) then we decided to clean out all the closets in the house! We ended up throwing out like 8 big bags of garbage, which we just love. We get so excited to clean and get rid of things no one is using. We worked on the bedroom a little bit too getting it ready for my extended stay a la hotel Nocelli...

On Saturday I went with Lucien and Adrian to their eye doctor appointment. Lucien hasn't been checked in 5 years (I know it's long, but we didn't realize!) and Adrian's teacher said he was showing signs of needing them. So later this week we'll go pick them up, and I'll put up pictures of the boys and their new looks! I love Lucien's new glasses, and Adrian's make him look like a little man, I can't wait to see them.

Saturday night Lucien's parents came over and took us out to dinner at the Outback. It's so nice to get out and get my fill of stores and restaurants before the transplant because it's going to be a long time before we can go to these places again.

On Sunday Lucien had a show with Beatlemania in Harrisburg Pennsylvania. I asked Mya and Kathy to baby sit in shifts so that I could go along to the show. It was a three hour drive each way, which was fine because it was really good quality alone time just Lucien and I. The trip had its ups and downs of course. We got into a small fender bender when someone backed into us at a rest stop, and cracked our bumper – great, just what we need right now! But on the flip side, we did hit up the Sonic Drive In and devoured some of their out-of-this-world burgers. We love Sonic, but they don't have any near us.

The show was a lot of fun; it was great to feel in the swing of things and in familiar settings. It really made us forget for a few hours about everything going on and things felt 'normal'. It was a beautiful breezy night near the river, the perfect night to be outside. It was great to see the guys again and catch up with them. The show went great and was a lot of fun. It was strange, but nice for me to actually get to sit and watch the show, instead of running around like a chicken dealing with all my normal Stage Manager duties.

This week I have a few tests in preparation for the transplant. Today I had a pulmonary function test, which I passed (Whew!). Tomorrow is a heart test in the nuclear medicine department and Wednesday is a bone marrow biopsy which unfortunately I will be awake for. Thank goodness for Ativan!! That's all for now, I will update at the end of the week!!

Journal - July 13, 2008 (Sunday)

Hey Everyone! Well, here we are the night before I get admitted for the hospital stay for the transplant! We had a wonderful week trying to fit in all the activities and things that we love to do before I head in.

I sat at the front desk all week and got to get a lot of work done, which I was really happy about. I guess I'm a true workaholic because there's nothing better than answering the phones, talking to students and scheduling, I really miss working. It was great to see everyone and catch up.

Adrian started his summer preschool this week, so Lucien was able to bring me to all my tests and appointments. The pulmonary one went good, I passed it but it was hard! The Muga scan (heart test) went well, and the bone marrow biopsy went as well as that ever could. I was pretty looped on Ativan, 3 mgs to be exact, but it was still awful. By Thursday we were done with all the tests and were free in the mornings.

Friday morning we decided to bring Luciana to Pier Village for a walk on the boardwalk. She loved it so much, she was pointing to the ocean, watching the people on the sand and she fell in love with a little doggie we saw walking. We took her out of the carriage and let her hobble around on the boardwalk for a few minutes which was adorable because she's only been walking for about three weeks now. It was such a great morning out by the ocean, I'm so happy we went.

Saturday after we were done teaching, we hit the road for a shopping afternoon! We headed up to Freehold to the mall and decided to try out the new Cheesecake Factory Restaurant, which we had never heard of. We actually both hate cheesecake with a passion, but the menu looked good and the dinner was outrageous. After dinner we walked around the mall for a few minutes, we had some errands within the mall to do, like getting glasses adjusted and some other stuff. On the way home I really wanted a coffee coolatta (MOCHA!) so we stopped for a Dunkin' run.

On Sunday, we went and got the boys, little Lucien and Justen at around noon. They will be staying with Lucien all week for their vacation and to help with Adrian and Luciana. We had such a great day. Lucien grilled an amazing feast of *everything* you could imagine. We had burgers, hot dogs, shrimp, potato skins, buffalo wings, coleslaw, corn, and grilled chicken. We ate so much, that I really am amazed we didn't all just pass out after dinner! It was another beautiful day, so we took out the kiddie pool for a few laps. It's a shame we couldn't open the big pool this year, but that would have been too much work with everything going on.

So... I'm getting admitted to the hospital tomorrow (Monday) morning at 9 am and I'm sure it'll be a busy and tiring day. Lucien and I are nervous this time, because we know this is what we've been waiting for and also that these weeks coming will be harder to get through. But we're ready, and just thinking ahead to when this is all over and life resumes.

July 2008 – Getting some restaurant and shopping time in with the family just before getting readmitted for the bone marrow transplant hospitalization.

July 14 (Monday)

It's show time, people. I'm back admitted again, this time for the main event. I walk into the hospital, back to the familiar unit of the BMTU with my head held high. My room this time is positioned right in front of the nurse's station – I am the highest risk patient this time around. This is the final battle in my war against Leukemia... my mindset? Bring it on; let's do this, get it over with and move on with life! I unpack my bags of jammies, Crocs, lotions, notebooks, my laptop and my digital picture frame full of photos of my babies. It takes me only minutes to move into my room, and then I wait. What comes next?

I have Nurse Ramona today who's usually in charge when it comes to administering the Chemotherapy in preparation for a transplant. She brings in a calendar of the month of July which is labeled with all sorts of numbers, drug names and dosages. In her Jamaican accent, she explains my treatment plan for this month.

SUN	MON	TUE	WED	THUR	FRI	SAT
JULY -	14 ADMIT	15 DAY -7 BUSULFAN	16 DAY -6 BUSULFAN	17 DAY - 5 BUSLUFAN	18 DAY - 4 BUSLFAN	19 DAY -3 CYTOXAN
20 DAY -2 CYTOXAN ATG	21 DAY -1 Start Prograf ATG	22 DAY 0 REINFUSION (BMT)	23 DAY +1 MTX	24 DAY +2	25 DAY +3 MTX	26 DAY +4
27 DAY +5	28 DAY +6 MTX	29 DAY +7	30 DAY +8	31 DAY +9	AUG 1 DAY +10	2 DAY +11 MTX
3 DAY +12 Start Neupogen	4 DAY +13	5 DAY +14	6 DAY +15	7 DAY +16	8 DAY+17	9 DAY +18
10 DAY +19	11 DAY +20	12 DAY +21	13 DAY +22	14 DAY +23	15 DAY +24	16 DAY +25

CHEMOTHERAPY:

Busulfan – (Injection) – Treats certain kinds of Leukemia, and is also given to prepare the body for a bone marrow transplant. This medicine is very strong, like all medicines used to treat cancer and is injected through a central line or port. Before given this drug, you will be given medicines to help prevent vomiting and other side effects. May cause anxious feeling, headache, loss of appetite, skin rash, stomach pain, trouble sleeping.

Cytoxan (Cyclophosphamide) – (Injection) – Treats certain types of cancer. This medicine needs to be given on a fixed schedule, do not miss a dose. Drink extra fluids so you will pass more urine to keep your kidneys working well and prevent bladder problems. May cause itching, hives, swelling, trouble breathing, blistering, peeling, red skin rash, blood in your urine, painful urination, fever, chills, cough, sore throat, nausea, vomiting, weakness or yellow eyes or skin.

Methotrexate (MTX) – (Injection) – Treats several kinds of cancer, including cancer of the blood, bone, head, neck, lung and breast. This medicine is given via a shot under your skin, into a muscle, into an artery or into your spine. Side effects include itching, hives, swelling, tingling or soreness of your mouth or throat, trouble breathing, blistering of skin, vomiting, diarrhea, seizures, confusion, sores or white patches on your tongue, lips, mouth or throat and weakness.

Prograf (Tacrolimus) – (Oral) – An immunosuppressant drug which lowers your body's immune system so your body does not see a transplanted organ as an invader, stopping your body from attacking the transplanted organ. This drug may increase your risk of developing serious infections, cancers or transplant failure.

ATG (Anti-Thymocyte Globulin) – (Injection) – A special antibody used to treat graft-versus-host disease in patients having a stem cell or bone marrow transplant. Is administered via the central line directly into the blood stream. Side effects include difficulty breathing, heart palpitations, dizziness or lightheadedness, flushing, itching, rash, hives and chest pain.

This round of chemotherapy is much stronger than the treatments I've received before. This is actually the Preparative Regiment Treatment which includes the highest doses of Chemo to destroy diseased cells and blood-forming cells in the body before a transplant to make room for the new cells to flourish. This chemo literately eliminates the immune system so it cannot attack the donated cells you receive during the transplant. You only would ever receive these high doses in preparation for a transplant; never just during a normal treatment. With this high level of chemotherapy, they cause much more severe side effects, but also are able to destroy more diseased cells. Things are about to go downhill fast, or as one of the nurses explains it, "We're basically going to get you as medically close to death as possible, to allow your new marrow cells to flourish and take over for a fresh start; a new beginning of life." ... gulp.

Once my new central line is in my neck, which takes up most of the first day, we're ready to get this show on the road. The first few days of Busulfan are pretty uneventful. I spend my days watching TV and surfing the internet to try to keep busy. By day - 5, Thursday, I'm starting to feel the effects of the chemo through my low energy. Even the simplest things like watching TV require too much effort, so I choose to sleep instead. When you get Busulfan, they also give you Ativan to prevent nausea... but this has the complete opposite effect on me and I find myself not able to keep anything down.

My blood counts have started to drop, quickly too. This is what we want to happen. We need this harsh Chemo to clean out my body as much as possible to make room for my donor's cells. Everyday into treatment, as the numbers plummet, so does my energy and overall health – but not my spirit. Chemo can't take that away.

LAB RESULTS   NOCELLI, SHERI   10:38 A.M.
CHEM PROFILE   REF RANGE   07/14/08

	REF RANGE	
WBC	4.0-10.0	3.3 (L)
RBC	3.9-5.2	3.48 (L)
HGB	12.3-15.5	11.4 (L)
HCT	36-44	33.3 (L)
PLATELET CNT	140-440	219

LAB RESULTS	NOCELLI, SHERI	5:56 A.M.
CHEM PROFILE	REF RANGE	07/15/08
WBC	4.0-10.0	2.0 (L)
RBC	3.9-5.2	3.05 (L)
HGB	12.3-15.5	10.0 (L)
HCT	36-44	28,9 (L)
PLATELET CNT	140-440	176 /1000 (L)

Journal - July 19, 2008 (Saturday) Day -3

Hey Guys! Sorry for the lack of updating this week. It's been pretty uneventful, pretty much me in the room by myself playing Nintendo DS and watching bad TV. As the week putted along so did the better part of my health, I'm really weak and have been either sleeping or being nauseous most of the time. On Day -7 through -4 I got a Chemo called Busulfan, along with Busulfan they give you round the clock Ativan to prevent seizures. Of course the Ativan is what's making so physically ill. Saturday and Sunday I got a drug called Cytoxan with ATG, Monday will be a 'day or rest' still getting ATG and Then Tuesday the 22 in the infusion of my new cells.

It's been a little bit of a lonely week, even with Lucien here visiting; I slept through half the time. I just have no energy. I'm too tired to get on the phone, or to play guitar or even sometimes to watch TV.

Before I close off for today though, I want to the Raike Family for helping us out on our tropical jungle we had taking over the back yard, And to Tracy who took care of the weeds along the driveway. All these things help up so much, can't imagine how to ever thank everyone. Again, words along cannot express how thankful we are and always will be.

Well, it is late and I have no brain right now with all these typos and stuff, what can I say, I'm waiting on my new marrow! The doctors are optimistic the way my health is pulling through and as far as anyone saying if they think this will cure me, we keep hearing "It's the most aggressive treatment, and we have colleagues up and down the east coast very interested in your molecular deformation type of Leukemia." Not always the most encouraging things to hear, but what's left but to fight, hope and pray to get healthy and back to my family and friends.

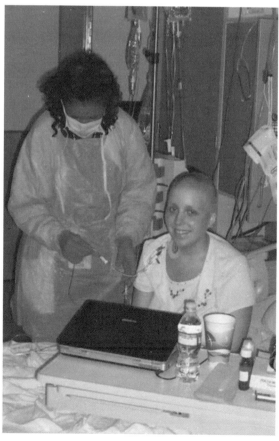

(Above) Getting chemotherapy in preparation for my bone marrow transplant.

July 22 (Tuesday) Day 0

Today is my new birthday. Today I receive the cells that will give me a new chance at life.

Doctor Ayers has explained to me the whole process of a bone marrow transplant; it's such an amazing feat of medical coordination and invention. My donor could be anyone, male or female and live anywhere in the *world*. When you join the national bone marrow registry, you open up the possibility to save a strangers life no matter where they live or who they are. Legally, the donor and I cannot know who each other is until two years post-transplant; so until then, I can wonder about who that person is. Whoever they are, they have been undergoing testing for weeks now in preparation to make sure their body is fit enough to donate. Everything is time aligned just right for the transplant, so yesterday my donor was in a hospital somewhere in the world, having their cells harvested. Those cells were then transported in a cooler overnight to New Jersey for me. My chemotherapy and my donors harvest had to be perfectly scheduled to coordinate, for me to receive the transplant today on Day 0.

The actual transplant takes about a half hour from start to finish, and actually is just like any other blood transfusion. The nurse brings in a white foam cooler, opening it up to reveal a clear bag with red liquid stuff inside – the new cells. She checks and rechecks the numbers and information on the bag with my hospital bracelet to make sure this bag is mine before hanging it up on my IV pole. She hooks it into my line, and the transplant is officially in progress. Nurse Ramona stays with me through the entire transplant process, checking my temperature and blood pressure every ten minutes. She routinely asks me how I am feeling. I feel fine, actually. Between the chemotherapy and other meds, I'm exhausted, but I feel fine otherwise.

During the process, the nurse, doctor and I talk about the process. I question why the bag of cells says "O" as the blood type... I thought I was A+? They explain to me that HLA and blood typing are two separate processes. Since they look at HLA for bone marrow transplants, it doesn't matter if the donor and recipients blood types match. Eventually, over the course of a few weeks or a few months, my old blood type will disappear, and I will officially share the same blood type as my donor.

After about a half hour, the transplant is finished. That was a breeze! What was all the fuss about? Everyone tells me how great I'm doing, keep up the awesome work. I feel awesome... until the evening comes around and I develop a fever. This is alarming to the doctors since I am already on antibiotics which the fever is spiking through. The night nurse comes in and takes a blood culture. Cultures cannot be taken from the central line like normal daily blood tests, so she has to use a needle. I cry, but not with my usual intensity... I'm just too tired to full on freak out right now.

In the morning, the fever finally goes down, but I am officially wiped out. I'm starving, and craving steak, hamburgers and popcorn from home, but I can't keep any food down anyway. I'm at the point where I just keep a bucket at the foot of the bed, because everything I try just comes back up. Because of this, I'm progressively getting weaker.

Journal - July 24, 2008 (Thursday) Day +2

Hey Everyone! Well, here we are on "Day +2" which means I had my transplant on Tuesday July 22. The transplant itself is a very uneventful process; it took about a half hour at the most. It was really just like getting a blood transfusion. The only difference was that the nurse and the doctor stayed in the room the whole time to monitor it.

That night however I did end up with a fever, so there was a lot of blood work and feeling awful. The day after I still had a fever which they were worried about because I was already on antibiotics, so that meant I was spiking through the antibiotics which is not good. The fever went away eventually, but I'm still feeling awful today. It's been impossible for me to keep any food down. I am hungry though, and craving all kinds of foods from home, I am so done with hospital food!

This morning I feel a little better, I really hope it stays this way and I don't start feeling crappy again. My hair is growing back really fast, and my eyebrows are really filling in again. I'm happy that it's growing back, but at the same time it's kind of a pain because the hair on my head will have to be washed now. It was nice and fuzzy but now it's starting to feel a little greasy after growing for two days.

That's about all that's going on, hopefully I start feeling better. I've really felt too awful to talk on the phone, even to Lucien sometimes at night which is hard because usually I wait all day to talk to him. I miss being home more than I can even say, I miss the kids and Lucien so much. I can't wait to get home and back to normal life. All I want is to be home, work, see my family and be normal.

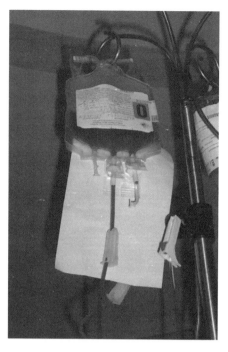

(Above) The bag containing my new bone marrow cells!
(Below) July 22, 2008, this is me getting my bone marrow transplant

July 25 (Friday) Day +3

Things are moving along great, the doctors and nurses are thrilled at how I'm holding up through this whole process. I'm a diligent patient and listen to *almost* every bit of instructions I'm given. I'm drinking as much water as I can to stay hydrated, wash my hands after everything, and brush my teeth several times a day to ward off infection. With my platelets so low, they have me using a strange version of a toothbrush; it's actually a sponge attached to a stick. After every brushing, I have to use medical grade fluoride mouth wash which comes in an amber bottle. I have to use this mouth wash after every meal as well. I hate brushing with this stuff, but whatever it takes to avoid infection I'll do.

LAB RESULTS   NOCELLI, SHERI   6:00 A.M.
CHEM PROFILE   REF RANGE   07/25/08

	REF RANGE	07/25/08
WBC	4.0-10.0	1.1 (L)
RBC	3.9-5.2	2.53 (L)
HGB	12.3-15.5	8.6 (L)
HCT	36-44	24.0 (L)
PLATELET CNT	140-440	36 (L)

Lucien visits over the weekend, but it's different than any other time he's come to see me. He has to shower and change into fresh clothes before he comes up to the hospital. Before he comes into my room, he has to dress in a sterile robe over his clothes, wear plastic gloves and a mask to protect me from germs he's carrying from the outside world. He can only hold me through this shield separating us – I miss human contact with my husband. Most of his visit he spends watching me sleep. When I am awake, we joke around about the stupidest little things. We hold hands and watch TV when I can stay awake. When the nurses are not looking, he takes his mask off, and kisses me on top of my head.

Sunday morning, I get hit with a severe nose bleed which lasts for ages. For an hour Lucien brings me tissues and paper towels for me to use. When it finally ends, he wets a towel to clean my face and my fingers of the blood. After all of this commotion, I am weaker than ever. All I can do is sleep, which is killing me inside that he is here to visit me and I can't even keep my eyes open.

He is gallant through this whole thing, and never leaves my side even when I am sleeping. He holds my hand the entire afternoon as I drift in and out of my extended nap. Just knowing he is next to me fills me with comfort and absolute harmony.

Just as he's packing up his things to leave, my nose springs a leak again only worse than before. The nurses are worried since my platelets are so low. We start the same routine we did this morning with him bringing me an endless supply of tissues. He calls his parents who are waiting at our house to drop off the kids to tell them he's going to be late; he wants to stay with me until my nose stops bleeding. Patiently we tend to my nose; I'm quickly losing what little energy I have left. Tears start streaming down my face, "I'm so sorry to make you late, you can go if you want. You really don't have to stay because of this." My words are lethargic.

Lucien smiles through his paper mask and rubs my head, "I'm not leaving you like this. Just breathe and relax, it's all going to be okay. I'll get home when I get home." He assures and calms me. I take a deep breathe, and together we wait for my nose to stop. By the time it subsides, my eyes are heavy with sleep again. He lowers his mask, kisses me on my forehead and encourages me to sleep. I follow his urge, and close my eyes with him still sitting there – the first time in all these months that I haven't watched as he left my hospital room.

I'm not sure when, how, or why but things have gotten really bad at lightning speed. I have constant fevers which fluctuate between 102 – 104. Even Tylenol can only bring them down to 100 for a short time before they skyrocket again. I have non-stop chills which turn to sweats with the flick of a switch. The nurses bring me 4 or 5 extra blankets when I'm shivering relentlessly, then I kick them to the floor in a hot sweaty fury of warmth. I'm throwing up constantly, even when I haven't eaten a bite. My mouth has developed a mass growth of a white film, like a sheet of blisters covering my tongue, inner cheeks and the roof of my mouth. I can't eat, drink or speak without excruciating pain. I nod or shake my head in slow movements when the doctors and nurses ask me questions. The technicians have switched to taking my temperature by putting the disposable thermometer in my arm pit to avoid irritating my mouth sores. With all of this madness, I am so worn down that I can barely make it to the bathroom, resulting in my very own potty commode next to my bed.

By Tuesday I am literately a blob on my bed. Everything is a blur. All I know is that I am lying on my left side with the head of the bed at a fifteen degree angle. I can open my eyes slightly, but that is the only bodily movement I have control over. I cannot lift my head from my pillow, I can't move my hand or fingers, and my legs are dead weights – I feel paralyzed. I think there are people talking in my room, but I can't be sure what they are saying, all of their words are a jumbled frequency I can't decipher. They come over, one on each side of me and turn my body to lie on my back, gently using their hands to guide me. The nurse on my left is talking to me, but I don't hear her through the fog my brain is engulfed in. I feel her take my arm, lay it to the side and wrap a tourniquet around it. I feel the cool sensation of the alcohol pad as she disinfects, and as she starts the blood draw all I can do is close my eyes and breathe through it – so weak I can't even produce a tear, a whimper or a frown. She finishes, puts a bandage and places my arm at my side. "Would you like to go back on your side, sweetie?" I can't answer; I can't even nod my head. As if she knows what I wish I could say, she turns me back to my side.

The whole day goes on like this. I have no sense of time passing, except that it's the same day because there is still light coming in the window. As night approaches, I start perspiring with fever. I still cannot move; it feels like I am lying in a puddle of sweat. The nurses keep tending to my IV pole, adding and removing bags, hanging glass bottles of antibiotics. They arrange my call button in the palm of my hand with my thumb over the button in case I need them, but I can't use it, it's too difficult to make the connection between my brain and my thumb. Therefore, when my IV machine beeps with a line occlusion or air in the line, I lay listening to it beep, beep, beep until finally someone comes in the room and notices it alarming.

LAB RESULTS CHEM PROFILE	NOCELLI, SHERI REF RANGE	5:00 A.M. 07/28/08
WBC	4.0-10.0	.3 (L) **
RBC	3.9-5.2	2.39 (L)
HGB	12.3-15.5	7.8 (L)
HCT	36-44	21.9 (L)
PLATELET CNT	140-440	26 (L) **

** Result reviewed by smear

Wednesday brings no change. They decide that it must be the central line in my neck that got infected, and want to remove it. Transport comes to my room, but I cannot move to the gurney, I am still an immobile pile of myself on the bed – still on my left side from the night before. Several men congregate around me, each grabbing an end of my sheet. On the count of three, they hoist me through the air on my sheet and place me on the gurney. I moan with every movement; the only communication I have. They bring me downstairs to special procedures.

I get rushed right into the room, no waiting around in the hallway this time. Immediately, the doctors and nurses fuss around me, removing the central line. They clean up my neck and place a large bandage where the line used to be. Now, they take my right arm, extend it on the plank and strap it down. Oh shit, you've got to be kidding me. It's one thing to go through this crying as my coping skill – but to be forced through this with no outlet of emotion is a complete hell. All I can do is lay there, unable to move and endure every stabbing needle, poke, prod, slice and stitch. It takes them forever to find the right spot again. Just like last time, they have to try twice to get it right and when they finally finish two hours later, my arm is stained with deep, dark black and blues from the trauma. I may be laying there silent and still, but inside I am SCREAMING in an unimaginable broken down, beaten up tone of pain and suffering. All I can do is lay on the gurney, and stare at the ceiling with no release of feeling whatsoever.

Transport brings me back upstairs to the BMTU. Getting wheeled by the nurses' station I hear them comment in a shocked tone at the massive bruise encompassing my upper arm. Once in my room, the same group of men comes around to lift me on my sheet back onto my bed. When they lay me down, my head is facing my table… this is when I notice that my cell phone is gone. My eyes dart left and right, I see my notebook, pen, lotion, mouth wash, water… no cell phone. My breathing picks up rapidly; my heart is pounding so hard I swear it's going to jump right out of my chest. My phone is my only communication to the outside world… it's the only way I can call Lucien. I can't use the room phone, because our home number is considered long distance and it would cost a fortune to use every day. My breathing becomes labored and the next thing I know, I dart up into a complete upright position on the bed. Everyone in the room starts to panic around me since I haven't moved in days. I'm gasping for air, but am choked, unable to get a breath… my heart feels like it's skipping beats, I feel like I am going to suffocate to death right here and now.

In one swift motion one nurse raises the head of my bed to an almost right angle, another pushes me back to lean on it and a third nurse puts an oxygen mask around my face. They direct me to calm down, to try to breathe. Through the mask I am muttering over and over and over, "my phone… my phone… it's gone…" It's a miracle that they can actually understand me. One of the nurses goes over to the table and looks for the phone. She looks all over the shelves and drawers before announcing her findings that I am right. The phone is gone.

"Someone on the staff must have stolen it while you were downstairs, sweetie. I'll put a claim in for you, and we'll get your room phone hooked up in the meantime. We'll figure this out, but for right now you need to calm down. You had a panic attack. We'll help you get everything sorted out. Right now, think about slow, even breaths." She sits on the edge of my bed, and coaches me through my breathing for a few minutes. Once I've steadied my breathing, I start to doze off from all the commotion. The nurse lowers the angle on the bed, but leaves the oxygen mask on me for the remainder of the day while I sleep.

In the evening, I talk to Lucien on the hospital line for a little while. It's so difficult to speak with the sores overtaking my mouth, but I am able to tell him that my phone was stolen. I spend most of the conversation listening to him as he tells me stories about what the kids have been up so, and some funny things some of the students said or did throughout the day. We call it a night early since I just don't have the stamina to stay awake.

LAB RESULTS   NOCELLI, SHERI   6:00 A.M.
CHEM PROFILE   REF RANGE   07/28/08

WBC	4.0-10.0	.1 (L) **
RBC	3.9-5.2	2.24 (L)
HGB	12.3-15.5	7.3 (L)
HCT	36-44	20.0 (L)
PLATELET CNT	140-440	25 (L) **

** Result reviewed by smear

The morning arrives, and while I have gained a little mobility in my body, my throat is aching with sores and blisters. I cannot swallow food or water, take pills or even speak. When Doctor Ayers comes on his morning rounds, he decides to make some adjustments to my treatments to help me through this. He puts in an order for IV nutrients to be infused and changes all of my oral medications to injections. He also decides to put me on steroids to help me deal with all of my ailments. He goes on to tell me that he is very happy with my progress, and that many of the symptoms I am experiencing are actually signs that the transplant is working.

A little while later, Nurse Mary Ann comes in with a large clear plastic bag full of white liquid resembling milk. She hangs it on the IV pole, hooks it up to my line and explains, "This is TNA, or total nutrient admixture containing glucose, amino acids, lipids and some vitamins and minerals. Since you're having a hard time eating, this will supply you with all the nutrients you need but will bypass the processes of eating and digestion so that you get what you need." I nod, showing her I understand.

When Lucien calls on the hospital phone at night, I can't even speak a word. Without any explanation, he understands completely. We spend an hour on the phone with him talking to me about his day, telling my stories and talking about anything he can to keep the silence at bay. When he says goodnight, and that he loves me, I can't even respond with anything but a faint "Mmhmm".

Journal - August 1, 2008 (Friday) Day +10

It has been a very hard week, and still is. This is the first time I have had the energy to pick up the computer since last Thursday. It all started Sunday morning with one of my famous hour long nose bleeds. The day went downhill from there, we had a nice visit, then in the late afternoon I started getting really weak and right before he was supposed to leave I got a second nose bleed. Lucien was great a stayed an extra hour with me until it stopped, even though it through off the schedule to pick up the kids and everything. From here, every day of the week got worse and worse. I think next started the high fevers, constant fevers ranging between 102 -104 coming down to 100 for a few hour with Tylenol. This went on literally all week, and fingers crossed I made it through last night and half of today at around 97 degrees. I had awful chills all week, changing quickly back to sweats from the fevers, vomiting everything, then the other end of things started going crazy. I got so weak that I can't yet walk to the bathroom, I have a stupid little commode thing, it's that bad. There have been times I have not been able to sit up without being lifted in my bed from being so weak. Wednesday they decided to take the central line out of my neck thinking that it might be the cause of the infection and place a new one in my arm – everyone that knows me knows that this is the most torture I go through in here. And this was the worst ever. It took them 2 hours, and two tries to get it right. I was a mess. *Then*, I get brought back to my room and my cell phone was stolen. This was enough that I think I had my first ever panic attack, I couldn't breathe, they were running around to get me oxygen, it was awful. Thursday hits, bringing along a sore throat, so bad that I cannot drink, eat, take pills or speak. That hasn't changed today, so they are starting me on IV nutrients. I also have been put on steroids to make me stronger. The doctor says to hang in there; I am really wrapping up the worst of it. Some of the things I am showing are actually sign that the new cells are starting to grow. My white cells are going up right on target, so he keeps telling me I'm doing great and to hang in there.

It's been crazy, not getting on the computer or being able to talk to anyone. When I had a cell phone I saw everyone calling but didn't have the strength. Now I can't even speak to Lucien if I call him from the hospital phone. He knows though and I call and listen to him, he's been so supportive and amazing. This turned out long, but there was a lot to say! Hopefully things starting turning around now.

LAB RESULTS   NOCELLI, SHERI 6:00 A.M.

CHEM PROFILE	REF RANGE	08/02/08
WBC	4.0-10.0	3.2 (L)
RBC	3.9-5.2	2.77 (L)
HGB	12.3-15.5	8.7 (L)
HCT	36-44	24.0 (L)
PLATELET CNT	140-440	48 (L)

LAB RESULTS CHEM PROFILE	NOCELLI, SHERI REF RANGE	6:00 A.M. 08/05/08
WBC	4.0-10.0	15.9 (H)
RBC	3.9-5.2	3.17 (L)
HGB	12.3-15.5	10.0 (L)
HCT	36-44	28.9 (L)
PLATELET CNT	140-440	172 (L)

Journal - August 5, 2008 (Tuesday) Day +14

This week has been a lot better so far. Once they started me on the Steroids, everything slowly began to get better. By Sunday night I could start to eat again, and people could understand me if I tried to talk. The fevers are all gone, and the doctors keep telling me how well and quickly my blood counts went up. I found out today that they're letting me go home in 5, possibly 3 days! That was shocking to me, but so exciting. Of course I'm really nervous to go home, I know things are not ready for me yet, and it's a lot of pressure on Lucien to get everything ready. Luciana is a handful in the mornings for him to handle and try to clean for me on top of keeping the normal household running; this is a stressful week for him.

I'll update as soon as I hear anything else about going home. It'll be so amazing to be home. I know there's many weekly doctor appointments in store, but I'll deal with that to be home with my family.

August 6 (Wednesday) Day +15

The steroids have boosted my recovery faster than the speed of light. The sores in my mouth are going away, I am able to eat soft foods and drink on my own again so they've unhooked the IV nutrients. I can speak again – you don't realize how much you've missed communicating until it's taken away from you! I can move around again and am even able to make it to the real bathroom instead of the commode sitting in the middle of my room (where anyone can walk in while you're going!)

Doctor Ricci is on rounds this week, and comes in this morning with a mischievous grin, "So, today we're going to play a game. We're going to unhook all of your IV lines and get you on all oral medications. We'll monitor you this way for a few days and if all goes well, we should be able to bust you outta here by Saturday. What do you think of that plan?" He flashes a crooked smile.

"Let's do it!" I exclaim in pure surprise. I am shocked, I mean, Saturday? The goal was to be home by September and here we are at the beginning of August! This has to be a dream! I call Lucien immediately on my new cell phone he brought me over the weekend and tell him the news. For him, this means some major work on the home front. We've been advised to completely clean out the room I'll be recouping in. This entails dusting, vacuuming, steaming the carpet and washing the curtains. We've had several air purifiers donated by our generous friends and clients, so I can have one going in our bedroom as well as the waiting room. Lucien spends the next few days finishing up everything for my possible weekend arrival home. He scrubs down the bathroom, gets my shower seat ready, sets up a microwave area in our bedroom... basically he transforms our bedroom into a satellite hospital room.

I get unhooked and have free reign of the room without carting a pole around with me... such sweet freedom! I take advantage and spend zero time in bed all day, instead watching TV from the couch and indulging in some people watching perched on my window seat. I can totally deal with being here till the weekend if I'm not hooked up to the dreaded IV pole! At night, Lucien and I chat like little kids on the phone, excitement dripping from our voices. We wish each other good night and turn in for the evening.

Doctor Ricci comes in super early the next morning, with that same silly grin on his face, "So, how'd you like to sleep in your own bed tonight?" I think my jaw actually hit the floor. "You did great yesterday, so let's get you outta here kid. I have to say, in all my years, I have never seen any patient be released by Day 16 after a bone marrow transplant. You truly are one of a kind; looks like that rocker defiance came in handy." He laughs at himself for a second, and I laugh along. "The nurses will get all of your medications from the pharmacy and teach you what you need to do. They usually have a few days' notice, but I think they can hustle to get you home. I want you to remember something though… and that's that you're probably going to have to come back to the hospital within a few days. Your immune system is still very low right now, and you're highly susceptible to all kinds of viruses and bacteria. I'm not trying to burst your bubble; I just want you to prepare yourself. Ninety nine percent of patients released after a transplant return within a few days for treatment inpatient, and they're not even released as early as we're letting you go. So your odds are pretty certain that we'll see you back."

I nod my head acknowledging him, but as soon as he leaves and I am alone in my room, I say what I'm thinking out loud, "Not *this* patient doctor, *I'm* not coming back." I smile and reach for the phone to let Lucien know the new development!

The nurses zip around the hospital getting all of my medications from the pharmacy, discharge papers prepared and booking my follow up visit. I'm elated at the coincidence that Nurse Mary Ann is on duty today, and is helping me get myself organized. She prints up a clear instruction sheet of all my medications; showing me what the bottles and pills look like as we go through the list together.

SHERI NOCELLI
MEDICATION LIST
8/7/2008 (Day +16)
PROGRAF – (Tacrolimus) (Immunosuppressant) – dose depends on drug level** HOLD AM dose when having labs drawn – 8 a.m. / 8p.m. (dose upon discharge 1.5 mg twice a day) – NEXT DOSE 8 p.m. tonight

CELLCEPT – (Mycophenolate Mofetil) (Immunosuppressant) – 1000 mg twice daily (8 a.m. / 8 p.m.) – NEXT DOSE 8 p.m. tonight

ACYCLOVIR – (antiviral) – 400 mg twice a day (8 a.m. / 8 p.m.) – NEXT DOSE 8 p.m. tonight

VFEND – (Voriconazole) (antifungal) – 200 mg twice a day before meals (7 a.m. / 4 p.m.) – NEXT DOSE tomorrow morning

BACTRIM DS (antibiotic) – 1 tab twice a day on Mon-Thur only (8 a.m. / 8 p.m.) – NEXT DOSE 8 p.m. tonight

ACTIGALL (liver) – 300 mg three times a day (8 a.m. / 4 p.m. / 8 p.m.) – NEXT DOSE tonight 8 p.m.

PRILOSEC (stomach / over-the-counter) – 1 capsule daily (before a meal) – NEXT DOSE before a meal tomorrow

MAGNESIUM OXIDE – 400 mg three times a day (8 a.m. / 4 p.m. / 8 p.m.) – NEXT DOSE tonight 8 p.m.

AMBIEN (sleeping pill) – 1o mg nightly at bedtime as needed

HYDROCORTISONE 1% topical cream – apply to rash every 6 hours as needed

PREDNISONE (steroid) – 60 mg each morning and 40 mg each evening – do not take on an empty stomach (8 a.m. / 5 p.m.) – NEXT DOSE tomorrow with breakfast

ATIVAN – 1 mg every 8 hours as needed

ZOFRAN – 4 mg every 6 hours as needed for nausea

I also receive a lengthy package of discharge paperwork.

ADULT DISCHARGE INSTRUCTIONS
DIAGNOSIS: ONCOLOGY

Follow Up: Please follow up with Doctor Ayers on Saturday 8/9/2013 at 9:00 a.m.
Follow up lab work on 8/9/2013 as ordered
Medication: You are being discharged home on medication. Please review the medication discharge instructions

Weight: Obtain a scale and weigh yourself daily. Record your weight on chart and notify your doctor of a 2 pound or more weight gain in one day
Activity Level: As tolerated
Positioning: No restriction
Sex: Presently should not have sex
Work: As tolerated
School: N/A
Driving: None allowed until cleared by your doctor
Hygiene: No restriction
Travel: Consult with primary MD
Nutrition: No fresh (uncooked) fruits or vegetables. No pepper or spices. No unpasteurized milk, cheese or dairy products. No luncheon meats. Do not eat raw fish (sushi). Do not eat rare meat or meat that is undercooked.
Elimination: Avoid constipation and straining for a bowel movement. Drink 6-8 glasses of water a day. Notify your doctor if there is blood in your urine, strong odor or you are unable to urinate.
Protection: Help yourself recover from treatment during the first few weeks after chemotherapy. Take your temperature twice a day. If you have a fever above 100.5 or feel warm, flushed or itchy call your doctor. Avoid people and crowds whenever possible. No dental work is permitted. Apply sunscreen SFP-15 or greater and wear long sleeves, hats and pants when sun exposure is possible. For prolonged Neutropenia, consult your oncologist before taking Tylenol, Aspirin, Motrin, Advil, etc. No fresh fruits or vegetables. No plants. No cleaning up after pets. Avoid people who are sick or have been recently vaccinated. Plan activities and incorporate rest periods into them. Allow for daily naps, walking is the best exercise.
Due to low platelets counts, there is an increased risk in bleeding: Do NOT use razor blades. Use a soft toothbrush and do not floss.
NOTIFY DOCTOR:
- Temperature over 100.5, shaking or chills
- Redness, swelling, pain, odor or drainage from any wounds or catheter sites
- Shortness of breath, cough or difficulty breathing
- Painful bowel movement
- Sore throat or swelling of the throat

- Chest pain, burning when you urinate, new skin rashes, blisters or burning skin
- Loss of appetite, nausea, vomiting
- Onset of mouth sores
- More than 4 watery stools in 24 hours, pink colored urine, black or tarry stool

FALL PREVENTION:
Remove area rugs, throw rugs, place light and telephone near your bed, use nightlights, keep stairways and hallways clear of clutter, consider placing handrails near toilet and bathtub

I sign on the discharge paper, and I am a free woman.

Journal - August 8, 2008 (Friday) Day +17

Well, how's this for an update... I'm home! I'm on day 17 after the transplant, and I'm already home! On Wednesday the doctors took me off of all the IVs I was getting, and switched me over to pills for everything. I figured hopefully by Saturday I'd be able to come home, as it turns out, the doctor came in Thursday morning and said, "So, how'd you like to sleep in your own bed tonight?" I was floored! So all day Thursday the nurses were amazing and went crazy trying to get me all my meds for discharge. It was a lot of work for them, they usually have at least a day's notice to get everything rolling, but they made it happen! Lucien came in the morning and took all my bags which was great, and then his parents picked me up at about 6 at night. I walked out with my little (big) bag of meds, and boom! I'm home!

It's really funny because my mind thinks I can do everything normal, like just run up the stairs, or simple things like that. But when I walked in and tried to climb the stairs, wow! My legs were literally shaking and I had to hold the railings really tight to keep my balance. I got right in the shower, what a great feeling to be able to shower!! I really needed to because my hair that grew back is now all falling out again and it is so itchy! It's like cat hair getting in my eyes, all over my clothes, it's awful. So I'm trying to wash away as much as I can, I mean, if it's gonna fall out then let's just get rid of it.

It's wonderful to be home, I'm staying in the bedroom for the most part, because I can't go in the waiting room at all right now. So, that's the update! I'm home, feeling pretty good, just really tired. Taking 14 prescriptions multiple times a day, and I wouldn't trade it for the world. I'll update more often now that I'm home, I have about two to three doctor appointments a week, so I'll let everyone know how the progress is coming along.

Journal - August 11, 2008 (Monday) Day +20

Things are going really well so far! It's so wonderful to be home, and seeing the kids again is just amazing. They both changed so much in a few weeks. Luciana had a huge smile on her face and started saying "Mama" repeatedly when she first saw me – that was great. Adrian gave me a big hug and said, "Mommy I missed you so much." I can't believe how well he is communicating; his speech has gotten so much better this past month. He started rubbing my head, feeling the hair that is starting to grow back again and told me he likes my new feathers!

Saturday we had a nice barbeque complete with all the foods I haven't been allowed to eat forever like tomatoes and lettuce on the burger and coleslaw! So good. Of course, I have a little mucus on my tongue that hasn't gone away yet, and it really changes the flavors of a lot of foods. Some things taste really good, and some are just nasty. I'm eating a lot anyway though, because my appetite is through the roof from the steroids.

Sunday we did something that I don't think we ever did before. We lounged in jammies all day watching TV on the couch, a first for us. I even pulled together enough energy to do something very out of the ordinary – *I* cooked us dinner. That's right, my usual specialty is Macaroni and Cheese out of the box, but all the time in the hospital watching food network inspired me to cook! There's nothing I want to do more than have a Sunday of cooking and the kids helping and running around. Lucien does all the cooking here, so he was really happy to have a day off and we had a nice crock pot Roast for dinner (it was my first meal ever, so I'm allowed to cheat with a crock pot). That really wiped me out though, I was exhausted and don't think I'll be venturing into the kitchen anytime soon; I need to slow down and rest. I'm still really weak, going up the stairs takes a good minute or two, I have to go real slow and hold both railings for dear life.

My doctor appointments both on Saturday and today went really well. They lowered my steroids today dramatically, so we have to watch and see how I react to that. In the office they were all amazed that I went home on day 16 after the transplant and was sitting in their office on day 20... They kept telling me I looked great, so that was encouraging. I'm still really ultra-high risk for fever, rash, and all kinds of other problems, so I have to be so careful. Some of those things are out of my hands if they happen, if I get any graft vs. host disease, so we're praying I handle everything well. On a side note – I think everyone knows I'm a huge Brett Favre fans... don't know why, I just love watching the guy. When I found out he was coming back to football last week, I immediately wanted a football jersey in the green bay colors (they're classic Favre, come on!) and now we have Brett the Jet! I can't believe he's in New York! I'm hoping I get to make it to a game, even though he's in Jet uniform, he's Favre! So here are some pictures of me today wearing my Favre fan gear! Enjoy!

Journal - August 13, 2008 (Wednesday) Day +22

Time for some ups and downs, of course. Things were really great the first few days home, and then on Tuesday I started to get some ailments. I woke up in the middle of the night with excruciating pain in my knees. I had read about joint pain, but you really don't know what that means until you're going through it. It had me in tears, no position would help, Tylenol did nothing (as usual), it was awful. In the morning I needed Lucien to walk me to the bathroom, practically carrying me, I just was unable to use my legs. I spent about a good half hour pacing really slow holding onto the bed and that loosened the joints up enough that I was at least able to move around. The pain was there, dull all day, and then got worse at night again.

I also developed this burning rash on the palms of my hands. It made it impossible for me to do anything; I couldn't even open my pill bottles. It was one of the things that I was supposed to call the doctor about if I noticed a rash developing, so I called. They told me first, that the joint pain is very common, and that if it continues this painful then they will give me a prescription for a painkiller or something like that. About the rash, they were pretty concerned; we need to see if that is graft versus host disease or something else. So they scheduled me today for a ...... skin biopsy! Once I heard this I was devastated all the rest of the day, I was a mess.

So Wednesday morning Lucien and Luciana brought me in, and Lucien held my hand while I cried away during the biopsy. It wasn't that bad, but I don't want to do that again anytime soon. They took blood while I was there and gave me the pain killer prescription for the joint pain. Now I don't have to go back until Monday.... thank goodness! Some time off from there will be really nice.

Other than that, nothing else new. Luciana and I are spending a lot of time together. Mostly me looking at her from far away because I still am not going near the kids and if I do, I shower right after. Which reminds me, I want to thank whoever it was that bought me the wonderful shower seat. I had it on my Amazon list, and usually when things ship, I see who sent them. But on that package, the packing slip didn't say who sent it. Whoever you are out there, I can't thank you enough, I use that every day and couldn't shower alone without it.

Alright, I'll keep updating! Hopefully things start to look up a little bit now.

August 13 (Wednesday) Day +22

I wake up at 2:30 in the morning crying in excruciating pain. My legs ache like I can't even describe; I try to move them, but they are stiff as wood. I lay here crying, not sure what else I can do – why are they hurting like this? Lucien stirs awake to my whimpers, even though I've tried to keep them quiet to let him sleep. "What's wrong, where does it hurt?" he's on immediate alert as he jumps immediately into a calm but genuine panic mode.

"My legs," I murmur, "they ache so bad, I can't even move them, it hurts so much." I'm just flat out crying by now. Lucien takes the covers off of me and starts massaging my knees, calves and feet doing all he can to make the pain go away. I sob as the agony takes over my whole system; I have never felt such a nagging relentless pain like this. For what seems like an eternity, Lucien rubs my legs into the night, until I finally fall asleep through my tears.

This morning is a complete repeat of the middle of the night, as I wake up in a fit of pain. Hearing me, Lucien wakes up and I ask him to help me get to the bathroom. He comes to my side of the bed, tries to lift my left leg but stops immediately as I bellow in pain. He reaches for my both of my legs this time, scooping one arm behind my knees and his other arm behind my back. Slowly, he lifts me to a sitting position on the edge of the bed where I rest for a minute grimacing in pain. He comes behind me, supporting me by wrapping his arms around my chest and hoists me into somewhat of a standing position. Together, we hobble gradually towards the bathroom with Lucien holding most of my weight. We finally make it the fifteen feet to the bathroom where he sits me on the toilet. How humiliating, screw the pain – I can't even walk myself to the bathroom anymore.

When I've finished, Lucien assists me back to the bed where I sit on the edge, my legs stiff and throbbing beneath me. He has to go get Adrian ready for summer camp, so I am left alone to sort this mess out. I figure that maybe if I can get blood flowing that maybe I can work through the discomfort and loosen things up. I scowl as I turn my body facing the bed, standing myself up using the mattress as leverage. Finally in a standing position, my legs wobble under me like the Little Mermaid, Ariel, standing on the beach for the first time as a human. Using the bed frame as support, I pace at turtle speed… one leg, the other leg, one leg, the other leg until after a half hour or so, I feel somewhat strong enough to let go. Slowly but surely, I make my way across the room without any support – mission accomplished, legs are weak, achy and stiff but at least they're somewhat functional.

As the day goes on, my legs feel a little better but I develop a horrifying rash on the palms of my hands. The entire inside of my hand is beet red, and looks like one humungous blister covering the entire surface. It burns, itches and scowls my hands – making the smallest of tasks absolutely impossible. I can't use the remote control, open my pill bottles, turn a door knob, use a fork or grab toilet paper – everything I touch feels like ten thousand razor blades piercing my skin. Rashes are on my list of "call the doctor if…" so I call Doctor Ayers cell phone to tell him what's going on. He calmly assures me that this is all part of the process, and that he will do what he can to make me comfortable. He explains that both of these symptoms, the rash and the leg pain are both graft-versus-host disease coming out in different ways.

Graft-versus-host disease is a complication which occurs after undergoing a bone marrow or stem cell transplant in which the newly transplanted donor cells attack the transplant recipient's body. In allogeneic transplants, where the stem cells or bone marrow tissues are received from a donor, the new cells regard the recipient's body as foreign, causing them to attack the recipient's body. Symptoms range in severity, and occur in either acute GVHD or chronic GVHD, both ranging from mild to severe. Acute symptoms in the first three months after a transplant can include diarrhea, vomiting, nausea, dry or irritated eyes, and skin rash, redness or itching. Chronic symptoms start after three months and can include dry eyes, vision changes, dry mouth, fatigue, chronic pain, muscle weakness, skin rash, shortness of breath, vaginal dryness and weight loss. Doctor Ayers explains to me that while graft-versus-host is uncomfortable, it's actually a good sign after transplant because it means that the new donor cells are gaining momentum and "taking". It shows that the donor cells are stronger than my weakened cells – he is happy to hear signs of graft-versus-host. On the flip side of the coin, if the leg pain doesn't subside or gets worse, he will prescribe prescription pain killers to help. The rash he is more concerned about, so he schedules me for a skin biopsy to make sure that it actually is GVHD and not something else.

Life post bone marrow transplant is a lot of hard work; I am very diligent about following all the guidelines I've read about online about staying well after a transplant. I do not go anywhere near our downstairs since it is essentially a waiting room for a hundred young students every week, wouldn't dream of using the downstairs bathroom, and avoid door knobs like they carry the plague – after all, to me, they do. I shower every single day to rid myself of any possibility of germs. After each shower I feel like I ran a mile – they are so much work! I can't shower by myself standing, so I sit on a shower seat while I soap and wash my "feathers" which are starting to grow back in with baby shampoo. I use a brand new towel after every shower and put on fresh jammies. When I go to my doctors' appointments, I wear a face mask and plastic medical gloves to protect myself. My daily pill taking is like a part time job, and eating is easier said than done with everything tasting pasty to my white mucus coated taste buds. I don't go near my children – I only admire them from across the room. It's too risky; is it worth one hug if a possible consequence is hospitalization? The baby sitters still come every day to take care of the kids, since I can't yet care for them. Not only am I too weak to tend to them; I'd also rather enjoy them from afar then to be separated from them again – soon enough I'll be well enough to cuddle, squeeze and kiss my babies.

Journal - August 19, 2008 (Tuesday) Day +28

Things are puttin' along pretty good. The rash on my hands got better for a few days, then on Friday I woke up with it the worst it's been. It's really hard because I couldn't open pill bottles, cut food, type, anything. It was really frustrating and painful. I used a whole tube of Hydrocortisone cream over the course of Friday and by Saturday morning my hands were much better. I do have a faint rash on my arms that is what they biopsied that I noticed over the weekend started to spread everywhere. It doesn't itch, but it's there. Because that seems to be spreading, and also the mucus on my tongue started to spread to my cheeks and lips, the doctor upped my Steroids really high to try to kick all of this out. I was taking 40mg in the morning only, now I'm on 60mg in the morning and 60 in the afternoon. It is confirmed from the skin biopsy that I have Graft Versus Host Disease, which really is to be expected since my donor was unrelated. But if we stay on top of it, then we should be able to keep it under control. Because I have it, my blood work Monday was a little off, my Liver enzymes were high and my Platelets were pretty low, but they told me that's because of the Graft Versus Host Disease.

Honestly, the Steroids are bothering me a lot, because they make you gain weight first, but mostly because they puff up your face so much. It's really upsetting when you look in the mirror and it looks nothing like you. I know when I stop the Steroids the puffiness will go away, but it's still hard to face people knowing that I look so different. I guess though if I have to look like I do in order to stay home and strong and out of the hospital then that's a fair trade off.

It's so wonderful being home. The kids are just amazing and do more amazing things every day. Yesterday was Adrian's birthday; I can't believe he's 5 years old already. We couldn't tell him it was his birthday though, because he would have been looking for a cake and party. He'll get all of that this coming weekend though. He did love his birthday cards in the mail, he looked at me and yelled, "I got mail?!" he was so excited and made me read him the cards 10 times.

Other than that, I'm still trying to find foods that taste good to me. The mucus in my mouth masks the real taste of everything. Some strong flavors come through, and some things are downright disgusting. Like I can't stand dip, hot fudge, apples, ketchup and a ton more. It's just gross! But there are some things that are so good that I'm just going back to like Salads with Italian dressing, Provolone and Olive Loaf sandwiches on Wonder Bread, steak, sweet corn on the cob, pop tarts and ice cream. It's so random! I keep trying new things, if I don't like it I don't eat it, that's all!

I'm a little stressed too, because starting the first week of September a couple of the babysitters are not able to continue. I'm not really sure what we're going to do yet, because I'm not allowed to take care of the kids until I'm at day 100, and I'm only day 28. I think in two weeks I'll be able to handle Adrian when he gets home from school in the afternoons, but I'm worried about the nights with the baby. I can't lift her, so there's no way I can get her up from her nap and feed her, and I'm not allowed to change diapers, so if I have to watch both kids until Lucien is done working, I don't know how it will happen. I have a few nights covered, but there's a few that I need to find someone to come over from about 5 – 9 while Luciana is up. I just hope it works out; it's just stressful worrying about how it's going to work out.

Journal - August 25, 2008 (Monday) Day +34

I can't believe another week has gone by! Today I am day 34 already. I had a doctor appointment today, everything looked okay. I'm still waiting for them to call me back about the blood work to see if we are adjusting the Prograf (that the drug that suppresses my immune system). They did tell me to not take another drug today called VFend until I hear from them, because that could be what's making my Liver enzymes be off. But we won't know unless I don't take it to see what my body does, I do need the pill though. So it's really just a test I think. They also took blood today for a really important test which we will get the results back in about 10 days. I'm anxious for the results; they will show what percentage of me has become the donor cells. What we want to see is 100% and no more of my old cells. This is really important and I think I'll get more anxious as we get closer to next week for the answer.

Other than that, the week had minor complications here and there. My hands feel much better, but now since Thursday they've been peeling. All the skin that was blistered is just flaking off. It doesn't hurt, but it's really annoying and very disgusting. *Very*. I'm extremely tired, last week I think I did too much. We didn't have a babysitter one night, so I figured I could watch the kids for two hours while Lucien taught – big mistake. I'm completely not ready for that. I just need to make sure I'm covered at nights, because I'm nowhere near ready to handle both munchkin's. I think I'm pretty covered now heading into the fall.. I only need someone to help on Tuesday nights from 5 – 8ish. I can handle the 8-9 hour I think. It's just the dinner hour and the time around it. I have one week to find someone.

I want to thank the wonderful people over at the church. They keep amazing us with all of the help. Last week they brought over a new backpack full of school supplies for Adrian who will be starting Kindergarten (I can't believe it!). Lucien and I were in awe and Adrian is so excited to start school with his new Spiderman backpack and supplies.

It was also the little guys birthday on the 18th, so we had a small but awesome birthday party for him on Saturday. My parents and brother came down from New Hampshire to visit and Lucien's parents came down. We blew up balloons, had a great Barbeque and a wonderful day. I think this is the first year that he really understood that it was his birthday; it's so amazing watching him grow up so fast.

After the party Adrian played with all his new toys, and my parents, brother, Lucien and I tried out the XBox 360 (Thank you so much to the families who pitched together to get this for us, it has been the biggest stress reliever, the best medicine there is!) Beijing Olympic Game – what a riot! We were all rolling on the floor laughing for hours. It was the best night, and just felt like everything was 'normal' for a nice chunk of time.

The weekend went really fast, but slow at the same time. It was wonderful, I haven't had that much fun in a very long time. Now I'm excited for tonight, because we're done teaching a little early, so we're going to put together our coffee table and end tables that we had bought in January and never had a chance to build. I'm sick of tripping over the boxes, and I want somewhere to put my drink in the living room, so I am VERY excited to get these things built. I'll update again during the week, everyone please send out prayers this week that the test comes back all donor cells and none of my old cells. This is such an important test we're waiting for. Again, thank you to everyone for everything that you are doing for us and our family!

(Above) Celebrating Adrian's birthday! This is one of the rare pictures I allowed to be taken while I was getting bigger from the Steroids.

Journal - September 1, 2008 (Monday) Day +41

Well I'd certainly say that this was the summer that didn't happen for us! I can't believe its September. Here I am starting to think about changing curtains and decorating for fall, when I really haven't even seen my own house since February when I first got sick and shipped off to the hospital.

The week went well with its normal ups and downs. I had a couple nights of really bad joint pains in my knees and ankles again. It's so severe that nothing, not even my narcotic pain killers can help. Those nights of course I don't sleep at all, so the days are really hard to get through, I'm so tired. My hands are doing better, still peeling but I've been using Eucerin creme and that has been helping a lot. Dry skin became an issue this week, my legs turned to elephant skin out of nowhere. That's the crazy thing about these random little ailments is that they happen so fast and so severe, there's no warning signs. I'm trying to deal with them the best I can as they come. The hardest thing still is my big poofy face. It's even bigger than last week. It's embarrassing for me, so I don't let anyone see me.

There's not too much else going on here. We went through the house a little bit to see if there was anything we could try to sell, or eBay for some extra money. There's a few baby things Luciana is done with that we're going to bring to the consignment shop, hopefully they will sell. For some reason this became the toughest financial month for us. I think everything caught up all these months to now. Example, the mortgage was due today on the 1st, and we have literately nothing for it. At least it's the new month, and hopefully by next Monday we'll have enough to overnight the payment. It's just very scary, I'm always a pay on time person and when it's the bills that really count, I get nervous. It's a stressful week for us just on a financial mental level.

On a good note, the kids are great. Adrian starts school on Thursday. I'm really happy that the bus will be picking him up and dropping him off right in front of our driveway again. I was worried how I was going to get myself to a bus stop to get him, but now that problem is solved. They usually honk, and I can just come out and get him. Luciana seems to be a little under the weather, but not sick. She's not been sleeping too well and is cranky so we're thinking it's a tooth. But man, does she have a nasty cranky streak when she's not feeling right... gee, I wonder where she gets that trait from?

September 3 (Wednesday) Day +43

Cabin fever is taking over my life! I've gone from living in a tiny hospital room to living in a bedroom; a step up, yes, but four constricting walls just the same. I feel like getting out into the world, so Lucien and I decide to take a trip to A.C. Moore to kill two birds with one stone – fresh air, and maybe supplies for a mini project to keep my mind busy. I'm SO excited to get out of the house *not* for a doctor's appointment! I stand in my closet throwing clothes everywhere searching for something cute to wear. Unfortunately, due to my massive Steroid weight gain, I'm limited to moo moos these days... ugh! I pick out my butterfly print potato sack reminiscent sun dress, a bright yellow purse, a green striped head scarf, orange Crocs, lime green hoop earring, a khaki cloth face mask and my clear plastic medical gloves – ready to hit the town! We pull up to the shopping center, park and Lucien suggests I go take my time to pick out what I'd like while he gets Luciana out of the car seat.

The sun on my face, the breeze flittering my dress – I feel amazing! I stroll through the parking lot with a long lost confident pep in my step. Until I trip on my own feet right in the middle of the road. As I head face first towards the pavement, I throw my hands out in front of me to break the fall before touching down with a forceful thud. I freeze in this position for a good 15 seconds before fumbling my way back to my feet. The plastic gloves are all broken and ripped revealing bloody scratches on my hands. People are staring at me; a lady gets out of her car, hollering over to see if I am okay. Nodding my head at her, I turn back towards our car. As I open the door to get in, with Lucien looking over in concern, I break down in tears, "Never mind, can we just go home? I can't even walk, never mind go in the store." I stare at my bloody and bruised hands in my lap and just weep in defeat.

"Let's get you cleaned up, with some new gloves, and go back inside. There's no reason to get so upset, I'll help you. What good is going home and giving up going to do?" he encourages. He's right, what good is it to give up and go home. I take a deep breath, calm myself down and laugh.

"I probably looked pretty funny falling on my face with this crazy butterfly dress, mask and gloves," wiping my tears, I manage to find humor in the moment, "okay, I'll try again." With a smile, I get back out of the car and wait for Lucien and Luciana so we can go together – just in case I topple over again, so he'll be there to help me.

Journal - September 3, 2008 (Wednesday) Day +43

Today I had my doctor appointment and everything looks really good for the most part. The big news is that the blood test they did last week to see what percentage of my blood has become the donors. We wanted to see 100% donor cells and 0 of my own, and that is exactly what we saw! This was good news and everyone is really happy to hear this. As far as the rest of my blood work, my platelets are dropping which is not a good thing. They were at 70 last Monday, and down even more to 45 today. Usually once I reach 30 I start getting those nose bleeds. So we're on the watch now to see what happens. They said that the numbers could be dropping because of the Graft versus Host Disease, but if they continue to drop as of Monday, then they will probably have to check my marrow with a biopsy to see what is happening in there.

We also have lowered my Steroid dose from 60mgs twice a day down to 40mgs twice a day. The reason for lowering it is because my knees and legs have become very weak. I actually made a total fool of myself yesterday walking to the car and literately fell down flat on the pavement. My legs just gave out. Luckily I landed on the palms of my hands (which are now two big black and blue hands). I was okay, didn't bleed but today I am so sore. My arms, legs and hands are just a mess. The doctor was really concerned about the fall, and said it could be the Steroids making me weak.

On a side note, Adrian had his Kindergarten Orientation this morning, so Lucien brought him. He got to meet his teachers and see his new school. I can't believe my baby is starting Kindergarten tomorrow. I had to get all of his paperwork together today, label his backpack and everything and I have to make sure I have fresh batteries in the camera for the morning. He's such a big boy! I can't believe I'm the Mommy of a Kindergartener, where is the time going.

Journal - September 8, 2008 (Monday) Day +48

Hey Everyone! I had my doctor appointment today, back to the Monday schedule it looks like. I was in and out of there in about an hour which was awesome. My platelet count stayed where it was from last week, actually I think it was 45 last week and was 48 today. (Really that is no change). But since it didn't go lower, there are no tests to do, just to keep watching the numbers. My skin was a little red today they thought, and they're not happy that it's not evening out by now. They also want to get me off of the steroids as quick as possible, which I am thrilled about. The only reason I'm on the Steroids is because of the skin problems at this point. So they're going to have me go to a Dermatologist and also to get some kind of Ultra Violet light therapy that will heal the skin. They said it's like standing in a tanning booth. I'm all for that, to get off of these Steroids! I can't stand the poofy face. I know I keep saying it, but it bothers me that much.

So Adrian started school Thursday. He was so excited. The poor thing though, they messed up his bussing and sent him to the wrong school! They transported him then to the right school which was good, and he really probably didn't realize what was happening. He had a great two days, loves doing his homework and is happy to be going.

Over the weekend we had some good restful family time. I was a little extra weak this weekend, and had a lot of really bad joint pain in my knees and ankles through the nights for some reason. So the lack of sleep made me extra sluggish. We did some fun low-key things though. We got to make popcorn in the air popper for the first time with Luciana. She was so excited, it was great. Both kids were running around the kitchen like crazy.

Sunday we celebrated kickoff weekend of football! We ate like maniacs, and got to see all three games. I suited up in my Favre jersey and everyone else got decked out in Cowboys (I still don't have any Cowboys clothes... maybe for Christmas I'll ask for some, I feel so left out!) We had fun tossing mini footballs around and watching the games. It felt like a normal Sunday which was just what we needed.

Journal - September 15, 2008 (Monday) Day +55

Another week gone by. I can't believe I'm a little more than 50 days past the transplant. It's going so fast, and I'm so thankful that so far I haven't had to go back to the hospital. I know I could have to if I get a fever or another complication, but making it this far is huge to me.

My appointment today went well. I don't know how the platelet levels are because the results didn't come back while I was in the office. The doctor said my skin looked better and not to call the Dermatologist just yet, and we'll hold off on the whole ultra-violet light therapy thing which I am happy for. That would have been like going to a tanning booth three times a week for a half hour without the tan. It would have been a lot of traveling. I still might have to do it if the skin doesn't clear up, but for now it's on the side burner. We also are going to lower the Steroids again by very little, because over the course of the week I got a little weaker by the day, and my hands have been shaking pretty bad, sometimes I can't even write or hit the right keys on the computer — it's super frustrating. Hopefully lowering the Steroids will help.

Of course, Luciana and Adrian are sick with runny noses, coughs, and just feeling lousy. And of course, as much as I avoided them all weekend, I got sick too. I have a really bad sore throat, runny nose and just feel awful. The doctor thinks it's viral, but said firmly to call if I get a fever. Great. Hopefully I get better; I have to rest and drink a lot of fluids to try to get this to go away quick.

Other than that, the week went really well. I have some auctions on eBay of things from around the house to try to raise some money towards the bills. I also want to thank a wonderful woman who I met on Free Cycle. I put up an add there that I was looking for a treadmill if anyone had one they weren't using, since I am supposed to be walking for exercise but I'm not allowed in the sun, I really needed a treadmill. Well she emailed me and offered hers and is dropping it off tomorrow morning. I can't thank you enough for your generosity towards a stranger. Thank you to everyone who is supporting us, the meals, the financial and babysitting support, you are all in our daily thoughts and we are so thankful for everything everyone is doing and continues to do. Things are still so tough for us, just because I'm home there's still so much craziness involved with everything from the doctor appointments to the bills, the kids and the cooking. I think the beginning of the year is when things will start to turn around for me recovery wise, when we start weaning off of some of the meds. I hope it starts to normalize by then anyway.

Journal - September 18, 2008 (Thursday) Day +58

Things are good here, or stable I should say. The kids are still sick, Adrian is a little better, but Luciana is actually getting worse. She had a little fever last night when she went to bed and her nose is getting worse. It's been working out where the babysitters are able to be here when the baby is up so I haven't gone near her in days (that is so hard! I just want to squeeze her little legs and hug her!). I unfortunately am still sick too. I have a cough now which gets worse at night, and I am so wiped out from the moment I wake up that it's impossible to do anything but watch TV and sleep most of the day. I think it's going to take me some extra time to get over this little sickness because of my nonfunctioning immune system. I hope it's not too long, it's so upsetting to feel weak again after I was doing a little better for those couple weeks.

Journal - September 22, 2008 (Monday) Day +62

Happy first day of fall! I love this time of year, the weather is so beautiful. Hopefully I can get out and enjoy some of it under a shady tree or something. It would be nice to get the kids outside a little before the cold comes too. And I can't wait to decorate for Halloween! This is my favorite time of year, since as everyone knows I go curtain and decorating crazy! I love it.

My appointment today went fairly well. My platelets last week doubled which is good, and I don't know what they did today yet. The doctor said he would call me and let me know how everything looks. I told him he only had to call if something was wrong or pills have to be changed, but he said he would call either way, he thinks I should know too if things got better. He really wants me off of the Steroids, so he's lowering my dose again starting Friday I'll go down to 40 mgs a day. He said he's lowering them much faster than is usual, I guess that's good and means I can handle it. I like that they are aggressive with things, it makes me think that they are confident I can handle it.

On the flip side, he does want me to meet with the Dermatologist to see if they agree that I should do the ultra violet light therapy for the skin graft versus host disease that I have. It's not getting better or worse, but the doctor thinks we should address it in case it decides to get worse. So I have to set up that appointment and we'll see what they think.

The weekend was awesome, we had Lucien's boys stay over, and it was Justen's birthday, he's ten years old already. So we had a little birthday party for him. I made him a Basketball cake, which was cute and Lucien's parents ordered some pizzas. Later we all played the Olympic Games on the Xbox, and then Basketball on the Xbox which was great. Little Lucien and I were on the same team in Basketball and won, which was amazing considering I never watched one Basketball game in my life!

Other than that, the little munchkins are good. Adrian started potty training for nighttime Saturday, which is of course not going too well. He woke up wet Sunday morning and woke up Lucien and I at 4 am Monday morning because he wet the bed again. He's 5 though, and no matter how tired we are, I want Adrian night trained. Luciana ended up getting a fever Thursday so I had to stay far away. She went to the pediatrician on Friday and now she's on an antibiotic, a nasal decongestant and two different fever reducers to alternate. She's looking much better today though, but my doctor told me to stay away still, I have to be really careful. And now I will close with a thought for all you football fanatics out there regarding, what else, but the lovely Sunday night game... How Bout Them Cowboys? !

Journal - September 29, 2008 (Monday) Day +69

Fall is in the air, and I love it! This week was great, we got to open the windows, turn off the air and get some fresh air into the house. For me, that was so wonderful after being in cooped up spaces for so many months. There's nothing like fresh air and watching the curtains move in the breeze, I'm enjoying every second of it. It's the little things in life that bring me so much undeniable joy these days!

I did have a doctor appointment scheduled for today, but was unable to get a ride. So I have to call and reschedule for another day this week. So, no medical updates there. I know the doctor won't be happy, he really wanted to see me today to monitor my skin and the graft versus host disease since we lowered the Steroids last week, but I couldn't get to north Jersey today any way I tried to make it happen.

My legs got a little stronger this week, maybe that's due to the lower Steroids. We also had lowered another drug called Prograf to try to stop the shaking that I have in my hands. That didn't work; I still shake like a leaf. Everyone sees my hands going and tell me, "Wow, look at you shaking!", but I don't even notice it all the time anymore unless I'm trying to eat, write or type or something. And of course, I was sick a little last week, and now over the weekend it got worse. I have a bad cough now, runny nose and am really tired (more than usual) and really sore. It feels like the flu, but it's not. It's awful! The cough keeps me up all night so I'm extra exhausted and end up sleeping all day. I hope it goes away soon.

Other than that it was a crazy week home wise too. Adrian is having trouble in school so we were on the phone with teachers and emailing them back and forth all week. Ah, the fun little parts of being a Mommy that they don't tell you about! Luciana just does her thing, walks around demanding what she wants... and getting it. Over the weekend we decorated the waiting room for Halloween. I love it! This is my favorite time of the year; I go bananas with the decorations all the way through the New Year. I handmade all these little black bats and we hung them everywhere, set up a display in the bay window with my Halloween tree, and there's pumpkins everywhere. It's such a fun atmosphere, and just puts a pleasant feeling in the house. Fall is the best! Makes me want to bake an apple pie... or maybe just buy one at the store, I'm too tired to bake! I will update after I do get to the doctor this week.

Journal - October 2, 2008 (Thursday) Day +72

So I finally got to the doctor yesterday from rescheduling from Monday. It was a chaotic visit though. There are several different areas of the building that the doctors rotate where they are on different days. Two people sent me to the wrong area apparently where I waited for an hour before someone realized. I knew I wasn't going to see my usual doctor because he was on rounds in the hospital, but I was supposed to see his nurse. So anyway, I get to the right place, they do my blood pressure and weight (all the fun stuff), but I did lose a pound this week! yay! We do the blood work... ugh... and then I wait for the nurse, who is nowhere to be found. Someone comes in the room then and says, "I looked into everything and it looks like you had a 9 am Pulmonary Function Test over at the hospital because of your cough." Nice of someone to tell me that.

Anyway, to shorten this story a little, I said no, I will not be doing that test today, my ride will be here in a half hour. The nurse came in and checked me out, she said my platelets last week went up to 93 which is good they are starting to go back up. She looked at my skin, and doesn't think it looks bad so she called the doctor and told him that I don't need to make a Dermatologist appointment just yet (awesome news). I do have a cough that I've had for about a week. I caught it from Luciana, so I know that's what it is. They are concerned that it could be Graft Versus Host Disease of the lungs, so I have to keep an eye on it and let them know if it gets worse. Other than that, they said since it is Wednesday already, I don't have to come back on Monday. I do have to call though and tell the doctor how I am feeling on Monday, and he'll probably lower the Steroids over the phone at that point. Then, I don't have to go back in until the Monday after! (Which is Columbus Day, so I have to call and see if they are actually open).

So that's how that went! Nothing too new other than that. I'm getting ready for my Mom and Aunt Carole to visit this weekend, that's going to be a lot of fun. I'll also try to get some pictures on here of the Halloween decorations in our house; I go crazy in the waiting room with new curtains and decorations everywhere. I love this time of year and decorating like a crazy woman. It's so much fun.

Journal - October 7, 2008 (Tuesday) Day +77

Hello everyone! Well, no updates as far as doctor appointments this week since I have the week off from going! That's exciting because it means I must be doing well. This week I am much stronger, although I have had some days with bad joint pain. My skin even looks like it is clearing up from the rash a little bit. My favorite part though is that my poofy face and belly from the Steroids seems to be going down a little bit.

So I'm sure by now you've all seen the info about the Beatlemania Benefit Concert on the main page. The night is being hosted by the church – we are working together to get all the details straight. The show will be held at the Middletown High School South Theater. Lucien and I are super excited that this event is able to take place; it's really going to be such a fun night to have everyone we love in one room just partying and having a great time. Lucien and I will be performing a 30 minute opening act, performing some songs from Deal With It as well as some other songs. I miss performing so much, I can't wait to get on stage and sing for everyone!

So mark your calendars, November 8th and buy your tickets! You can buy them at several locations which I will list on the site, or you can buy them at our music school. They are $30 general admission. So please purchase your tickets and spread the word! If you'd like some flyers to give out or hang at your place of work, let us know and we'll give you some to pass around. So tell your family and friends and let's fill that Theater!

I will continue to update this week when I hear anything from the doctor. He is supposed to call and tell me to adjust some of my meds (hopefully lower the Steroids again!). I will also update with any new information about the Benefit Beatlemania Stage Show Concert! It's going to be great!

Journal - October 9, 2008 (Thursday) Day +79

We have a lowered Steroid dose announcement! (This is major good news to me!). Instead of 40mg a day, I'm taking 40mg and 30mg, alternating every day. I wish it was just 30 every day, but eh, I'll take what I can get.

I am feeling much better this week, much stronger. I can walk across the room a little faster and the stairs are a little better than turtle speed now. I am even starting today to be back in the waiting room and taking care of phones and scheduling of the business. Lucien is thrilled about me going back to my duties and taking it off his plate! He thinks he might react though and answer the phone accidentally by habit... it has been 9 months of him juggling his job and mine, I don't know how he did it.

So I am right now in the waiting room on the regular computer, not a laptop for a change, as I write this. It's exciting to be able to work again. I can't take a check or money from someone's hand, they still have to put it in the "payment box" to be safe with the germ factor, and I can't touch the doorknob or anything, but I can sit here and answer the phone! I can't take care of the kids totally yet, as far as diapers, and lifting Luciana in and out of her crib is impossible. So I still have babysitters coming to help me with the kids at night. I'll start slowly maybe one night a week at a time taking care of the kids. I just need to make sure I'm strong enough that I don't fall down the stairs carrying the baby or anything (don't laugh, I tried over the weekend and that almost happened!)

Things are going awesome for the Beatlemania Benefit Concert. There are several local papers that are interested in covering our story and the event itself, and there are a few radio stations that are advertising for us. We are really excited, and are rehearsing our opening act. It feels good to pick up my Acoustic again (ahh.. my beautiful Fender Malibu!) Anyway, tickets go on sale officially tomorrow, Friday the 10th. Please spread the word and tell everyone you know about the show! If you're in for a lesson you can ask us for some flyers, we have a ton of flyers to give out that you can give to everyone you know. Our goal is to sell out, so if you can help to make that happen, that would be awesome! I'll update again soon!! Love to you all!

Journal - October 13, 2008 (Monday) Day +83

Time for an update! It's great to be back at the front desk again, taking back over the phones and scheduling. I love it, and so does Lucien! It's a big load off of his shoulders that he doesn't have to worry about all of that, and he shouldn't have to because it is a whole job in itself. It's been great seeing everyone; I can't believe how tall all of the younger students got over the summer!

I did see the doctor today. It was a short visit, which was really nice. They did blood work like usual, and I didn't hear anything from them today, so that means everything was probably fine. He didn't say anything about my skin, so that must be good, and he was happy to hear that I am stronger this week. I did have some strange leg pains over the weekend, but my friend Mya and I (yes, she IS a nurse, so she has reliable information) came to the conclusion that it was something to do with the muscle and not being used to walking around being as physical as I have been. There was a medical term for it, but I can't for the life of me remember it! That pain got about 50% better today, so hopefully tomorrow it won't be as bad.

Anyway, the doctor told me to lower the Steroids again starting Friday to 40mgs on day and 20mgs the next. He said as soon as we get to every other day, the symptoms will dramatically get better. Yay! I hope that means the poofy face and belly too, because I want to look half way decent for the Benefit Concert! We'll see, maybe if I drink a little more water too the poof will go down. Only time will tell.

That's all from here, for the most part, uneventful. We're just getting ready for the Benefit Concert. We do so many Beatlemania shows in a year, that we are far from excited over (they are a lot of work for us), but this one is different because it's local and all our friends and family will be there. We're really looking forward to it! If you're planning on coming, we are recommending that you get your tickets in advance, because they are already going fast and they just went on sale this week. This is great news of course, but I also don't want anyone we know to lose out if you are planning on coming. I'll update later this week on everything, thanks for checking in!

Journal - October 21, 2008 (Tuesday) Day +91

I went up to the hospital yesterday but I didn't see the doctor, it was only blood work that they did. That's a good sign I'd say, but it would have been nice to not have that done either. But I was only there about a half hour then came home. I haven't heard anything from them about the results, so usually no news is good. The only thing I am dealing with right now is that my eyes are getting very bad over the past couple weeks. I used to have perfect vision; I could find the backing to any earring in any carpet! But a few weeks ago they started getting blurry a little bit, and lights at night bother me *a lot*. I think the doctor said he wants to send me to get them checked, which would be great, because it's getting hard to deal with at this point.

The weekend was a lot of fun. Lucien had a show in Philadelphia on Friday night, so Mya stayed with me to help me with the kids. We ended up having so much fun doing all juvenile "sleep over" -esque activities! I worked on her plastic canvas pumpkin while we watched a crazy movie, we played X Box for a long time then topped off the night after the kids went to bed with caramel ice cream sundaes. It was like being 13 again!

Saturday Lucien had two more shows down in Philly, so the kids went to stay with his parents, and I was able to go to the shows with him. It was a really cute theater, and since he had played there the night before, he knew there was a lot of space away from the people for me to stay in the back of the room. It was really good to see the guys again. The show was a lot of fun, there were some different production songs that we don't always get to do so it was cool to hear some different tunes.

It was a nice early night, we were packed and out of there by 10:30 and on our way home. In the car we went over the songs that we'll be performing for the opening act at the benefit concert. I think we might have figured out the song we'll end with, but we have to get the guitars out and see if it jives well. Oohhh.. What could it be?? The suspense!

Journal - October 27, 2008 (Monday) Day +97

Hello everyone! What a week / weekend / day it's been! I'll start with the news of the day from the doctor's office, which of course is a little good news, and a little "eh" news. The good news is that the Steroids got lowered again! Now they're 40 mgs and 10 mgs alternating every day. That means in another 10 days, I should be able to stop taking them on the every other day! I'm really excited about that. The other good news is that I only have to go to the doctors officially every other week from now on! That's because this coming Thursday, the 30th is my official 100 Day post-transplant mark. That is a huge milestone, and everyone is congratulating me already on reaching it so well. The nurse I saw today even said that my blood counts this whole time have been rock solid. Let's hope it stays that way! Now the news that I'm less than thrilled about.. I knew it was coming... they scheduled be for another bone marrow biopsy. Ugh!!!! I dread that, the anxiety, the pain, the grogginess from the overload of Ativan that I get for the next 24 hours... oh I dread this. The fortunate thing is that it's not for two weeks, so it's scheduled for the Monday after the benefit concert. I am really nervous already about the biopsy though, I just have to try to not think about it.

The week here was crazy, Luciana had a runny nose that probably wasn't anything bad, but could turn into something bad if I caught it, so I had to stay clear away from her. But the kids are doing well; it was one of those weeks where I feel like they both just sprouted!

That's on my end; the weekend was pretty uneventful minus the fact that Saturday was Lucien and my 5th wedding anniversary. We spent it just the way we wanted to, with the kids! We had a good quality family weekend and I wouldn't have wanted it any other way. Other than that, every spare second we have we're spending on preparing for the benefit. Remember to tell everyone you know to come see Beatlemania Saturday November 8th!!! We're never ever local so now's the chance to come see the show! Not to mention the opening act that Lucien and I will be performing, songs from the album Deal With It that we released in February. Gather all your friends and family of all ages and come see Beatlemania!! I'll update soon! Love to everyone!

PS – Has anyone secretly arranged for Brett Favre to make an appearance yet???? :) kidding :)

October 30, 2008 (Thursday) Day +100

Today I celebrate a huge milestone... the 100 day post-transplant mark. After a transplant, life is all about setting mini goals and celebrating like a maniac when you reach them. Patient survival rates are calculated using the 100 day, 1 year, 3 year and 5 year milestone markers. I have been a statistic since my diagnosis day, but now I am celebrating being a statistic in the "100 day" club! Every day is an adventure as I still deal with so many side effects from the medications and as well as the graft-versus-host attacks which are random, arriving often swift and without warning. I am stronger by the day; am able to walk almost as fast as my brain thinks I can, am starting to depoof from my Cabbage Patch round dimply face appearance and have started reclaiming my life. My priorities are clear; keep getting better, spend every second with my children and husband, and work on living a healthy lifestyle to keep cancer out of the equation for the rest of my life.

New battles arise periodically. Lately, my eyes have been having many issues including sever light sensitivity, blurred vision and pain like a swarm of beach sand in my eyes. When I look at the couch or any piece of furniture, it is double... almost with a halo of itself surrounding it. The overhead lights in the waiting room office are unbearably bright, my computer screen feels bright as the sun and by around 5:00 every night, I'm in so much ocular pain, all I can do is lay in bed with my eyes closed. After the kids are in bed at night, Lucien and I usually watch TV to unwind, but even this has become impossible. Instead I sit on the couch with him, and listen to the TV with my eyes closed to stop the burning irritation.

These are all things that are included in the cosmic payment I have to make for being alive. Chemotherapy and bone marrow transplants are harsh medical warzones that I had to battle through. It is a ruthless process, but it you make it through, you earn the ultimate prize – your life. In exchange for that, you have to deal with the side effects of the strong drugs and treatments your body is put through. I would gladly take these side effects, and deal with them the best I can, because you know what? – At least I'm alive.

Journal - November 3, 2008 (Monday) – Day +104

It's November! Where is time going?! Halloween was Friday and was so much fun! We took the kids out Trick or Treating for as long as I could last which was just about an hour. Not too bad! Adrian was Buzz Lightyear from Toy Story and Luciana was a pink poodle. They had a really good time; I wish I could have lasted longer for their sake. Adrian could have gone another hour, and I wish we could have. I was just so exhausted; we had to cut the night short.

No doctor's appointment this week! It was so nice to wake up on a Monday and not have to truck up to the cancer center! Not that I don't love everyone there, but being home for those four hours was a lot better. I'm feeling pretty good this week, just realllllly tired. I don't know if that's from the lowering of the Steroids or the time change or what. I do have a good feeling that I am *perhaps* doing something very typical of myself, and over doing it. I think I'm taking on way too much since this is the week of the big Benefit Concert! I'm super excited, and a lot is done, but there's so much that has to be done too. As stressful and exhausting as it is, it's really gratifying and I can't wait until Saturday. Lucien and I have some surprises planned that *no one* knows about, not even my mother and not even the queen of getting things out of me, Mya! Nope, no one knows our surprises!

Well, if I don't get a chance to update again before the weekend, see you all at the show!!!!!!!!!! Love to you all!

Journal - November 5, 2008 (Wednesday) Day +106

Everything is coming along nicely for Saturdays Benefit. Everyone is coming to me and asking how they can help which has taken a huge load off of me to get everything ready. The raffles are going to be a lot of fun! There are a few I sure would like to win if I was allowed to enter!! :) It's going to be such a wonderful weekend, I'm so excited to have everyone who we love in one big room together for a such a fun night, it's really like a big party. A lot of my family is coming down from New Hampshire for the weekend, and they will be helping out tremendously Saturday night. Then Sunday morning I think we're planning on going out for a nice brunch before they head home. Then, of course, Sunday the Jets are home, so I know we'll have the game televised, and what a way to wind down after all this running around but with a Brett Favre football game?! I'll have to get all dressed in my #4 jersey, it's a shame it's a Packers one though, I'll have to update and get a Jets Jersey eventually. It's really the perfect weekend; I don't know what else I could ask for!

So this is probably the last update I'll make until the middle of next week (since I have the bone marrow biopsy planned for Monday morning, I'll be out of commission for two days or so). So I'll put up lots of pictures and details from the benefit concert then, and until then, I hope to see you all there on Saturday!!! Love to you all!!

Journal - November 11, 2008 (Tuesday) Day +112

Lots of updates today! I'll start with my doctor appointment yesterday (Monday). First they did blood work, which they always get the very first time... well, wouldn't you know it took them three times to get it? I ended up crying my eyes out all through the blood work which hasn't happened in forever. Thus began my worst visit ever. They did tell me to lower the steroid dose again, which is awesome! But next was the bone marrow biopsy.....

I had to lie on my stomach, and already at this point I was hysterically crying and shaking. They poked around looking for the right spot then cleaned the area. By the time they were starting to numb the area, I was already a wreck and there were nurses holding my legs down. How could I help it?! All those little needles, my worst nightmare and it hurt! Then came the big one, Lucien says this needle looks like a corkscrew. I was in more pain than I can remember since childbirth. I was screaming so loud, and crying so hard, everyone was trying to calm me down, and Lucien just kept telling them, "There's nothing you can do, just keep going". And they did. Finally it was over. The head nurse looked at me and addressed the room, "I don't care what anyone says, in 6 months when it's time for another biopsy you get put to sleep. No one should have to go through this much agony. Never again!" She was insistent that everyone hear her, and I sure am relieved. So the rest of the day and night I slept right through, with Lucien waking me up for dinner. Today I am still SO sore, it hurts really bad to just get to the bathroom, and sitting aggravates the area really bad. It's just awful and I don't wish a biopsy like this on anyone.

On a much happier note, the Benefit concert Saturday night went unbelievably well! We had our usual "sound check" problems, this time though it was a power issue with the theater, if it weren't for my father being there and figuring the whole issue out, it would have been a enormous problem!

Lucien and I performed the opening performance of the show. We played songs from our latest album Deal With It (if you don't have it yet, stop by iTunes and see what you're missing!). We performed Deal With It, Message For Peace, Childhood Friend. Then I stood and sang my version of Fleetwood Macs Landslide. Then the big surprise of the night, the band came out and we did

Give Em A Fight. The crowd went crazy, it was awesome! Give Em A Fight is the perfect cancer battle song! It took a lot of energy, stamina and guts to get on stage this soon after a transplant. Mostly, it was very difficult for me to get on stage in front of all those people looking as round, chubby and different as I do right now from the steroids. However, I have to admit that getting on stage again and that before show adrenaline was the best medicine in the world! I've missed the stage so much, it was incredible to be back!

The Beatlmania Stage Show, of course, went without flaw, it was great and everyone had a great time. We had a lot of fun joking around backstage too doing impressions and just having a good time. Thanks Jon, Jess and Joe for helping to make this night extra fun! You guys are the best!

After the show we did the usual meet and greet in the lobby and got to personally thank a lot of people for coming, the line was so long though that we didn't; get to see everyone. The night was great, everyone had a wonderful time and if you want to see more pictures from the night check out the Beatlemania page of my site! Thank you to everyone who came out and enjoyed the event with us! We love you all!!

Performing the opening act of my Benefit Concert a big accomplishment for me to have the confidence to get on stage with my Steroid appearance.

(Above) Uncle Dicky and I calling the raffle winners at my benefit concert.
(Below) Posing with my parents after the concert. This picture is still difficult
for me to look at, this was one of the few times I allowed pictures to be taken
while I was poofed up on Steroids.

HEMATOPATHOLOGY REPORT

PATIENT NAME: NOCELLI, SHERI
YOB: 1984 (AGE 24)
GENDER: F
PHYSICIAN: AYERS
REPORT TAKEN: 11/10/2008
REORT RECEIVED: 11/10/2008
SPECIMEN(S) RECEIVED:
 Bone Marrow Aspirate
 Bone Marrow Biopsy
 Cone Marrow, clot
CLINICAL HISTORY:
AMP STATUS POST ALLOGENIC BONE MARROW
TRANSPLANT
MICROSCOPIC DESCRIPTION:
Peripheral Blood:
CBC: WBC: 8.5, RBC: 3.67, HGB: 12.7, HCT: 36.9, MCV: 100.5,
MCHC: 34.5, RDW: 13.8, PLT: 253
DIFFERENTIAL (%): BANDS: 1, SEGS: 74, LYMPHS: 14,
MONOS: 8, META: 1, BASOS: 1, MYEL: 1

PERIPHERAL BLOOD COMMENTS: Mild red cell macrocytosis
and occasional tear drop cells. Rare metamyelocytes and
myelocytes. No circulating blasts seen.

MARROW DIFFERENTIAL (%): Erythroblasts: 35%, Blasts: 2%,
Neutrophils: 54%, Eosinophils: 1%, Basophils: 1%,
Lymphocytes: 5%, Monocytes: 1%

ERYTHROPOIESIS: Slightly megaloblastic maturation
GRANULOPOIESIS: Normal complete maturation
MEGAKAROCYTES: Unremarkable morphology
LYMPHOCYTES: Not increased or atypical
PLASMA CELLS: Not seen
OTHER: Myeloid to erythroid ratio of about 1.5:1
CLOT SECTION: No particles seen

BONE MARROW BIOPSY: Touch Preps: Adequate - Cellularity:
40%
BONE MARROW COMMENTS: Decalcified bone marrow biopsy
shows trilinear, maturing hematopoiesis. Megakaryocytes are

adequate in number, but include a few dysplastic forms. Hemosiderin deposition is present.

FINAL PATHOLOGIC DIANOSIS:
Peripheral Blood – Macrocytic Red Cells

BONE MARROW – NO EVIDENCE OF RESIDUAL LEUKEMIA

Journal - November 17, 2008 (Monday) Day +118

I just got back from the doctors, and have updates. First, it was funny when I got there, the nurse who does my blood pressure and weight was all excited to tell me that he had thought of having them try this numbing spray stuff that they use in pediatrics before blood work, so I was like, sure! Let's try, I'm game! Turns out it didn't do much of anything, but hey, it made for some fun banter.

Then the doctor came in and checked out everything like my mouth and rash (which is gone) and we talked about what meds I'm on and doses. We talked a little but too about the results from the bone marrow biopsy last week. There are no traces of Leukemia in the bone marrow at this point, which is awesome news. However, he's a little concerned because I am not 100% donor, I'm 95% donor cells and 5% my cells. What this means is that we have to wait until the end of the week to see another result from the tests, if the abnormal cell is still present in me, then that could mean the remaining 5% is bad cells and will need to be possibly treated. If there is no evidence of the cell malformations then the remaining 5% of my cells might not be bad.

In the meantime while we wait for those results, we are going to lower the steroids now dramatically faster. Last week I was on 40 mg every other day, now we're going to 30 every other day and next week down to 20 every other day. The doctor said that sometimes getting rid of the steroids and Prograf meds will allow the donor cells to reach 100%. I really hope this works, because if it doesn't he said I will have to "get another dose of the donor cells" which to me sounds like another transplant. But I'm trying not to jump to any conclusions and I'm hoping that getting rid of the steroids will do the trick.

Over the weekend, we had little Lucien and Justen visit. It was Loosh's birthday, he is turning 14, so we got him a Dallas Cowboys shirt and I made him a football cake. (Actually he helped me make it!) Then he and I decorated the whole house for Christmas! (We had to because of our schedule this month, so it's up early, and I love it!) All three trees are up, the village is done, the curtains are changed, and he helped me do everything! All "daddy" Lucien had to do was put the angel on top of the tree and the lights in the tree.

The rest of the weekend we played x box, we have a new game someone gave us (thanks Roy!!!) with these piñata gardens, it's so much fun! I stayed up with the boys until 1 am playing it Saturday night and we were up bright and early playing again on Sunday! Then Lucien beat the boys over and over at Madden Football, and then little Lucien kicked all our butts in Archery in the Olympic game. We had a great time, it was an awesome weekend!

Journal - November 26, 2008 (Wednesday) Day +127

Happy Thanksgiving everyone!! Well, a day early, but I won't be around the computer tomorrow, so no better time than the present! We have so much to be thankful for this year and so many friends and family to be thankful towards. Thank you to everyone, every single person who has gifted us with your love, support, prayers, time, and meals, absolutely everything. I am thankful especially that I am with my beautiful family for the holidays; to be in our home, living life as close to normal as possible, enjoying every word out of my children's mouths, every little expression on their faces, and the amazing feeling of kissing them goodnight, and seeing their bright little angel faces in the morning. I'm thankful to sleep in my own bed, with Lucien's arms around me every night holding me tight and keeping me warm, his good morning hug when I sleepily come downstairs in the morning and our couch time together every night when we're done working. I'm thankful to be working again, talking to all of my friends, all of our clients, doing the scheduling and phones. It's great to be back to work, and back to life. There's nothing like these simple things, nothing at all as wonderful as these very simple things.

We have no more news from the doctor yet, but I will post on here as soon as we know anything else. I don't go back until Monday morning, but hopefully he'll call before then with some good results. All we can do is hope and pray at this time, and that's all we're doing.

Have a very happy Thanksgiving everyone! Enjoy your Turkey and mashed potatoes, I know I will! I'll just be missing one of my mother's amazing pork pies (mmmmmm!) but I can look forward to that on Christmas!!

Journal - December 1, 2008 (Monday) Day +132

Whew, what a week! Or... half a week since I've written on here I think. Thanksgiving was wonderful; it was low key and just a lot of fun. We spent it with Lucien's parents, just the 6 of us. Some family stopped in at different parts of the day which was nice to see everyone, but no one stayed very long. Dinner was fabulous and then we all sat around watching the Dallas Cowboys kick butt!!

The weekend was a lot of fun. Friday night Mya and I played some mad Piñata Garden on the Xbox 360, it was a blast. That game is so addicting it's not even funny! Then Saturday I went with Lucien to Philadelphia where he was performing with Beatlemania. We had a lot of fun, we always do, and it's always fun to see people we don't see all the time.

The two shows went great, but it was a really long day. At least we were home fairly early, 12 on the nose! A babysitter had watched Adrian and Luciana all day, she's great with them, and they love her so much. All Adrian talked about all week was the babysitter coming on the weekend. And Luciana is talking up a storm herself! She's 19 months old and has already started saying phrases like, "It's stuck", "This is down!", "Baby go?" and a few others. She's amazing. We watched Rudolph the Red Nosed Reindeer Sunday for the first time with the kids, and they were both glued to the TV, even though Adrian had a hard time looking at the Bumble snow monster! Very cute.

This morning was my doctor appointment. Lucien and Luciana came with me today. Luciana was afraid that *she* as seeing the doctor, and kept saying "No okay!" when we told her it was okay! We did get good news that at this point there is not only no sign of Leukemia, but there is no sign of the molecular abnormality either. This is major! But we have to keep a close eye on my percentage of me and donor. If it goes to any more than 5% of me in there, then we will have to act on it more aggressively. Let's hope that lowering the steroids will bring it back to 100% donor!!! This week I'm on 10 mg every other day and next week I drop to 5 mg every other day, then that's it on the prednisone!!!

That's all for now, I'll update as soon as we have results on the blood tests they did today!

Journal - December 8, 2008 (Monday) Day +139

Ah, the most wonderful time of the year... bitter cold, 10 layers of clothes, wet socks... it's a blast! I do love this time of year though. Not too much went on during the week, but the weekend was a lot of fun!

I starting making 'test' batches of Christmas cookies. I quickly realized that I'm waaaayyy too weak to make dough, and told Lucien right away I'm going to need a hand mixer if I'm making Christmas cookies this year. So I got a little hand mixer at Target and I love it so much! The cookies came out awesome too, they're cut out as stars and candy canes with homemade royal icing! It was my first time making cookies like this, so they're a little rustic looking. I think they'll look better next time I make them.

Unfortunately, we lost our beta fish, Seaside, this week. I was upset because I had him about 4 years. I had won him on the Seaside Heights Boardwalk and he lived with us a long time. So, Saturday night we took the kids to the pet store to pick out a family pet beta together. We picked out a beautiful purple, red, and blue colored fish and some fresh food for him. When we went outside from the store it had started to snow big beautiful snowflakes! Lucien had Luciana, and I was holding Adrian's hand and asked him what he thought we should call our new fish. Immediately, he said, "We should call him Salmon". And that's his name! Adrian was so excited to get Salmon settled into his bowl and feed him. It's his first pet really, so he can't stop talking about him!

Adrian's school has been amazing through this time, very understanding, accommodating and helpful. They had asked us to have the kids make up letters with some things they would like for Christmas and send them in. The staff all pitched in and collected all these amazing gifts for the kids for Christmas! Lucien went and picked them up this morning, and when he came home with everything, all wrapped and ready Christmas I was overwhelmed! It's so amazing and I'm so excited for the kids for Christmas. I'm so happy they are getting toys, because I wasn't able to afford too many. I got them mostly clothes they needed, some puzzles, books and movies so now they have more fun things for Christmas morning!

His school even gave us a Turkey that we froze until Christmas and a Shoprite gift card which we will use tomorrow for diapers. To everyone over at the school especially Adrian's teachers thank you so much for everything you have done for our family during this season, Adrian and Luciana had just as tough a year as Lucien and I, between adjusting to babysitters, traveling to their grandparents every week, change of routine, not spending time with me for so long, it just makes me want to give them the best Christmas ever! And with everyone's help that we've received, they will have a perfect Christmas.

I also have to thank everyone at the church again for everything you are doing to help us through this time. It amazes me that people continue to open their hearts to us and I will forever be thankful for that, because even though I am sitting in my familiar spot at the desk working, taking care of the kids mostly on my own and seeming to be 'back to normal', I'm definitely not. I just don't want to log on here every week and complain about my ankle pain, or extreme tiredness or any of that, because it's a time to be thankful for the positives. And we would not be able to keep this household running just yet without the help that all of you are continuing to offer. I do still have a ton of prescriptions, medical transportation, and things like that, so we are close, but not quite there on getting caught up. And for all the help, support, and prayers I can never ever thank everyone enough!

Journal - December 16, 2008 (Tuesday) Day +157

Well it's about time for an update I think! Sorry I missed the normal Monday update, but I was so tired yesterday, I spent a lot of the day in bed resting. I did have a doctor appointment yesterday in the morning. Lucien and Luciana came with me to bring a tray of cookies to everyone in the office, and of course a special bottle of wine for my doctor for Christmas.

The appointment went very well, and we got the news that we were all hoping and praying for... <u>I am back to 100% donor cells</u>! He said though that this is something we will be watching constantly for a while, but at least it went in the right direction right now! This was the news we were looking for heading into the holidays. We had a great visit with him and ended up talking about Christmas traditions more than anything else! He did tell me to be careful with the Christmas Eve Italian fish feast, so I'll make sure I stick to safe fish! I asked him if for this time we could stretch my next visit to 3 weeks instead of 2 because of the crazy holiday schedule, and he said that we could as long as I called him if I noticed anything different! I was *very* happy about this!

Over the weekend we had Loosh and Justen over to celebrate our Christmas with them. Saturday morning I did a little photo shoot with them near the tree all dressed up, then Saturday night we had Grandpa's famous Italian sandwiches for dinner, then opened presents! We gave the boys all football stuff of their teams, Giants and Cowboys, which they love and have fun with. The boys gave Lucien a really cute ornament for the tree, and they gave me (with Lucien (Daddy's) help) my very own personalized Cowboys jersey so I'd have it for Sunday night's game.

After our mini Christmas celebrations we watched Rudolph and Santa Claus Is Coming to Town. Adrian is still afraid of the Bumble; the poor thing! Luciana loves the movies and sits through them both mesmerized.

On Sunday little Lucien and I made sugar cookies and gingerbread girls and boys. He loves helping me in the kitchen, and he really does help out a lot! He's 14, I can't believe what a little man he is. Sunday we all spent playing the X Box, we have such a good time playing that, its fun when we play a game that we all can compete on. It makes for some funny moments.

This week should be pretty uneventful, hopefully. I've been very, very tired, to the point that if I don't sleep in until 10 or 11 every morning, I just can't make it throughout the rest of the day. So Lucien has had to do all the errands and banking and stuff, because I just need to rest in the mornings. But anyway, other than that, everything is good. I'm of course wearing my new football jersey as much as I can this week to support the boys! I love it so much, it even has my number "84" for the year I was born! Quite a win we had Sunday night I must say! I've said it before, and I'll say it again..... How 'bout them Cowboys!

Journal - December 29, 2008 (Monday) Day +170

Merry Christmas everyone!! This is the longest I've ever gone between updates, so there's a lot to talk about! The week before Christmas was nuts getting our house ready for guests. I couldn't travel to New Hampshire this year, so my Mom, Dad and brother came to visit us. They got here late Tuesday night and that was the kickoff of Christmas! For the first time in history, we only worked Monday and Tuesday last week, and took the rest of the week off. It was so worth it!

Christmas Eve was a blast. We went to Lucien's parents and exchanged gifts. This was the first year that I got to experience the Italian Fish Dinner on Christmas Eve. There were 5 fish dishes throughout the dinner; it was so different and delicious. The kids got huge magnadoodles, which they love, Lucien got a nice shirt, and I got leopard print Crocs! They're by far the coolest I've ever seen!

At about 7:30, we started to hear sirens outside in the distance. Everyone started running around getting their coats and hats on, because this meant Santa was coming by soon with the fire trucks! I was like a 4 year old; I was so excited to see this. I was jumping up and down, screaming and waving.... it was kind of pathetic, but so much fun! Of course, they sped by at about 50 miles an hour, we heard a "Ho Ho Ho" and that was it, he was off! (I guess to start delivering presents!)

We headed home, singing the Chipmunks Christmas the whole way! Once we got home we put out some cookies and milk for Santa, and Adrian wrote a really sweet letter to him too.

Christmas morning was the best! We woke up, got the kids and came down to open stockings! I got lots of makeup that I needed because my makeup was a year old, I didn't wear any all year, and some other really cool stuff. We took a break for breakfast and then dove into opening! We went steady opening gifts for a few hours. The kids had a lot of presents to open since we had donations from Adrian's school, the church and friends and family even sent some extra gifts for them this year. I was so happy for them to see their excitement over all their new clothes and toys. I was especially happy for all their new clothes since they were both outgrowing everything they had.

Lucien and I got jammies, some books and dvds. I got some jewelry that I had been eyeing up at the Fossil outlet when it opened, and a new bathrobe because I had forgotten my old one at the hospital, some bath goodies, a pair of clogs, canisters for the kitchen, a toaster. Lucien got some converse, a new cordless drill and typical stuff like bracelets and a belt. Then everyone started acting funny, and the next thing I know, rolled around the corner into the living room comes a purple Marshall Amplifier half stack!!! I had been eyeing this up for years!! I needed an amp for the tour coming up this year (the Deal With It Tour), and I was going to use one of Lucien's old amps. But boy was I floored when I saw this! It's limited edition, Marshall, and the amp of my dreams! This was the best Christmas present ever!

It was just a fantastic way to wrap up this crazy year. Christmas was always a big deal in my family, we always start talking about plans in August, and we're absolutely nuts and insane about the whole thing. But this year was that much more special, because when I was spending all those hours and days alone in the hospital, it was thinking about Christmas that got me through. My goal was to be home by Christmas, with my family, with my children and I was rewarded with that, and then some. I could never have asked for a better time, everything was just as I wished for all those months. And now, we're heading into the New Year with high hopes for life. We're reaching high this year, and we'll get there. We're so determined to do everything and I know we'll get every single thing accomplished. This year we're cleansed of the old and looking forward to the new. We've shed old skin, old relationships, stale partnerships and time of sickness and we're determined to enjoy a healthy, happy new year with our Tour coming up after a year of delay, a new album coming out in the spring, new business ventures, new partnerships and a new way of life. We're excited for 2009, looking forward to a wonderful year professionally and personally. I think after the craziness, we deserve just that, and with the drive inside both Lucien and I, I know we'll have a wonderful year. Because of all the help, support, donations, gifts and open hearts you've all offered through this year, we were able to maintain a positive outlook. We have been able to look forward to the bright future instead of dwelling on the things we've gone through and are still living through every day. We do it, live it and look forward, thanks to all of you, we love you all!

Have a merry, wonderful New Years, and let's all hope and pray for a happy, healthy year to come for everyone. Happy New Year Everyone!

As Lucien has been yelling from the rooftops, 2009 is gonna shine! ! ! !

(Above) Celebrating Christmas Eve 2008 at Lucien's parents' house. (Below)Christmas morning 2008 opening gifts with Luciana.

(Above) Christmas morning 2008 opening gifts with Adrian
(Below) Christmas morning 2008 totally surprised by my purple Marshall amplifier!

Journal - January 7, 2009 (Wednesday) Day +179

What another crazy week! Last Tuesday, Luciana tripped on a toy in the living room and hit her head on a coffee table. She had a really big wound that kept bleeding no matter what we tried. There was a nurse here at the time because her son was taking a guitar lesson, and she tried to butterfly the cut closed. It was in Luciana's hair line though, so that didn't work. And every time she cried, it would start really bleeding again. So I called my friend Mya, and she came right over to look at it. She thought it could use 2 or 3 stitches, so off to the ER we went! Of course that's the last place in the world I should be is an ER full of sick people, so I wore my mask and gloves. The staff there was wonderful and got us right into a private room and looked at the baby right away. It ended up she needed 6 stitches! They put the dissolvable kind which was awesome, and were really good with the baby. She didn't cry at all, she was a real trooper. I don't know what I would do without Mya, she's always there when I'm in a pinch, she's the best friend I could ever ask for.

The week went on pretty uneventfully thank goodness! We spent the weekend taking down the Christmas decorations. It didn't take too long, which was good because I was really worn down from the week and needed to rest a lot. Lucien had to keep yelling at me to get back on the couch and stop doing too much. It was really nice to see the house go back to normal!

I had my doctor appointment Monday morning. MAN is it hard getting up at 7:30!! The appointment went really well though, he said that all the new problems I'm having are to be expected with stopping the Steroids after being on them for so long. I've had swollen ankles, severe arthritis pain in all of my fingers at night and every morning, and a complete loss of appetite. The appetite is a lot like being pregnant, certain foods that I usually love are disgusting! And then I crave other certain foods... but anyway, the doctor said this was all normal. The only thing we're going to watch if it gets worse is the finger pain, it does really interfere with day to day activities, I can't even play guitar right now. Everything else looked really good though, and now I go back in three weeks.

I hope I have some more quiet weeks ahead. Lucien and I have a lot of projects we're working on right now though, so work is absolutely nuts. We even have a video shoot scheduled for a few weeks from now as we resume the Deal With It Tour, there are a few videos that were planned and put on hold when I was diagnosed, that we're scheduled to resume with now. It's really exciting, and we're really happy to get back to work 30 hours a day like usual. The only difference is that I have to sleep extra hours now to keep up my energy, but it's worth it. That and the chocolate flavored Ensure Lucien bought for me, I think I'll be ready to go into this crazy year!

Journal - January 19, 2009 (Monday) Day +191

Hey Everyone! There's not too many updates right now, because I didn't have an appointment today due to the holiday. The last two weeks have been okay, I'm still dealing with the major pain in my fingers, especially with all the snow we're having — the moisture seems to be affecting the pain. And I'm still dealing with the ultra-puffy ankles and extreme tired-ness. Today I tried to get up but had to go back to bed I was so tired. I didn't get up until 12:30 in the afternoon, which was scary because we had students coming at 1! I managed to pull myself together but it's been a tough day to get through.

Last weekend was really exciting for me. Lucien asked me what would make me really happy, since we were heading towards the one year mark of diagnosis. I knew right away what I would love, and that was to finish painting and decorating the foyer, waiting room and downstairs bathroom. So we painted the foyer a deep gold color, and I decorated it with some iron pieces like a table and a candle holder that I had in the bedroom. It's so pretty and inviting now! We also did the downstairs bathroom a deep red color. I absolutely love it! It's a shame I don't use that bathroom though because it's considered a "public bathroom". So I have to enjoy it by standing outside and looking in. Works for me! Next week Lucien is going to paint the waiting room for me, I'm so excited! We even sold our old waiting room chairs and got a great deal on blemished black leather chairs from a hotel supplier. So the makeover is costing us nothing, except maybe a gallon of paint. It's amazing, I feel so fresh by looking at the new decor, it's completely a new beginning for this year!

Luciana slept in her little toddler bed for the first time. She was so cute, she didn't move *at all* she was so afraid. When we went in her room after her nap she was laying there in the same spot and said, "Help me!" It was precious!

Everything is so exciting right now, I mean, it's just exciting to wake up in the morning and know that I have a full day of work ahead of me. I look forward to answering the phones and doing my job, working with Lucien's record company again as we prepare for photo shoots and video shoots coming up in the next few weeks. Yeah, I'm exhausted and worn down and dealing with my joint pain and everything, but my excitement to live my life again over rides all of that. The support from *everyone* and the kind words from our students week after week, really keep me going and put a smile on my face. And Adrian and Luciana are so amazing, their little faces are so beautiful and I just want to stare at them and sit with them all the time. They are my two little guardian angels, and I look forward to watching every second of them growing and becoming the amazing people I know they'll be. For all of this, life is wonderful and it can only get better and better from here.

Journal - January 27, 2009 (Tuesday) Day +199

Hey Everyone! Well I didn't end up going to the doctors yesterday, but I called and he said that he would call me back to reschedule later this week and not to worry about it. The only thing new around here is that I hurt my mcl ligament right above my left knee. It happened exactly one week ago, I woke up and was in a ton of pain! I limped around for a few days before finding out that it's a ligament injury. From what I understand, the reason I got it was probably from trying to do too much too soon on weak leg muscles. Leave it to me! So now I have a knee brace, and have to elevate and ice it every night.. Not to mention that I'm limping around... always something!

On the brighter side of things, Lucien finished the waiting room makeover for me this weekend. It looks so amazing, and just brightens my day to see the new color on the walls, I love it!

The kids are great, Luciana is saying so many new things, like "I'm sorry" "bless you" and "Ba-bie" (when I gave her a Barbie to play with!) She's something else. And Adrian was really funny with the painting going on; it must be really exciting for him too to see the new look after all these years!

Speaking of a new look, this is the first week that my hair is long enough for me to wear it out without a hat or a wig. Everyone says they love it! And I do too!!

January 2009 – My hair is starting to grow back in and my face is beginning to de-poof!

Journal - February 4, 2009 (Wednesday) Day +207

Hey Everyone! My appointment this week went pretty good. I've lost 10 pounds since I've been to the doctor which is about 4 weeks (way too long! I should go every two!). Everything else went pretty well. My potassium was on the high side, so we figured out what foods in my diet are causing that which is tomato soup and soy sauce... the only things I can get down right now! They told me to keep eating them anyway, because they'd rather see my potassium high that me to not eat. The other news from there is that I cannot dye my hair pink like I wanted too! I'm upset about this, but they said it could trigger graft vs. host disease again, and I do not want to go through that again! They told me to stick to wigs, so that's the plan!

Things are, as usual, crazy here. We're still trying to catch up financially, and it just seems we can't get there. There's always something going wrong. This week my printer bit the dust. Well, I use that every day for work, without a printer, I can't invoice any students, or print paperwork or anything. So I had to find an affordable solution which nothing is affordable according to our nonexistent budget. I keep forgetting that although I feel back to normal, I am not even close and I need to calm down and un-stress about things like this. I'm trying to, when I look at the kids, and Lucien when he's sleeping at night, those are special moments that really hit me, how lucky I am to be back home, and how lucky I am to feel like my normal self – as stressful as that can be!

This weekend we had a photo shoot to launch Lucien's new website look, usually the record company updates his website just prior to a new release, but this time it's a re-launch of last year's album Deal With It. So they ended up talking me into having photos too, and I'm so happy with their turnout! I'll post some here, of me with my orange Gretsch guitar, but check out Lucien's website to see all the new pics! I'm really comfortable now with my hair, I actually love it! I'm looking forward to this weekend too, because we're starting the video shoot for No Rest (from Lucien's album Deal With It). This weekend we're starting shooting for that, and the video should be completed in a few weeks and then all over the web and TV. It's exciting, and hopefully is a sign of things picking up in a positive new direction for the year!

February 2009 – Shot from website photo shoot

Journal - February 16, 2009 (Monday) Day +219

Hey Everyone! Happy Valentine's Day to everyone! We haven't celebrated it yet; I think I'll send Lucien to Target tomorrow to get a heart of chocolates 75% off!

I had my doctor appointment today, bright and early...! At least I knew who my driver from the medical transportation company was because I had him a few times now, so I was comfortable to sleep on the way to north Jersey. Everyone in the office at the Cancer center today was in a really good mood and all smiles, which was nice, cause I was pooped and wanted to be in bed! So I cheered up and was joking with everyone... it was fun. They asked me to wait around to see how my blood results were, and turns out everything looked really good!

The white, hemoglobin and platelets were all right where they should be. That is really good, because that means that my marrow is functioning and making blood like it should be. Awesome, awesome. Last week they did the test to see what percentage of donor I am, but those results weren't back in yet. The great news is that we're going to start lowering my Prograf. That's the med that makes me have no immune system, so I am really happy that we'll start lowering that. I take 2 mgs a day right now, and starting tomorrow I will lower to 1.5 a day. And with that the doctor said that I am doing a great job!

He was a little concerned about the reddish dark circles under my eyes, until I explained to him that I was shooting a music video yesterday and had to scrub off my eye makeup... I wonder how many times he's heard *that* excuse?? I'm guessing..... once!

We have finished shooting the video for No Rest which is reallllly exciting! We can't wait to see it done. We had a blast shooting, we really had a hard time holding back laughter we were having so much fun!

Journal - February 20, 2009 (Friday) Day +223

Happy Friday everyone! There's so much going on! I'm so excited for the release of our latest music video. It was so scary heading into it, because I'm still not 100% back to what I normally look like, so it took some heavy makeup and practicing in the mirror to make sure I was ready to perform on camera.

Lucien and I headed to the editing studio Thursday and Friday mornings to see how everything was going, and we are so excited for this one to be released. I think we'll go again Sunday for the last editing session then looks like the No Rest video will be released early next week!

This is really exciting for me, and I had to come on here and tell you all the fun news. It feels SO unbelievably great to be getting back to performing, it's the most invigorating feeling, and I didn't realize just how much I missed it!

Journal - February 23, 2009 (Monday) Day +226

I hope everyone had a great weekend. I know I sure did. We did nothing but spend family time together, and it was wonderful! Luciana might be getting close to potty training, so I was so excited when a mystery person left $35 worth of Target gift cards in our mail box last week, Thank you whoever you are!! I was able to use that to get her a little training potty as well as some household essentials too, like c'mon, you can't beat Targets price on Lysol disinfectant spray! Anyway, so part of the weekend Adrian tried to teach Luciana how to use the potty, it was really cute, and of course I have some embarrassing pictures of them for that... lol

And my really exciting news.... the No Rest music video from Lucien's album Deal With It is officially released today and all over the Internet!! So far, I've found it on YouTube, Vimeo and Metacafe. This is the fun part for me is seeing where his record company puts him all over the Internet. It's so exciting!!! It was super fun to shoot the video, and now it's just as exciting to see it published! Enjoy everyone!!!! and make sure you rate it, leave a comment, and send a link to all your friends to check out! Here are some screen shots of the video, I'm loving it!

February 2009 – Frames from the music video for "No Rest"

Journal - March 9, 2009 (Monday) Day +240

Well, spring is almost here! Or so I thought so until we got blasted with that snow storm last week! What a pain the snow was, we have nowhere to put it when it comes like that. But Lucien got out there and shoveled like a mad man and all was well. He even found a few minutes to make himself an igloo! Luciana wasn't too thrilled with it, but she's hard to please :)

I was supposed to go to the doctor last Monday but got canceled because of the snow. So I went today. I couldn't believe I dropped another 5 pounds, which actually they are starting to wonder why I'm still losing so much weight, so I guess we'll have to keep an eye on that. My blood results looked good from three weeks ago, and I haven't gotten any phone calls about today's results, so that usually means things are good. The doctor did say I was doing great, and to keep up the good work, which is what I always want to hear. We're not going to lower the Prograf again just yet, he wants to lower it really slowly, which is fine. Whatever is the safest way to go, I'm good with.

This weekend was warm enough that we were able to get the little ones outside for a little while. It was perfect; there was no sun so it was safe for me to be out without searching for shade. We got the kids bikes out and let them go up and down the driveway. Luciana will be 2 in May and this was the first time she's ever gotten on a bike. Actually, this was the first time in about 4 years that Adrian rode a bike too. It was so amazing to see their little faces having so much fun. Of course, we were very overly protective of them and hovering over them because it is so unsafe back there in our pavement jungle. As mostly everyone knows by now, my ultimate dream is to get grass back there for them to be safe and enjoy the outdoors. It's not fair that they missed a whole year of outside, and summer and all those simple things that children should enjoy. I'm determined to make it happen for them, to give them a safe place to run around and learn and grow in. They need that in their childhood.

I hope everyone is doing well, and enjoying this warm weather. Spring is almost here, and I think it is the most promising season, a season of new beginnings, of hope and of living life to the fullest!

Journal - March 12, 2009 (Thursday) Day +243

One Year Anniversary of Diagnosis

Today marks an important date for me, today is the one year anniversary of my Leukemia diagnosis. One year ago today, I was rushed to the hospital in north Jersey, and admitted on floor 4, the Bone Marrow Transplant floor. It was one year ago that our lives changed forever, I was whisked away from my children, my husband, my home, my life, and introduced into the world of blood work, gruesome procedures, chemotherapy, hourly temperatures, endless doctors and nurses, and hours of loneliness, helplessness and silence.

It's amazing that here I am one year later, sitting in front of my computer, All My Children is on in the background, Luciana is napping upstairs (a little under the weather) and things are crazy, in a great way. Life is almost, dare I say normal. Almost. How ironic that our first students today are two children of a nurse who administered Chemo to me during my treatments. Now today, she'll come in with her children, we'll have small chat, laugh a little and the day will continue. It's amazing to think, how much my life has changed in this year.

But, things are so exciting right now. There is this wonderful foundation based out of northern New Jersey called the Smile Forever Foundation. They financially assist families and individuals who are fighting cancer and autism. The director of Smile Forever is a friend of mine who I met online during my hospitalization, who underwent a Bone Marrow Transplant 3 years ago to treat her Leukemia. Today she is doing amazing things, directing this wonderful foundation.

I am very excited that we will be performing with Beatlemania at a fundraiser concert event in May. It will be a wonderful event for the whole family, so please tell all your friends and family and come out and support this wonderful cause !

GUARDIAN MEDICAL CENTER
INTERIM VISIT REPORT

DATE OF VISIT: 3/09/09
DIAGNOSIS: Acute Myeloid Leukemia
DATE OF TRANSPLANT: 7/22/2008
CURRENT PROBLEM LIST:
  Chronic graft-versus-host disease
  History of AML
INTERIM HISTORY: The patient returns to clinic today for further follow up with regard to her AML, status post a matched unrelated transplant. The patient reports of having an uneventful

past 2 weeks. No complaints today. The patient notes it has been approximately one year since she presented with AML.

CURRENT MEDICATIONS: Prograf decreased 3 weeks ago from 1 mg to 1 mg in the morning and 0.5 mg at night.

PHYSICAL EXAMINATION: Vital Signs: Weight is 141 pounds, blood pressure104/68, heart rate 103, and respiratory rate 16 and comfortable. Temperature 98.8 degrees. General: The patient is a pleasant, well appearing, young female in no acute distress.

ASSESSMENT: The patient continues without any clinical evidence of recurrent disease or recurrent graft-versus-hosts disease

PLAN:
1 – Graft-versus-host disease. We will hold her current dose of Prograf for two additional weeks. On
next visit, we will decrease her Prograf to 0.5 mg p.o. b.i.d. if there is no evidence of GVHD
2 – AML – The patient has no evidence of recurrent disease pending today's laboratory evaluation. The patient will return to clinic in 2 weeks' time for further follow up. She knows to call me if any new or alarming symptoms arise in the interval.

Journal - March 16, 2009 (Monday) Day +247

Another weekend gone by. Things are okay, although everyone is sick. The kids are both sick, I think it's just that they both have little colds, and nothing more. But it's a pain because I really can't take care of them when they're sick, it's way too risky for me. If I catch even the littlest cold, it could turn into something more severe really quickly and who knows what could happen from there. I feel so bad when they're sick, and I can't just hold them and comfort them.

The weekend was a lot of fun; we had Lucien and Justen (my step sons) visiting for the weekend. When we have them over is the only real time that we 'take off' from working, and really just lounge out and play video games and get nothing done – it's great. We celebrated my father in laws birthday Saturday. Here's me in my fantastic apron baking brownies for the kids. (I got laughed at a fair amount for my apron, but I like it and that's all that matters!)

We played Xbox most of the weekend. Sunday morning I got up really late out of bed, came downstairs and fell asleep for another 3 hours in the living room. I felt bad that I didn't get to game with them in that time, but I was exhausted for some reason. By the time night rolled around, I couldn't even help give the kids dinner, I was so exhausted and really not feeling good at all that I was stuck on the couch. We watched the HGTV Dream Home Giveaway, but didn't win... ah, next year I guess.

I can't wait for the nice warm weather to come around, even though I can't be in the sun, I can sure sit in the shade and soak in the fresh air, and just enjoy the simple things. That's what it all about when it comes down to it.   Life is amazing – especially with my new found love – the FAUX HAWK! I am loving short hair, it's actually very hard core rocker if you style it right!

(Above) March 2009 – Making brownies and starting to experiment in the kitchen.
(Below) March 2009 – Getting my faux-hawk on!

Journal - March 21, 2009 (Saturday) Day +252

Ooohh... intriguing, I'm updating on a Saturday morning when I'm usually guzzling coffee and watching garden shows on HGTV...

I have to update though, I got some pictures to post and some stories to tell! First off, I have to say, I'm so sick right now! I was up coughing all night, can't speak a word because my voice is history from coughing, but I really don't care and know I will get better soon. Life is too good right now; I know I'll get over this cold quickly.

So last night, my best friend Mya, came to the school PTA casino night with me. Lucien couldn't come because he had a Beatlemania show in Wayne NJ. The tickets were donated to us to go, so I asked Mya to come with me. We got all decked out, high heels, party dresses, shawls... all done up and ready to roll! It was so much fun to get all dressed up, what a great feeling! So we hit the road... a little too early of course... so we found a diner and parked out there for a minute.. ya' know, I like to be on time... but not too early either.. (This I inherited straight from my parents!). So we got there and Wow, the country club was beautiful.

So we walked around for a while, Mya was starving so she was on a mission for the spring rolls to come by, which they did occasionally. I figured out that if I stood right next to the kitchen door, I could grab off the tray before the waitress went out and the food got all breathed on (I'm still not supposed to have buffet or food that's out). So I stalked the kitchen door for a little while.

Okay, so we got our chips which were given to us with the tickets, and we hit the tables!! It was so much fun since it wasn't real money. If we happen to win chips, then we'd cash them in for tickets towards the 100 gift baskets that were there! Mya did AWESOME, that girl can gamble man, she did great. I only tried Roulette... I played Lucien's favorite number, 14, twice... and hit it right on twice!!!!! I've never gambled in any sense of the word... so that was so cool for me. So we won enough chips that we had like 12 sheets of tickets or something like that.

Then we had dinner, the country club was really accommodating to me, and made me a plate of food in the kitchen, since I'm not allowed the buffet. They brought it to me at the table and made sure I was comfortable. I can't say enough about how wonderful the wait staff was to me. Dinner was awesome, and then we gambled a little more. Then... we hit the baskets!! I wanted everything, there was a Pool Opening, A Coach Bag, Tiffany Earrings, an American Doll, A Disney Trip for Four.... I went around like a mad woman; I wanted to win SO BAD!!! I never win anything!

Sadly, one by one, a hundred baskets got raffled away to happy, jumping, smiling people, while I watched the Coach Bag go, the Pool Opening Go... everything I was wishing for. Then Mya and I were like, "Okay, so we didn't win anything, at least we had a good time." Then they announced they were going to raffle the super 50/50 winner. Mya and I had split a ticket.. so we got our ticket out and were staring at it... then we heard...

"The winner is, Mya and Sheri......." WOW!!! We JUMPED UP; she was in complete shock.... I grabbed her shoulders and screamed in her face... "Dude!! We won!!" and we hugged for like EVER. We won a BIG (seriously like, a huge cardboard check) for $5800, which we're splitting, we each went home with $2900. We were in SHOCK, everyone started hugging me (which I'm not supposed to do, ah well!) and everyone was so excited for us. What an incredible moment. I still can't believe it.

On the way home, Mya summed it up in the most amazing way (as we were driving past this awful stench of a dump.. ugh!) She said, "Sheri, just think where you were one year ago today." That thought was amazing. Last March Chemotherapy, a poor diagnosis, to one year later, the grand prize winner at a function like this... I never dreamed I would be living my life again so quickly. I am so thankful for every minute of every day, and I am so thankful that we won such an incredible thing last night. All I can say is that I am bringing my family to Kohl's tonight, and getting everyone their spring sneakers.. :) That means the world to me.

March 2009 – Casino night poker chips!

Journal - March 30, 2009 (Monday) Day +261

Well it's been a while since I've updated! Last Monday, I had my normal doctor's appointment, went through the regular blood work and all that jazz. But that night at around 6, the doctor called and said that he didn't like the results of my white count, that they had dropped by about half of what they were two weeks prior... which is not good. At all. So instead of waiting two weeks to go back, he said he wanted to see me in one week, We left it at that, but Lucien and I were on complete edge all week wondering why the counts had dropped, and if they were still dropping... two questions which I still don't have answers to right now.

So I went again this morning, just had blood work done and left. So I'm really on edge now, waiting to see if the phone is going to ring or not, and boy I sure hope it doesn't. I'd like to know why the white count dropped though, maybe because I'm still sick with this head cold. I'm not sure, but it's not a settling feeling. We're so on edge to see what happens, but trying to remain hopeful that things are okay.

So that's really about it for today, things were crazy only because of our nerves about my blood counts, but Sunday we had a wonderful family day... it was absolutely fabulous just to spend the entire day as a family. Now I think I'm going to decorate for Easter! I'll update if I hear anything about the blood results!! (But I hope I don't hear anything!)

Journal - April 13, 2009 (Monday) Day +275

It's been a long time again since I've updated on here, things have been really nutty! I'll start with today's doctor appointment and go back in time.. ! Today went well; my white counts are back to where they should be!!! All the prayers made that happen. I've been so worried about the low count from a few weeks ago, that hearing that news today lifted a ton of weight off my shoulders. We lowered my Prograf – now I'll only take 1/2 pill every day! I am so excited for that! The fewer pills I'm on, the closer I am to being done with this.

The past two weeks has been amazing. We've had such quality family time, which is all I want. Last weekend we had my step sons, Lucien and Justen over. We celebrated Easter with them, they got baskets, and we made Easter cookies all day. On Palm Sunday we got all dressed up and went to Lucien's parents' house for dinner. We had a beautiful day there, and got to see some family. It was a lot of fun. I really can't believe how big the boys are getting!

Easter weekend was very relaxing. Our tradition is to stay home in jammies just the four of us and do nothing fancy on Easter, and that's just what we did. Saturday night we got out and ran some errands. I was in need of clothes that fit (again). Because I am not yet back to the size I was "pre-cancer" but less than I was in November "steroid weight". I'm almost back into my shape, but not quite. So I had nothing to wear, no pants, no shirts, nothing that fits my current size. So we went to Marshals and I got some staple pieces to get me by. I hate buying clothes for myself; I always end up browsing the children's department!! I browse a lot and don't buy anything, like a quasi-shopaholic... maybe more like a browse-a-holic. Anyway!

Sunday morning we all woke up to our Easter baskets!! Luciana got lots of fun girly things like hair ties, and princess dvds, and an Ariel float for the pool, Adrian got Bubbles, Magic School Bus Books and a word puzzle (for my little puzzle nut that he is). Lucien got a Les Paul book that I got for him and some Snickers, his favorite, and I got my ALL TIME favorite... Cadbury Eggs (Full and mini size), Pink Peeps, and **blush** Yes, I got a Barbie for the pool... I'm such a kid it's not even funny!! But truthfully, I have a blast playing Barbie's with the kids, it brings me right back to childhood.

The egg hunt was amazing, the kids were so excited, their little faces, running around, I can't believe I didn't get this last year. I was in the hospital last Easter, and I never want to be apart from my children again like that, they were so happy, jumping and yelling for their eggs!

The rest of the day we went outside to get some landscaping done. Well, I'm not supposed to be in the sun, or get close to dirt or plants... okay, so I didn't listen to any of those rules. (I did wear a hoodie though, so my head didn't get any sun). Lucien did all the mulching, weeding, and heavy stuff. I started out by pruning the bushes... but all who know me know I do too much. I pruned to my heart's desire! I LOVE WORKING OUTSIDE, so I really took my time and did a great job. Was I done? Nope! Then I went over and laid some stepping stones in the rocks around the pool, which was leveling and digging and dirt and worms ... yep, everything I shouldn't have done. But I did it all with big smile on my face to be digging my gloves into the earth. I loved every second! Then Lucien and I put the kids to bed, pigged out on Easter candy and watched King of Kings... classic.

Fast forward to today... I AM SO SORE!!!!! I can barely walk; my thighs hurt so much, my hands hurt from the pruning, UGH! And forget bending over to pick anything up.... OUCH!!! I guess my body just isn't used to doing these things... and lesson learned, I have to take things in stride, and rebuild my strength... trust me, lesson learned!

(Above) Easter 2009 – Making Easter sugar cookies with the kids!
(Below) Easter 2009 – A squinty family picture

Journal - April 27, 2009 (Monday) Day +288

LAB RESULTS   NOCELLI, SHERI

CHEM PROFILE   REF RANGE   04/27/09

	REF RANGE	04/27/09
WBC	4.0-10.0	3.9
HGB	12.3-15.5	11.8
PLATELET CNT	140-440	278

LABORATORY DATA: Patient's differential shows 52% segmented cells, 28% lymphocytes and slightly elevated monocytes at 15%, and 5% eosinphils.

Well I went to the doctor this morning, and looks like everything is looking good! Of course, if there is anything wrong with the blood results he said he would call me later, so I hope the phone doesn't ring. I showed him a little mole that is starting to grow, because I had never noticed it before. He said he'd like me to see a dermatologist, and that since I had Leukemia I should plan one seeing on once a year from now on. (I like that he's thinking ahead, it feels promising!). So the appointment was mostly uneventful, the way it should be. He did get a little upset that I was in the sun this weekend and said he has to tell me firmly no sun... I guess that was wrong of me. I just miss the sun so much! But I need to start listening... He also said that in July when we reach the one year of my Bone Marrow Transplant date, then we will have to start all of my immunizations (which were all wiped out with the transplant, that's why I have the immunity of an infant). I literally have to get every immunization again; diphtheria, tetanus, Haemophilus influenza type B, Streptococcus pneumoniae, Poliovirus and influenza (annually).

I got home and was SO exhausted; I really needed to go back to bed. Lucien was moving a plant on the back porch and I went to tell him I was home. Wouldn't you know, I closed the door behind myself and yeah, we were totally locked out! Luciana was in the living room watching TV and we were locked outside with no key. So Lucien tried to get the door open (with no success), and I walked over to the church, the ladies in the parish center were kind enough to let me call Lucien's parents (they have a key) but they couldn't help because they live an hour away. So they called the locksmith to the tune of $90 later to get back into the house. Lesson learned. That was a very expensive lesson straight out of the grocery money! Smooth move on my part.

Anyway, the weekend was amazing. We did something we've never done in more than 7 years; we took a personal day on Friday. We spent the whole day in New York City, which was fun because I've personally never done the touristy NY thing, we're always performing or working and there's no time. We had lunch, then went to some of the shops. We hit up the Hershey shop, and the M&M superstore. We are huge M&M fanatics, so we loved, loved, loved that. We got the kids some little matchbox cars named after different chocolates it was pretty cute. We went to Colony music store which had the most amazing selection of sheet music, Lucien took forever, he was like a kid in a toy store. We went to the American Girl store since we were there, to pick up Luciana's birthday present that everyone is chipping in on. She's getting the Bitty baby twin, so cute it looks just like her!! The store was amazing, I felt like a little girl in there... so amazing. We walked in Times Square, and just took everything in.

The night ended with seeing Chick Corea and the Five Peace Band in the Rose Theater at Lincoln center. We had great box seats (since I can't sit too close to anyone due to germs and my low immune system still). The show was absolutely amazing, Chick was great as usual, and I loved the drummer's style, it was great. After the show, we went backstage and talked with Chick for a few minutes, and had our picture taken with him. It was awesome to hang with him, his music has been so comforting to me through this past year, and Lucien has been studying his music for close to 30 years, he was and is Lucien's inspiration when it comes to his jazz fusion. It was an amazing night, and just what I needed to get out and live life.

Over the weekend we spent a lot of time with the kids outside (in the sun, which is what the doctor was upset about). The Lincroft Little League had a parade down our street which the kids loved to see right in front of our house! Then we filled the kiddie pool so they could cool down in the heat. I can't believe it's not even summer yet!

Getting touristy in New York City at the Hershey and American Girl stores.

April 2009 – Starting to get outside with the munchkins.

Journal - May 18, 2009 (Monday) Day +309

Another few weeks went by all full of complete craziness... seriously it's been a wild few weeks. So I'll start with the medical update. I didn't go to the doctor last week, I missed my appointment. So I went this morning. It had been three weeks since I was there which wasn't too good, I know. We did blood work today, which I haven't heard anything back yet which is usually good news. He reminded me again that in July I have to start getting my immunizations all over again (this is not something I'm looking forward to!) so I said, "Well, that's not until July so let's not think about that yet!" I told him about a light rash I had in between visits, it was on my arms and chest, and was a lot of little tiny bumps, I couldn't see them and they didn't itch so the general opinion is that it was a little heat rash. The good news is that we lowered my Prograf again, now I'll take .5 mg every other day. This means I might be off the Prograf in a few weeks!! Exciting stuff. I go back to the doctor in two weeks now. Hopefully I will handle the lower med dose just fine.

What a crazy few weeks. For starters, the pictures we took yesterday on Sunday. Once a year I make sure we get family portraits taken and we also got Luciana's birthday pictures done in her princess birthday dress! I'm so thrilled with the pics!

Mother's day was amazing... I woke up in my own bed, in my own house, to my beautiful children... Adrian handed me a little gift bag. I opened it to find a necklace, called the Journey necklace (I'm wearing it in the pictures). Along with it Lucien had helped him write a note "Dear Mommy, This necklace is called Life's Journey. Every time you wear it remember the Journey you've been on, and the Journey ahead and that we need you to help us on our Journey. Love Adrian Luciana and Daddy" .. It was SO sweet. The note Adrian wrote, made me love it and appreciate the meaning so much.

That's how the week started... then it all tumbled down when our central air stopped working. We had to wait a week for it to even be looked at! Yikes. So we did what we could, we fixed part of it but left the rest to be fixed when we can pull it off. So right now we're lucky it's not scorching outside yet, but at least the kids have ceiling fans in the meantime!

Other than that, I don't want to harp on the negatives; I'd rather share the positives. So this coming Saturday is the fundraiser for the Smile Forever Foundation, who helps NJ families afflicted with Cancer, Autism and other disabling diseases. Please come out and support a good cause! This is open to kids of all ages, is a completely family friendly event. Lucien and I will be performing the opening act as well, so please come on out and enjoy a fun night of the Broadway show Beatlemania!!! Hope to see everyone there!!!!!!

May 2009 – Family photo shoot

Journal - May 28, 2009 (Thursday) Day +319

Well, Here I am a year older!! My birthday was Tuesday, and I'm 25 years old. It's so amazing everything I've experienced in my 25 years... and I am so thankful to be here celebrating my first birthday after transplant... I am here, feeling good, with my family, and that is the only gift I need.

Saturday we had a big show in Demarest NJ, a benefit concert for the Smile Forever Foundation. The show went really well, it ran like a well-oiled machine, no stress, lots of fun and very successful, the foundation raised a lot of money, and that makes me so happy that they did so well. The guys were great as usual; I always look forward to hanging with the guys. With Frank (stage tech) and Mya (stage hand/ merch), it was like a big family event more than work which is the way it should be! My mother and brother also were able to make it down from New Hampshire to see the show, which was awesome, I love performing for my family whenever I can. Lucien and I performed the opening act, doing songs from Deal With It. It was a lot of fun, and I'm so, so happy that everyone that was there from the cast and crew are like family, it just makes it so much more enjoyable.

Sunday was a blast; we had a small joint birthday party for Luciana and myself. Mom and Scott were here (Dad was sick and had to stay home.) Lucien's parents came down, Kathy and Mya and Joe too (our neighbor). It was really small, which is all we could handle really but a lot of fun. My brother helped us get the stairs into the pool, and then he jumped in. I couldn't help it! I missed swimming SO much, so I jumped right in! And yes, it was freezing, but so worth it!! We had a nice BBQ, then cake which I made for Luciana. After cake, we got Luciana into her Birthday gown while she opened presents. I love this dress and wanted to see her in it as much as I could! She got great presents from everyone, thank you everyone for everything!!! (And for my presents too of course!!) Her big gift was the American Girl, Bitty baby twin; she's so cute with dark brown hair and pigtails. Luciana loved her right away and started walking around the house with her in the stroller. It was perfect, just what I had hoped for.

It's been a crazy week otherwise with regular craziness, which I won't get into – it'll all work out. I'd rather not think about some things, and just keep up on the positives. I am just looking forward to the weekend, and hoping that things stay good and calm. I go to the doctor on Monday, so I will update then!

Performing at the Smile Forever Foundation Benefit Concert

May 2009 – Celebrating Luciana's birthday with a BBQ!

Journal - June 15, 2009 (Monday) Day +336

I didn't realize it had been so long since I've updated!! Things are going fairly well, I have been weaned off of the Prograf completely for about a week now, which is really amazing, I'm so happy about that. One pill down... lots more to go! It's been crazy here. We've been swimming (which is something my doctor doesn't actually approve of, but told me I can still do if I'm really careful, stay out of the sun and tell him right away if I feel anything afterwards like ears, throat etc.) So that's the plan. Of course over the past two weeks, no matter how much sun block, even at 50 spf, that I put on, I got a really nice tan (which is actually not good!). So this morning when I saw the doctor, I just came out and said, "I apologize for the tan, I really tried not to get it!" I mean I was literately floating in the pool under an umbrella... so... I don't know how I ended up with this tan, but it sure is even and nice!

Last week I did something else I've been told not to, and that was to go to Adrian's school for the Kindergarten show. I'm so happy that I was able to go, I've never been to any of his school functions ever and he was so happy. Before they started I went out in the hallway where I saw the kids lining up. I saw Adrian walking by and I knelt down, grabbed his face between my hands and said "Look Adrian, Mommy is here! I'm here to see you sing!" and it clicked, and his face changed into a big smile and he yelled, "Mommy you're here!"...oh my goodness the poor little guy, I've never been there. He was so cute, singing the 10 or so songs, then he came and sat with us for the Kindergarten slide show; it was really cute. Afterwards everyone starting mingling and things got really crowded, so I covered my face and bolted to the nearest exit to get out of the room, and Lucien returned Adrian to his teacher and explained that we had to go because of me.

It was also the church carnival last week... another situation I should not be near, but the kids could see the rides from their bedroom windows and we could hear people screaming on the rides and the "announcer voice" every night bellowing through our house all night. So the kids knew something was going on. So Wednesday night Mya and her daughter came over and we brought all the kids over while Lucien was teaching. It was so much fun! And not too crowded. Adrian and Mya's daughter were cute, they went on a bunch of rides together, and then I joined them on the Tilt a Whirl. It was a lot of fun. I felt bad for Lucien, so we went back for a little while on Friday night and got to put Adrian on some more rides. It was not the safest situation for me to be in, but the kids had a really good time and that's what means the world to me.

Other than that, we've just been recording a lot for the new album. I've been slaving over getting the artwork ready since I've been commissioned by Lucien to do all the art work which will be a mix of acrylic pieces and pointillism. I feel like there's so much work to be done! But it's all fun and I'm happy to be such a big part of the project.

I saw my doctor this morning, and everything seems to look fine. He mentioned I should start making yearly visits to the dermatologist, OBGYN and eye doctor just as I would later in life, but to start now for early screening. So I have to work on that. My appointment went well, but the doctor was running really late. It ended up when I got outside, my medical transportation had left me there... so I was stranded. I called Lucien who thank goodness was around and he had to cancel some meetings and stuff to come and get me. I was really upset that I had been stranded there. I'm really tired and wanted to get home to rest, and there I was shipwrecked. So I sat outside on a bench, watching people coming and going, trying to figure out who was the patient and who was the visitor; not too hard since I know what to look for. My leg fell asleep and when I saw the van pull around and stood up, fumbled and twisted my ankle.. ahhhh... what a morning!!!!!!!!!! I need to make something really positive happen today, because I really need to turn the energy around into something good. Hopefully this week goes smooth and we get a lot done.... and it's only Monday!

LAB RESULTS   NOCELLI, SHERI
CHEM PROFILE   REF RANGE   06/15/09

	REF RANGE	06/15/09
WBC	4.0-10.0	10.4
HGB	12.3-15.5	11.7
PLATELET CNT	140-440	275

LABORATORY DATA: Segmented cells are 33%, lymphocytes are 9%, and eosinophilis are recorded as 49%. Chemistries are within normal limits with the exception of mildly elevated potassium of 5.1. Protein is 5.4, alkaline phosphatase mildly elevated at 117, LDH 152, and magnesium 2.0
ASSESSMENT: This is a 25-year-old female status post matched unrelated transplant now off immunosuppression with a rising eosinophilia.

August 16, 2009 (Sunday)

I have only one excuse for not updating this page is so very long, and that is.... that I've been too busy living every second of this summer to the fullest. Against Doctors orders, I am tan, swimming constantly and enjoying the outdoors as much as possible and it feels wonderful!

July 22th was my one year anniversary of my Bone Marrow Transplant. I wanted to get on here and write an entry about "how far I've come" and this and that, but truthfully I was so busy, I just didn't! One year is a huge milestone; my doctors say it should be treated as another birthday. The nurses, my friends, my family, our clients, everyone congratulated me on my one year, it was really sweet, and I can't believe it's been that long since I've even been in the hospital! I am down to every other week as far as doctor visits, which is a nice break in between. But with the one year mark, all of this celebration comes with negative points I am dreading. I have had to go for many "one year tests" (and have more scheduled) from Bone Density Scans to check my bones to Pulmonary Function Tests (breathing tests to check my lungs functioning ability). I am supposed to start getting all of my immunizations again as of last month. Luckily, my doctor has postponed them since anything with needles is a very stressful event for me and things have been very stressful this month as it is, which he could see, so he told me not to worry about them, that we'll start the shots in the fall.

Along with the one year, other problems have occurred, which is to be expected after what my body has gone through. I am officially post-menopausal at the ripe old age of 25. While this has been a nice little perk, other side effects come with this since my body doesn't make enough estrogen anymore, like now we are watching like hawks for Osteoporosis, and other problems most women don't worry about until they're in their 50s. At least the hot flashes are over! I haven't had one of them in about a month, so that's very nice since it's so warm now in August! I am having trouble with my knees, which I am going to have to make an appointment with an Orthopedic Specialist (I think that's what it is) and will probably need physical therapy. On top of that, while I am enjoying summer, I did suffer an injury in the pool (karma maybe since I'm not supposed to be swimming???), Adrian jumped on my back, and his bony little knee hit my tailbone full force resulting in either a sprained or broken tailbone (not sure on those results just yet!) – It's painful though!! I'm taking this as a sign of brittle bones and preparing myself for the worst as far as that bone density test goes (I'll get the results on Monday).

About a month ago, I also tested positive for a virus called CMV or Cytomegalovirus. It's a common virus that infects most people at some time during their lives but rarely causes obvious illness. CMV infection can become dormant for a while and may reactivate at a later time. In normal people with normal immune systems, this is no big deal really, but for me, with a weak immune system can quickly turn into chickenpox, infectious mononucleosis or other serious things like that. It was a fiasco getting the medication for that, an anti-viral medication that my horrible insurance wouldn't cover. And I needed them, because otherwise this virus could turn into something more serious very quickly.

Now on to the positives! Summer has been amazing. Last year when I was hospitalized for the whole summer, all I wanted was one thing. To sit in the backyard with my family and watch the kids play. That's all I wanted, and this year, I'm doing it as much as I can! We had my step sons, Lucien and Justen for the entire month of July. It was a lot of fun, we swam a lot, played X Box on rainy days, went to Dorbrook park a few mornings which was fun. We ate a lot, played a lot and just had a lot of fun. In June (right in the middle of the whole CMV diagnosis, I even went up to New Hampshire for a few days for my brother Scotts High School Graduation (this was highly against doctors' orders as well, and I was lectured that I had to call and come to the hospital in North Jersey at the very first sign of fever or infection). It was a wonderful little visit to see my family and cheer on Scott on his big day!

Last week was Adrian's 6th birthday party; I can't believe my little boy is growing up! He had a Beatles birthday with a Yellow Submarine cake. He had a great time, and asked me immediately when was his 7th birthday going to be.

Yesterday we went up to Staten Island because Lucien had a Beatlemania show. It was right on the beach, which was great, I was so happy to have a chance to get near the ocean! It's literately been years. We had a lot of extra time to soak in the ocean, check out the street fairs all along the board walk and just hang around. It was awesome to hang out with the cast and crew; they're always the best group to be with. It's really the most fun and completely stress free group of people to be with, they're our extended family really.   It's always great to catch up with Alan and Jess, and of course Joe. He's great, just as crazy as Lucien and I with having Purell and Germ X available at all times.

Life is moving so quickly again, almost as though this cancer never was here and never stole a year of my life. It's also a big part of who I am today, how I live my life, how I approach things I do and how I do them. It has made me soak in my world around me in a new view and with new appreciation. And through all this, is how I sometimes, for a minute, forget that it was ever running through my veins. How it was ready to claim my life, and instead has only made me stronger. I still worry sometimes, as I'm looking at my hands, or showering, or doing my makeup, if it could be secretly building inside me again, preparing for another battle, but then I stop and realize that that's part of its war plan is the scare tactic – so every time that thought comes to me, I quickly shake it off and move on with my day, because I've fought the battle before, and I'm not about to waste another minute not living my life.

(Above) August 2009 – One year post bone marrow transplant, and celebrating by reading in the park – it's the simple things in life!

(Above) Celebrating my brother Scott's high school graduation!

September 24, 2009 (Thursday)

Time for an update! I know it's been so long, but as usual things have been crazy. So much has been going on in life, and medically, so it's really just been consuming so much time to take care of everything around here.

Last month I started getting my immunizations. Since my bone marrow transplant, my blood is actually my donor's blood, and has grown from the little amount in one IV bag to fill my bloodstream. So, this blood is fresh, I'm basically a one year old (okay, maybe 13 months?). Just as any infant needs their immunizations, I do too. And it's horrible!! You'd think that after everything I've been through, I might be a little better around shots... not true! Didn't happen. I am permanently and forever petrified. My doctor actually was very sly with me, and didn't bother to tell me that I had shots until I went in for my checkup, which was great because I had no time to worry about it really. The first three I got were Haemophilus Influenzae Type b (Hib) Vaccine, Hepatitis B Vaccine and Pheumococcal Polysaccharide Vaccine... and there were tears... many! I'm at least able to now warn the nurse (although they know I'm coming... I got a reputation!). I tell them, "I need a private area to do this, I need to recline or lay down, I'm going to cry, it's not you, don't stop, just please do it fast and get it over with.." then I cry like a little baby and go home miserable! I had to return a week later to get two more, which were Tetanus and Diphtheria Vaccine and Polio Vaccine... yup, same routine, cry and go home miserable.

I had to also make a separate appointment with my OBGYN, who I haven't been to since after Luciana was born, and I have to bring to him my bone density scan results. My oncologist slipped a little, and said, "I want you to make an appointment with your OBGYN to talk about how to treat your Oster..o.. I mean low bone density." SO.. I take this as ... I think I *do* have Osteoporosis. We shall see, I will be going to that appointment next week. He was also pretty concerned... and kinda freaked out by the horrible crunchy sound my knee is still making, and making louder each week.. I think he called it a Crepitus sound or something like that... it's great, he gets all tweaked out whenever I bend my knee... I get a kick out of that!! So unfortunately I am still awaiting answers on the knee, we don't know exactly what is causing the cracking in it, it doesn't hurt, it's just "really not right" as my doctor put it..

Life is nuts! Adrian started the 1st grade, which is an adventure in itself. He has some rocky moments, but so far he's doing much better than he has in the past years, so I do have a really good feeling about this school year for him. Little Diva, Luciana is ruling the castle with a vengeance. Everything is "hers", she's bossy, rude, in charge and a princess all at the same time... oh, and she's only 2. I don't know where in the world she inherited all that from.. :::bows head in shame:::::

Lucien and I have been working like crazy on his new album EvoLucien. So far, even I'm blown away by it. I'll routinely sit back, listening to play back after a session and just be awestruck by the songs. The artwork is coming along as well; this is a big project for me. It's a concept album, with a 24 page booklet.. So to go along with all this is a lot of artwork, mostly in pointillism to depict the images he is painting with the music. I'm really excited to see the final product.

So, things are moving along, it's been crazy, with all the shots, the knee, the bone density... but at I'm happy to be home and happy to have the opportunity to live this crazy life! I take all of these things in stride, because it sure is a long way from where I was a year and a half ago.

October 12, 2009 (Monday)

Hey everyone! I can't believe fall is here, and the leaves are falling. I can't believe I've been home for over a year, and how almost normal things seem these days.

The doctor gave me 4 weeks off from going to see him for blood work, which is a huge milestone of sorts. I think part of the *real* reason though, is because he is on rounds in the hospital until next week and it's a pain in the butt for him to have to come to my checkups... ha-ha... so I lucked out. I'll probably get to go to every three weeks starting next time which still is better than every other like it was.

Last week I had my appointment with the OBGYN. I had a regular checkup, which he thinks will probably come back a little abnormal due to what I went through, but that we shouldn't be totally alarmed by that either, that we should expect it. He was shocked to hear what I went through, since I haven't been to him since right after the baby was born. He looked over my bone density scan results, and started writing all over the paper, circling things and writing notes (I'm assuming this was not a good sign) because then he looked up and said, "You know you have Osteoporosis right?" Wow... what a way to find out!! I mean, I had a hunch that I did, but to find out so bluntly was still shocking. Basically, I have the bones of a 70 year old... so I have to be very careful or I can easily break or fracture a bone. He ordered blood work, and when those results come back, we'll put those with the bone density numbers, and come up with a plan of treatment. I think I can't get anything aggressive like Boniva (you know, the Sally Field commercial), since we don't know how drugs like that would interact with the meds I'm already on, so it will probably be dietary supplements, exercise and physical therapy. Only other medical news is that next week I also have to get three flu shots... yay. I'm not happy about this!!!!

I have been going crazy selling things on the Internet, Lucien parted with some equipment, and I sold some things we could live without on Ebay which helped to a bill or two last month. It's really rough right now, and we're just trying to do anything we can to pay the bills... everything from selling things, to extra hours, to cutting services.... even the kids Halloween costumes. We thought of the cheapest thing... rock stars!! Adrian wants to be Ringo, so all he needs is to use one of Daddy's wigs, some drumsticks and he's good to go! And Luciana is going to be a punk rocker, with her pink leggings, beaded jewelry and a microphone, all things we have already! Desperate times call for desperate measures!! But the munchkins will never know :)

This weekend my parents and my brother came down to visit, which was awesome. It was so needed to have a weekend of laughing, gaming and constant fun. What a stress relief to forget about the bills, the craziness, everything. We really needed it. I have a really good feeling that this week will start to bring positive things and be as stress free as possible. Things have to turn around sooner or later, and it can't be any later than today :)

(Above) Halloween 2009 – A family of punk rockers... and a random Cowboy and Beatle! At least we had a theme!

November 11, 2009 (Wednesday)

It's been so long since I have updated on here! Things are okay, it's been a little crazy this month... the munchkins have been back and forth on being sick, which is difficult because I can't go near them when they're sick. It's especially hard when Luciana is sick, which she's been off and on, but this week is the worse for her, she has a fever, runny nose and is ultra-cranky… it's hard because I can't wipe her nose or change a diaper (although I've done it in pinch, I put on medical gloves and do it, even though that's a huge risk).

Last week I was pretty sick myself. I started with a really bad cough, which I still have, but it only at night now. I was sleeping most of the day the starting the Sunday after Halloween (which ya have to be pretty sick for when there's 4 kids running around, playing games, being nuts etc). I had really bad chills, and did get a temperature of 99 point something which **thank goodness** went away after a few hours. If that had stayed, I was surely going to have to be admitted to the hospital. I'm still so so so tired, and have a night cough, but there hasn't been any fever since last week.

Monday I had an appointment with my oncologist up in north Jersey, which went okay. He wasn't too thrilled with the fact that I was sick, and coughing so much, and we had a big debate about the H1N1 immunization… he's not thrilled that I'm not getting it for the kids, but Lucien and I have very strong feelings about the whole thing, and did a lot of research and are very comfortable with our choice. Then came the fun part.. ugh.. they told me I had to get 2 immunizations (childhood ones), then come back next week to get more. SO… I asked if they couldn't just do all 4 while I was there because it's a big ordeal for Lucien to drive me up there on a Monday morning, with all the traffic, it takes us an hour to get there, and we're rushing because we have to get Adrian on the school bus first. So I'm always late. I used to have medical transportation which was so much better, I was there on time, and Lucien could work for the four hours that it takes for my checkups. But we ran out of funds for the transportation, so we've had no choice but for Lucien to bring me, which is a pain, he can't work for that time, and he has to sit with the car running the whole time (so much gas!) to keep the dvd player on so the baby doesn't scream for 4 hours... good times. Anyway! SO the Doctor agreed to give me all 4 which is a big big big big ordeal (for me). I cried like a baby, literately, it took 2 nurses, it's my biggest fear in the whole world is needles, so I was sobbing, which only made me cough more... when they were done, they were hugging me to try to calm me down, and insisted I drink water before I leave... they must dread when I come in! So I now have the immunizations to Polio, Tetanus and Diphtheria, Hepatitis B, and the Haemophilus Influenzae Type b (Hib) Vaccine... yeah... all that.

So, the next day, I get a phone call from the doctor regarding the blood work... this is never a good sign!! Turns out that my Potassium levels are sky rocketed, so high that they are worried about my heart! Now, this has happened once before so I'm trying not to get all worked up over it... but I am getting repeat blood work done tomorrow morning to see if it was a fluke or if there's a problem. They said that if it is still high, then I will need to start a medication for that immediately.. (just what I need... more pills). I did also have to start taking twice a day OsCal (Calcium with D) to treat my Osteoporosis until the OBGYN decides on a treatment. On the positive side of things, we have lowered my CellCept (this is one of the medications that causes me to have no immune system) by half! I was taking 4 doses a day and now am lowered to 2 doses a day.. that's the good news.. :)

I will try to update on the Potassium levels and what we have to do for that if it remains high. All I know is I want to feel better, I want to start concentrating on the holidays coming... I can't wait for my family to visit, and for the cozy season to come..

December 17, 2009 (Thursday)

I can't believe it's almost Christmas! It's so crazy to me that a whole year has gone by already. I love this time, I love the decorations, the festive mood, the tree, the movies, the music, everything about this whole season.

Medically, it's been a little crazy... I had an appointment this past Monday, which seems to be the schedule they were trying to get me on. Unfortunately, my sickness hasn't gotten any better in over a month. I think I've actually been sick closer to two months almost... I have a cough, runny nose, and a constant coughing up of phlegm and fun stuff like that. A day or two before Thanksgiving my doctor had called to see if I could come to get the H1N1 vaccine (which I still don't agree with at all), and I told him at that point that I was sick. So he prescribed an antibiotic, as well as Tamiflu just as a preventative measure. Of course there were all kinds of problems getting the antibiotic filled, and it took like an extra week to get it. I finished the courses of both of those... and I'm *still* sick!

SHERI NOCELLI

So when I was there Monday, they wanted to give me the H1N1... they had only received 100, and had saved one for me... (how lucky?). I told them I was still sick, and it was a big debate if I should get it. So, they decided to give it to me,.. (side note, I made it through without crying!! major accomplishment!). Then he wanted to schedule allllll these other tests to see what's going on, he wanted a chest x ray, and a catscan.... to which I had to basically refuse and beg to put off. The cost of these tests is so crazy, especially a catscan, so I begged to put it off another week or so, and he agreed.

Tuesday I got a call from the oncologist's office, saying that I need to come back for repeat blood work because my liver function test came back high. Great. The reason for this could be because I'm fighting a viral infection, or could be a problem post-transplant. So we need to see what's going on with that, and I have repeat blood work for that this coming Monday... something nice and festive to do Christmas week I guess...... ::sigh::

The cherry on the cake was when I got another call today from them.... turns out my antibodies in my system are really low, which is probably why I'm not getting any better. SO they want me to come up there and get an IV treatment of a transfusion of antibodies. It's basically like any other blood transfusion, only instead of receiving red cells, or white cells, I would be receiving the donors antibodies.... how long does this take? Oh, well, an hour to get there, an hour and a half to get going, 5 hours of transfusion and an hour home..... NOT exactly gonna work in my schedule too easily...... they did say that it could wait until after the new year, which is good, so I'm

332

hoping and praying that I can somehow recover and start producing some antibodies of my own!!!!

On the positive side, I'm so happy Christmas is almost here. I had a little photo shoot with Adrian and Luciana in their Christmas outfits... they did so good, and were so behaved! And I'm super excited to see my family next week!! I can't wait!!! I hope everything works out and I get better on my own, that's my Christmas wish!! If I don't get a chance to come back on here, Merry Christmas everyone!!! Love to you all!!!!! :) Thank you for another amazing year of being such loving and supportive family and friends!!

January 16, 2010 (Saturday)

Happy 2010 everyone!!! What a whirlwind the past month has been. First of all, Merry Christmas and happy new year to everyone!! 2010 has a lot of good in store, and I truly believe that. 2009 was cool, but it's time to move on to bigger and better and brighter things!

Health wise it's been a little rocky for me this past month. I was sick from Thanksgiving, until about.. oh, a week ago.. it was a virus that I just couldn't kick. The symptoms were a runny nose and coughing up mucus.. always fun! The good thing was that no one else could catch it, so it must have just been something everyone is immune to – except me! My oncologist tested my antibodies, and as it turned out, I had basically none (or a very low level) and told me I would need a blood transfusion of antibodies. Fun! Nothing like sitting for 5 hours with a drip when that's the last place in the world you want to be.

My liver function also came back with abnormally high function levels, so we had to do some repeat blood work a couple times, and adjust the meds by putting me back on the Cellcept. The function could be high from the virus, but we are watching because it could also be from long term graft versus host disease (with we are always watching for!). But, overall, for a year and a half post bone marrow transplant, I am doing fairly well! :)

Christmas was amazing this year, it was so much fun, and I was soooo happy to see my family again. We had a great time hanging out and playing games..hehe.. the kids were so precious waiting for Santa, just amazing, I love that time of year sooo much! We were very light on gifting this year, and the great thing was that no one seems to notice.. The kids were more than happy when they opened underwear or clothes... we tried to be extra practical!

The festive season had a downfall however... a few days after Christmas, once my parents were back home in New Hampshire already, my mom Diane suffered a stroke. She was smart though, (thats mom!) :) and drove herself right to the hospital (since she was driving when the stroke happened). She is doing well now, getting stronger every day. She spent a week in the hospital in Lebanon NH, then moved to a rehab center in Concord where she will be for at least 2 weeks. It's a long journey for her; she has to re learn how to do everything like walking, washing, dressing, writing, cooking, and basic everyday skills. She's a trooper though, and her spirits are high... like mother like daughter!

This year I will try to post more often on here about my recovery and all the details. This is such an important year... in July I will be 2 years post-transplant and do you know what that means.........???? If my donor agrees, we can know who each other is!!!!!! I'm so excited for that!!

It's been a long recovery with many, many forks in the road and twists and turns... but here's to getting on the highway and kicking all of the long term side effects of all the treatments I've had in the butt in 2010... Happy New Year to everyone, I love you all so much!!

March 10, 2010 (Wednesday)

It's been so long since I've updated on here! I guess that's a good sign, because it means I'm so busy with work and the kids, that I forget to come on here sometimes.

Things have been a little up and down health wise so far this year. I have been having a lot of blood results coming back with pretty high liver function results. This is something of concern, because it could be graft vs. host disease which is common after a transplant. It is when the new cells fight my cells, and can cause damage. I've also been having painful issues with my eyes the past few weeks. It feels like I have sand in my eyes, and as the day goes on, the pain gets worse. My oncologist wanted to see me right away when I called about my eyes to ask him what to do. He thinks it is graft vs. host disease as well, and that my eyes have lost the ability to produce their own tears, resulting in very painful dry eyes. So I am on artificial tears eye drops right now which Lucien has to put in, because I am the biggest baby and my eye clamps shut when there's a bottle coming at it. It's pretty painful though, and I have an appointment with a cornea specialist that can determine what's going on with my eyes. We shall see from there.

So, this Friday, March 12th is such a big date. It's the 2 year mark of my official diagnosis of Leukemia, and the day I was swept away to go live at Guardian Medical Center. I cannot believe it's been two years of living my life with the fight; it went so fast. I'm so thankful to be with my children every day. They are so amazing and are my little guardian angels every day when I look into their little eyes, I see these two little people looking back at me, not baby's anymore. They are everything. I would do anything for them.

Life is back in the fast lane, and I couldn't be happier. Lucien and I often forget about my battle, because we're so wrapped up in the day to day routine... until we get a harsh reminder of what we lived through, like my bi weekly oncologist appointment, or every time we put eye drops in, or every time the phone rings and the caller ID says "Guardian Medical Center".. uh oh, whys the Doctor calling? And our hearts drop until we are calmed by a simple question on the other end of the line.

It's crazy the whirlwind we've lived through in two years, and where we are now ... and I'm so thankful that the biggest problem I had today was that I had too much work on my to do list... it's amazing that life is sometimes back to "normal". I wouldn't trade this life for the world.

April 8, 2010 (Thursday)

Spring is here!! It's amazing to me that as soon as this warm weather arrived, and I took in my first deep breath of spring for the year, it immediately gave me a flash back of when I first was diagnosed and hospitalized, and that first time being released from the hospital after a month. I'll never forget taking those first deep breaths of the unfamiliar warm air, the smell of spring, after being stuck in a hospital room for 5 weeks. It's a hopeful smell, and wonderful feeling to be wrapped in the warmth of the sunshine, and knowing the spring is here!

And it is that memory that gives me the strength to take normal life "bumps in the road" in stride. This past month was full of mini mountains for our family – hurdle after hurdle, but I'll take each one of these tests from the world, and go step out on the back porch and breath in springtime air and know that everything will work out. – And oh, what a month it's been!

My eyes haven't gotten any better. At the beginning of March they started hurting like I have sand in them almost every day. The pain starts in the afternoon, and by the end of the day is so unbearable that I can't even watch TV some nights. So despite using artificial tears eye drops, they are not improving at all. My oncologist says this is probably a form of graft vs. host disease, and that I need to have them looked at by a specialist immediately. Well, I finally made an appointment for this Thursday.. (That's my version of immediately... 2 months) we'll see how that goes. I may need a medicated drop for them, but we shall see.

This Monday was the scare of all scares however. I went for my normal appointment in the morning, had blood work, saw the Doctor, and came home. When we got home (a 45 minute drive), there was a message on the machine "Sheri, you need to go to the emergency room or come back here immediately due to a level in your blood work"... woah.. So, we tried to stay calm, we lined up babysitters for the day, arranged for my friend Mya to drive me back up to north Jersey to the Cancer Center, and I packed a bag assuming that this would turn into an overnight stay.

I got there, and they immediately were waiting for me at the door, brought me into the room and did an AKG. My potassium level was reading a 6.8 – which is high risk for immediate cardiac arrest. They did the blood work and had me wait, telling me that I was probably getting admitted. An hour later the results were back and my potassium was normal – the original test was false. They explained that this can happen sometimes when they use a smaller needle, the blood can crystallize and give false reading... so.. I called my father in law for a ride home... and finally got back home around 6 p.m. What a scare... it was a feeling I haven't had to feel in a really long time, and it was horrible. I was so mentally exhausted from this whole day... but at least it was a false alarm. We're just about over the scare, but it took us a few days to move on from the "nerves". Now I'm **petrified** of the eye doctor appointment on Thursday... I'll update to let you all know how that turns out, and what this eye problem is that I'm having.

OH and the good news of the month... I'm off of the Cellcept for a whole week now. This means no more compromised immune system!! Hopefully my liver levels stay normal so I can stay off the Cellcept!! :)

May 20, 2010 (Thursday)

I'm so done with the eye doctor! If there's anything that's more annoying than being in the middle of two doctors who disagree on the way I should be treated for something, then please tell me about the alternative!

Today I had a follow up appointment with the eye specialist here in Red Bank for the severe chronic dry eye I've been dealing with since March. I went to him a month ago, and he put me on Systane 5 times a day. He said if that didn't work, then he wanted to put plugs in my eyes. Well, my oncologist, from his years of experience with bone marrow transplants, wants me to be treated right off the bat with Restasis. He says this is the proper treatment for what I am suffering from in my eyes. WELL, when I told the eye doctor this today, he replied with, "Well, he's not the eye specialist is he?"

Wow.. I mean c'mon, this guy completely just lost my business! I was there for 10 minutes, he didn't want to hear a word I said and I was done. Nice. So I'm going to have to call my oncologist back and just go all the way up to north jersey so see the Princeton specialist who deals with Bone Marrow Transplant patients all the time.

All I know is that I can't wait for the weekend just to relax and enjoy the beautiful sunshine and warm weather! There's something about the spring time that just smells like freedom to me.

July 13, 2010 (Tuesday)

I can't believe that time is flying as fast as it is. Summer is cooking this year (heat wise and time wise!) I had my appointment with my oncologist yesterday, and he was able to check my blood work results while I was still in the office, and everything looked great from white cells to hemoglobin levels... phew! This was a nerve wracking "in between time" because it was the first time that I didn't have to go get blood work done every two weeks and was moved to monthly. It's nice to not have to drive the early morning trek an hour to north Jersey all the time, but on the flip side, it's really scary not knowing what my counts are for a 4 week span. Turns out too, my doctor told me I don't have to come back for 6 weeks. Lucien and I are happy that I'm doing so well of course, but are scared to not have me checked for that long of time as well.

Of course, next week will be a massive milestone for me. Next Thursday, July 22 2010, I will be officially 2 years post-transplant. Along with this comes all these "two year tests" because of my clinical trial I did during Chemotherapy sessions. So yesterday they did an in office EKG and I have to schedule a MUGA Scan (a heart scan). I dread Muga scans, mainly because they inject a radioactive dye right into your blood stream. The rest is a breeze, it's just lying under a huge machine while across the room, you can watch your heart beating on a screen. For me it's the nerves with the needle, and the fact of the dye being radioactive that I can't stand the thought of. I have to schedule that test, and hopefully it will be fast and quasi-painless.

A few weeks ago, we also found out a really upsetting fact. We're not sure how it affects me or if it doesn't affect me, but either way it's unsettling news. The clinical trial I took part in during Chemotherapy included a new drug called Mylotarg (gemtuzumab ozogamicin) which was given as an injection in patient. I remember getting that one too, because it was given via IV push (where the head nurse administers it directly into your IV line, instead of the normal "drip" treatments). It was a drug being tested on patients with AML Acute Myeloid Leukemia. Well, a few weeks ago, the company who makes the drug Mylotarg voluntarily pulled it off the market because it was showing to cause more harm than good with the patient's heart and lungs even though it was showing promising results as far as attacking the cancer cells. So, of course yesterday I forgot to ask my Oncologist if this is something I should be concerned about or if this doesn't affect me. Either way – it's not a great thing to have this in the back of my mind that the drug was pulled off the market so quickly and voluntarily too. We'll see what this brings.

It's exciting that summer is here, and my step sons Lucien and Justen are here for over a month to visit. This is when summer really kicks in full blast and we can just swim and play games nonstop :) Well, and work too, but at least there's more fun involved! We had a blast (literately) on the 4th of July setting off small fire works in the back yard and we've also been to Sesame Place as well to enjoy some fun in the sun (which I got reprimanded for by my doctor.. oops!).

I also put a call into my transplant coordinator at the Cancer Center this afternoon to see how to start the process of finding out who my donor is. This is exciting but I'm so nervous too! ! I hope they want to meet me, because we both have to sign release forms and had to wait 2 years for this opportunity to know who each other is. I know my donor was a woman in North America, so who knows, maybe we could even meet! ! ! ! I want to thank her for everything she's given me in my second chance at life, and show her pictures of my kids and my family, and everything that's she's allowed me to have the chance to do in my life. I can't wait to thank her for her generosity, and extend our family to her... after all, we are blood relatives now!

July 22, 2010 (Thursday)

2 Year Transplant Anniversary

Today is my 2 year anniversary with my new bone marrow. It's so incredible to think that two years ago I was so sick, literately to the point of not being able to lift my head out of my hospital bed, and now today I've spent celebrating with all the fun little pleasures in life.... playing Rock Band with my step sons, eating lunch with all the kids, swimming in the pool, painting with my older step son, roasting marshmallows by the fire pit and sleeping in my own bed. I couldn't ask for anything more!

I haven't heard anything yet from the Cancer Center about finding out who my donor is, so hopefully things are running smoothly with that. I hope that they consent to us knowing each other. I want to thank them for everything they've allowed me to grow older to do and see, and for my kids to have their mother around in their little lives. I want them to know who they helped and thank them more than words can say.

In celebration for my 2 year anniversary, we booked a special dinner at Sesame Place called "Dine With Me" where you can have a buffet dinner (something else I wasn't allowed 2 years ago because of the germs), and while you're eating the sesame characters walk around, and pose for pictures and put on private shows. They even surprised me during the "Happy Birthday Song" by announcing my "2 year old birthday" and brought me over a rainbow sprinkled cupcake with 2 birthday candles! It was so much fun, and the kids, Loosh, Justen, Adrian and Luciana all had a ton of fun... almost as much fun as I did!

It was all I could ask for, and the perfect way to celebrate the two year mark of my new marrow.
In other news, my eye problem has gotten progressively worse this past week, with today being the actual worse day so far. My vision has deteriorated rapidly to the point of blurring and double vision. Reading the computer is a major strain and TV I can only handle with sun glasses because the light is so irritating. So I was able to make an "emergency" visit with a new Eye Specialist tomorrow morning in Edison (about 40 minutes away). Hopefully they can treat me properly and I can start to see normal again. 3 months ago I had 20/20 vision, so I can't imagine that this is normal to be so blurry all the time. I will update how that goes, and now I'm going to enjoy

the rest of my big celebration day! What's next on the agenda? Maybe more swimming... that's what life's about!

October 19, 2010 (Tuesday)

What a whirlwind life has been since I last touched base in July! So much has gone on, and life has whisked me into the express lane so much, that it was difficult to exit off and take care of things, like updating the blog! So, I have so many updates, both good and not-so-sure-yet too.

I'll start with the "eh" updates I think to get them out of the way and keep it real. I'll start with the "eye" issue updates. The doctor in Edison turned out to be great. He listens to what I'm telling him, and also was willing to work with my oncologist on a treatment which is what I was hoping for. He started me on

Restasis drops to help my eyes with tear production. I tried that for 2 weeks, twice a day and really it didn't help, and my vision got a little worse in that time frame. I went back, and he started me on another medicine called Bacitracin Ointment which is a gel like substance (almost looks like Neosporin) which has to be applied under the eye lid twice a day. It makes your vision VERY blurry, almost like you're looking through wax paper. This lasts 15 minutes or so, and then starts to dissipate. This ointment has helped me with a lot of the pain and has allowed me to get through the day with a lot more comfort. Unfortunately, the eye doctor seems to think this is not the "end all" cure for me (and upon my research, the Bacitracin isn't something you want to stay on for a prolonged period of time or it will cause new problems) and he has another plan. Plugs! Ah! He wants to insert Punctal Plugs in my tear ducts, which will supposedly stop the tears and moisture from draining. Great. This is planned for next week, and I'm less than thrilled. He wants to place temporary Plugs in the ducts which will disintegrate a week later. If they help, then he wants me to come in and get permanent acrylic ones inserted. Now, by permanent, you would think that meant forever. Naw, of course not. He said if you rub your eyes too hard, or pick at the corners, you could dislodge the plug and have to go back into the office to have it put back in. I am really not sure how all this is supposed to take place, seeing as though I can barely sit still for a regular eye exam. We shall see!

In August, while at Target buying school shoes for the kids, Lucien noticed a brown splotchy area on my shoulder. Well, needless to say, that completely crushed my Target shopping fix! I checked it out in the mirror and it looked dark brown, and shiny, almost like little scars. I'm always the first to make excuses, so I noted the fact that this spot lands exactly where I wear my purse straps.. hmm? So I showed it to my oncologist at my appointment in August. He said right away that he doesn't like the look if it, especially because the area is slightly raised, so he set me up to make an appointment with the dermatology department of the hospital. They made me an appointment for December or something crazy like that. So I figured it was probably just a routine checkup and nothing more. WELL, two days later I get a call from the Dermatologist office saying "Your Oncologist found out that your appointment was in three months, and said that was unacceptable. He'd like you to come in sooner. How's tomorrow with the head doctor?" (Okay, this was an alarming change of pace! Oh my God this can't be good!). So I went in the next day and after an hour of scrutinizing my various markings, they told me they wanted to schedule biopsies in two areas. One on my shoulder, and another one under my arm. AHH! Me + needles don't mix. It's my greatest fear in the whole world and this is no exaggeration. So I went in last Wednesday for the procedure. Needless to say, I was a complete nervous mess, so I took two and a half Ativan before arriving (do not try this at home, the regular dose is one!). The doctor who did the biopsy was great and fast, and a really sweet nurse held my hand and talked me through it. The Ativan helped so much, because I only cried the whole time (that's pretty good for me, usually there's a lot more drama with needles). So anyway, the interesting thing is that they didn't biopsy the first spot I was talking about, they did one under my left arm near the elbow, and another under the left arm right near the arm pit. The most interesting thing is that the spot under the arm pit has an identical marking under my other arm, so that makes me not so worried. I have the feeling that it could be some graft vs. host disease rearing its head again, and I just don't think that it's skin cancer... (This is my gut feeling anyway). So now I have stitches, which will get removed next Monday the 25th. The results of the biopsies are disheartening − the two location samples they tested show "thickened bundles of collagen aligned parallel to the skin surface are crowded in the reticular dermis" − AKA − I have Morphea Scleroderma. This is a thickening of the skin which can cause major complications over time, including scarring because the production of collagen becomes unregulated and out of hand, therefore abnormal causing excess collagen to be deposited in various organs and/or tissues of the body. This is something that we will just have to watch over time to see how it progresses.

We shall see. Oh and to add to the joy of my appointments on the 25th, I also have a regular checkup with my Oncologist that day where I'll be getting my MMR shot (since I'm 2 years old now), as well as the Chicken Pox Immunization as well. (Yes, expect more tears and drama from me!).

But you know what? I have some exciting news, which I know a lot of you have been asking me about since I've reached my 2 year milestone. The day after the two year mark, I sent in my "consent" form to find out who my donor was. A few weeks later, I got the letter in the mail I was waiting for, which introduced me to Kerry, my donor. On the form I was given her name, age, city and state, email address and phone number. It was so amazing to put a name behind my donor, and immediately I was on the phone calling my mom to tell her the news! My husband's first reaction was, "Wow, she's from Colorado? Maybe you inherited a skiing ability!" Well, I doubt that. Hahaha! After settling down from my excitement for about an hour, I knew I needed to contact her as soon as possible to "meet" her and thank her. I decided to call her instead of email, because I didn't really feel that thanking someone for my life through email was enough and I'm so happy I called. She's so sweet and kind and it was the best feeling in the world to get to know the person whose blood has allowed me to live my life. It's been wonderful getting to know her more and more, chatting through email and Facebook, and I'm looking forward to keeping in touch with her for many years to come and really, I've thought about it, and I think the best way to continue to thank her for her amazing gift to me and my family, is to enjoy life to the max, and life every minute to the fullest.

April 14, 2011 (Thursday)

Oh my goodness it has been WAY too long since I've gotten on here! I have not forgotten about all of you! I can honestly say that life has been that crazy busy!!! I've totally had ups and down's in the past few months, but now, as spring arrives, things are all looking great!

Most of the time I was actually sick with a "mystery illness"... it was a runny nose, cough, tired, sickness that lasted for about three months! Literately, I was sick from the day before Thanksgiving until late February!! We tried one round of antibiotics, a Z-Pack, but that didn't do anything. A week later we tried another, stronger antibiotic did nothing! Two weeks later, the doctor tried Leviquin AND a Z Pack at the SAME time (woah.. that's a cocktail!) and still, I couldn't kick this cold. SO, after a lot of kicking and screaming on my behalf, my oncologist made me come in for a blood transfusion of immune globins to raise my immune system since I just wasn't kicking this thing. What a horrible experience, I mean, my nurses were great, but being stuck in a hospital bed for 9 hours, attached to an IV pole sure did bring back some nasty memories. Thankfully, that did the trick and a few days later (and hearing some "I told you so's" from the doctor I finally got better.

Other than that, blood work has been looking great! So my appointments are getting more and more stretched apart... which is nice to not have to trek up to north Jersey every few weeks, but also a little scary to not have my counts checked. This stretch I'm on now will be an 8 week stretch... a little TOO long for my liking, but I suppose they have confidence that will be okay :)

On the home front, I have some wicked exciting news. After 8 long years of not getting behind the wheel, I've started driving again!! I felt like I needed to become more helpful when it comes to errands, and getting the kids around, and stop being "the patient". So I went and test drove some cars... I totally needed something SMALL, because I have zero perception of where a car starts and ends (ask my step sons, they'll tell you about the time I drove over the curb with them in the car, c'mon guys, let me forget about that!). SO, I ended up with the most adorable car, a green Nissan Cube!!! :::ahhh::: It's love :) It's been amazing to pick up Luciana at school, music blaring, singing my lungs out, and just feeling great! I love that I can run to the grocery store, or the bank, wherever (as long as it's not too far)... It's really been liberating in a sense. I was even able to sign up Luciana for Ballet classes, because I know I can get her there and back without asking Lucien to take more time out of his long work day.

I can't believe it's going to be May. More so, I am in shock that I'm going to be 27!!! I feel like an adult! Which I guess I should by now! It's just crazy, looking back almost 10 years ago, a 17 year old version of myself, falling in love with Lucien, making huge like choices, starting off in a one room apartment with some guitars, clothes, a bed and a plug in burner to cook on... to where we've come... two beautiful children who are the most precious gift I could have ever dreamed of, a loving husband who has been there and will be there and is my everything, my soul, my mate, my everything, my love, my complete life, a beautiful house with a lawn and a pool and a purple living room in a beautiful town, our music lesson business that is growing by leaps and bounds with the best clients in the world who make everyday fun to work for them, oh my god the list could go on FOREVER of all the amazing people, all the amazing things, everything that I am SHOCKED and THANKFUL for every single day... I constantly sit and think... "How the heck did a 17 year old kid get to right here, right now?" I am so lucky, and so proud of everything that we have achieved as a family in these short 10 years, and most of all, I am so thankful that I fought hard enough, and am here to see the fruits of all of our hardships and labors over the years. Man, we had to work for every single thing we own, every experience we get to live, and every dream we get to look forward to. I don't take one day, one minute, one second, NOTHING for granted. Every day that I can hug my children, kiss my husband and know that our family has an amazing limitless future to come, I am so thankful. I love you all! :::HUGS::::

February 15, 2012 (Wednesday)

I honestly have NO idea how a whole year passed and I didn't get on to blog or journal once! I guess that is a good sign for my recovery if things are that slow in the medical end of things. SO much has gone on since last April, all good thankfully!

Last year we added a few members to the family... 4 puppies! We have Francine (the Schnoodle), Gigi (the Shih Tzu), Pierre (the Shih Tzu) and Penelope (the Boston Terrier). They are like babies to me, which is funny, because I was getting the "baby" bug, and since I can't have any more children due to the menopause that my treatments put me into, the puppies are the next closest thing! I love them dearly, and it definitely feels like it was always meant to be that they're here. I've fallen head over heels for them! It's been a learning experience since I never had a dog before.

In our work life things are great as well. My husband's new album was released in November.

"EvoLucien" is doing awesome and we've been busy with promotions, music videos, interviews, touring, etc. It's a crazy roller coaster ride and I love every second of it. This album was extra cool for me even though I didn't get to sing or perform on the music end; the album is a concept album complete with a story line and a huge 24 page booklet. For this album, I was able to create 3 pieces of artwork for the booklet to illustrate the story line, so I spent months working on the three pieces in a tedious form of ink work called Pointillism (the entire picture is made of tiny dots). I spent hundreds of hours creating these pieces and am so proud of them now that they're published.

Medically speaking, things are smooth. My blood work has been perfect (in the words of my Oncologist). My eyes are the same with the chronic dry eye. I still have the tear duct plugs in, and I still have to use Restatis and Bactracim (ointment) twice a day, but without it I can't stand the pain of the dryness. I also had to visit the OBGYN this year because of other issues caused by the dryness of Menopause. The problem with this dryness is that I'm at a high risk of infection, so he wanted me to start an estrogen cream to moisten things up a little. I fully intended on using it until I read the fine print... "women who have had cancer previously are at a higher risk of developing uterine cancer, breast cancer, and other cancers when using this product.". Um, no thanks? Other than that, medically I am well :)

The kids are getting big; Adrian is in the third grade at Lincroft Elementary School. He also started Ballet this year and it has been amazing for him! It's great for him to work on focusing and controlling his body movements. Luciana is 4 and in her last year of preschool. It's depressing to think of next fall when she starts Kindergarten and she won't be home until 3:20 in the afternoon – I'll miss having lunch with her every day.

So, as you can see, life is pretty normal (as normal as ours can be!). I'm amazed that things are back to routine and am thankful every day for the chance to be here on this earth, with my beautiful children, my soul mate Lucien, and my little puppies... the whole deal. I breathe every breath of air with appreciation for this beautiful chance to live life to the fullest.

March 1, 2013 (Friday)

Another year has gone by at lightning speed! This has been a trying year in some respected, but super rewarding in others. I had a bout of Shingles which took me by surprise, but was manageable to deal with overall. There's not much you can do to treat Shingles, so I was on Acyclovir for a 10 day run, and then just let the Shingles run its course. My "rebel rock star" patient traits reared their head again with this... I knew I had Shingles, I could tell from the way it looked on my side. I also knew that if I told the oncologist, then I would have been subjected to a multitude of tests and possibly a hospitalization. Therefore, I chose to go to my primary care doctor (who I NEVER go to), and begged him to keep the Shingles between the two of us. He agreed, but told me if it got any worse or if I developed fever, then we would have to tell my oncologist. Sounds like a deal! So, he put me on an antibiotic and sent me on my merry way. By the time I saw the Oncologist a few weeks later, the Shingles were gone, but when I told him, "Oh yeah, I had Shingles a few weeks ago..." he flipped a noodle! He was like, "Why on Earth didn't you call me?! Shingles is serious!"... to which I answered, "it was no big deal!"... to which... he laughed hysterically. We have fun at least!

This year I had a development with my eye damage when I was forced into switching eye specialists; it ended up being a blessing in disguise. The new doctor did a whole exam and work up which revealed severe cornea damage (something that the first eye doctor failed to mention). Then the new doctor says, "You don't see as well as you think you do, in my opinion you should have been wearing glasses for quite some time now. I think a lot of the discomfort you are experiencing is from eye strain." I was shocked at this news, I mean; I thought my vision was blurry because of the dryness. So, I was prescribed glasses... and let me tell you, as soon as I put them on, it was a whole new world! The doctor was also concerned that because of the severe scratches and damage to the cornea that I was at a high risk of infection, so he prescribed a low dose antibiotic for a few weeks. There has been various other excitement, when he tried to change the ointment I use from Bactracim (ointment) to one that had another ingredient in it as well. I ended up having a severe allergic reaction to this new ingredient, and had to do a round of steroid eye drops to recover from the painful infection. I'm now back on the regular ointment and still the Restasis, which is working well.

My blood work thus far has been spot on, with all of my counts in the normal range. My Oncologist is encouraged by my progress, and always looks very happy with my status when I see him. I'm still on an every six week blood work and office visit schedule which is often for someone this far out from treatments. I cannot even begin to fathom that it has been 4 1/2 years since my bone marrow transplant – this just seems impossible, but amazing!

Life otherwise is incredible. The kids are so big. Adrian is in 4th grade and Luciana has started full day Kindergarten! My babies are not babies anymore, and I am so fortunate to be able to witness them growing into the mature pure hearted little people that they are becoming right before my eyes. We are up to seven dogs now... they are my little babies! We still have Francine the Schnoodle, Gigi and Pierre the Shih Tzu's and Penelope the Boston Terrier, and we have adopted Darla the 4 pound Yorkie, Mabel the teacup brown Boston Terrier and Rupert the 5 pound Maltese. Puppy chaos is wooftastic; I love every second of it!

Life is amazing and I'm eating up of it. The highlight of my year so far has been being able to see my idol, P!nk live in concert. When she was touring last time with the Funhouse tour, I was recouping, still building my immune system, and was not given the clearance to go to the concert. Heart = broken! So, with her new tour "The Truth About Love" you betcha I wasn't about to miss it! Lucien and I had front row seats... and she was amazing! Every musician has someone they look up to, as an "idol" figure, and for me, it's Alicia (P!nk). I was on cloud freakin' 9 during the whole concert, she is just so hard core and real. Her music was pivotal to me during my treatments, and helped me through some tough times. Seeing her in person was the experience of a lifetime.

As of August 2012 we have made a huge change in our lifestyle as a family. I was shocked at one of my appointments when the scale read that I was up to 170 pounds, and I started to do research on "diets". What I found instead is a new way of life, which is more than about losing weight, but is also a way of keeping your body healthy. Lucien, the kids and I all now follow a Paleo life style. The whole premise is that as humans, we should be consuming foods that are wholesome and real such as meat, fish, vegetables, fruit and nuts. The human body doesn't know how to digest and process all of the junk "fake" foods that our society is bombarded with daily such as sugars, breads, pastas, rice, dairy, and anything else that has been man made. By cutting all of this completely out of our diets, I have lost 25 pounds so far, and have never felt healthier in my entire life. We eat more quantity and quality foods than we ever did, and even more variety than ever before. We eat such a large variety of meats, vegetables and fruits, it's truly mind boggling. Many times I'm so stuffed; I can't finish what's on my plate. I've again become an improved version of myself. The kids, Lucien and I have survived this winter season without one cold of any kind... it's amazing how our bodies are stronger, leaner and all around healthier. Now, I've begun dabbling in the kitchen... I'm shocked to admit that I love to cook! I've started collecting these gorgeous dishes and bake ware from QVC called Temp-Tations which I am *obsessed* with. Between my bake ware collection and our new lifestyle, I have been inspired to start experimenting in the kitchen and it has swiftly become a passion. It has been a pivotal part of our year as a family, and keeping our bodies well. Our bodies are our temples, and to inject anything unnatural to our genetics makes no sense whatsoever. After everything I've been through, I might as well do everything in my power to keep my and my children's bodies in the healthiest shape possible.

(Above) Fall 2012 Pumpkin carving with the kids... and roasting the delicious pumpkin seeds at the end of the day!
(Below) Spring 2013 – Reinventing myself with a new punk hairstyle to celebrate my 25 pound weight loss.

July 22, 2013 (Monday)

5 Year Anniversary of Bone Marrow Transplant

I have an appointment with my Oncologist this week marking five years since my bone marrow transplant. I walk into his office with my head held high, smiling bright and emit a spectrum of positive light and love to everyone I pass. I sit in the waiting area next to a sweet lady who looks like she's in her mid-fifties, and I tell her I love her sandals. She lights up, "Thank you! I found them at Macys, they're Michael Kors and they're so comfortable." We go on to chat about fashion designers for a while before I'm called out back the nurse. I wish my new friend Loretta a wonderful day, and am elated when she expresses a heartfelt smile from ear to ear; mission accomplished, I've shared my energy and hopefully helped to lighten her burden for the day.

After my blood pressure and temperature are taken, I am led into an exam room to wait. I've been in this room before. In front of me, a movie starts playing as I remember the last time I was in this particular spot... I was here getting a bone marrow biopsy. Lucien stood to the left of the room, holding my hand as I lay on the table desperate for the torment to end... the right of the room was littered with white coats and blue scrubs as doctors and nurses anxiously tried to hurry to end my screaming commotion. I shake my head and this demon, this memory dissolves into thin air... I take a deep breath, and remind myself that was long ago. The door swings open and Doctor Ayers comes in with a smile.

"Hi, how are you doing??" he asks as he heads into the room. He places his tablet on the countertop and looks around the room.

"Looking for your wheelie stool? There isn't one in this room." I smirk.

"Yes! You got it, I'm lost without it...ahh.. what am I going to do?" he pretends to search around in panic as I laugh at the charade. "So, this is the big visit. Five years from your bone marrow transplant, this is an amazing accomplishment, you should be very proud of yourself." He leans on the counter in absence of his stool.

"I am. I can't believe it's been five years. I was 23 when I first came here, and now I'm an old lady at 29." I nod my head as I say this out loud, amazing myself at the reality of it all.

"That's right, and your kids were little, your daughter was just born and your son was in preschool. How old are they now?" he asks.

"I know, it's crazy... Luciana is 6 and is going into 1st grade and my son is 10 and will be in the 5th grade. I used to bring her to my appointments in her carriage, she was such a munchkin."

"Your daughter is a pip, she cracks me up. You'll have to bring her in this summer when she's off from school; she absolutely makes my day when you bring her in. What a riot." He laughs at the thought of Luciana as he starts walking over to the examination table. On cue, I stand up and hop on the table. Once I'm sitting, he comes to stand in front of me but pauses in front of the full length mirror, gives himself a once over and adjusts his lab coat collar.

"Oh my God, did you just check yourself out?" I bust out laughing, "Caught in the act!" I tease.

"Ah... well... Yes I did. You caught me. That's funny; my office upstairs has a wall of glass windows, and every single person that walks by checks themselves out. It's comical to watch." He nobly tries to change the subject as he shines the otoscope in my eyes and continues the conversation. "So how many dogs do you have now?" He shines the light in my mouth.

I automatically do my part, "Ahhhhhhhhhh" while he examines my mouth, then answer, "Still seven. No new puppies lately. I'm maxed out, totally done with seven! For real this time!"

He laughs at this, "That's what you said after the second, and the third and the fourth..." he puts the stethoscope on my back, I breathe in, and out slowly, and again, and again until he comes around and put the instrument on my chest to listen to my heart. This is all routine to us after all these years, like a practiced dance.

"They're all little though, they really only add up to one big dog... *maybe* one and a half!" I defend myself, but end up laughing along with Doctor Ayers at my lame attempt at justification. I lean back on the table and he puts his hand under my left rib cage. I breathe all the way in and as far out as I can

360

while he pushes hard pressure down on whatever organ he's checking.

"How are your kids enjoying summer, are you guys planning any fun vacations or anything?" I ask before breathing in and all the way out again for the second time.

"Yeah, we head down to the shore at Point Pleasant a lot with them, they love it down there." He heads over to the countertop and turns on his tablet while I dismount the table and just hang out standing in the middle of the room.

"You didn't ask me if my knee still crackles, do you want to hear it?" I taunt, knowing it makes him quiver like some people do with nails on a chalkboard.

"No, no, no, please that's okay! That's why I didn't ask, actually, I really don't need to hear it!. So, everything is looking good. You're doing amazing, I mean, you could listen to me more and not be in the sun, not work so much and go to the orthopedic to get your knee looked at, but you won't, so I won't bother saying it." He smiles, opens the door for me and walks me to the door leading to the waiting area. "Remember when I told you that in five years I'd be telling your story to patients for inspiration, well, here we are. Keep it up, you're doing everything right." He opens the door for me, "I'll see you in six weeks. Call me if anything goes on."

"You know I won't call you," I respond with a joking grin, "Thanks Doctor Ayers, I'll see you in six weeks."

SHERI NOCELLI

Looking Back and Moving Forward

I love to weed; digging my fingers into the Earth, soil getting under my nails, sweat dripping from my face. I love the rain, getting cleansed by the drops of untainted water as it runs through my hair. I love scanning XM radio and finding an old favorite song from childhood providing my mind's eye with a flashback of adolescent memories. I love waking up to the birds singing their high pitched opus in joyful chorus. I love running through sprinklers on a scorching summer afternoon. I love laughing and the hurt in my side when it's just too funny. I love watching my children sleep, sprawled out on their beds; their angelic faces dreaming of things only pleasant in nature. I love staring at my husband while he sleeps, with his mouth slightly ajar, his eyes closed to the fact that I'm studying his every breath. I love saying what's on my mind, speaking up, having an opinion, growing as a person, learning new things about myself every day. I love the little things, big things, obvious things, ridiculous things, amazing things and purposeful things. I have Cancer to thank for reminding me to cherish the world around me. I've learned so much, but am not naïve to the fact that there are mountains more to discover.

During my first inpatient hospital admission, one of the doctors one morning said something ludicrous to me, "After you've gone through all of this, all of the chemotherapy, treatments and hospitalizations... once you've beaten Cancer, you'll be a stronger version of yourself whose even better, more aware and more thankful of your life every day." I distinctly remember shaking my bald head at him and responding with immature attitude, "I'm already thankful for everything I have and am happy with myself – this is just a roadblock before I get back to normal life." The doctor acknowledged my opinion, but smiled a wise grin in response.

I was so wrong – and he was way more than right. There's no way I could have known then, that life could change and IMPROVE after Cancer. I survived this shit, and I damn well am going to live every moment like it's my last. I don't take for granted the smallest of things anymore. The birds, the rain, the sunshine, a good song – all of these things are the sparkle of life.

No matter how much you think you are the most perfect version of yourself, there is always room to improve.

I wear a simple stainless steel bracelet on my right wrist every single day which reads "All we have to decide is what to do with the time that is given to us." It's a quote from Lord of the Rings, but it's more than just some silly movie quote. It's become my life's mantra; it reminds me that every day is a gift. We are only given a short time on this Earth, and it is up to us how we live our life – it would be selfish to not soak in every moment with grace, gratitude, adventure and purpose. Every single day, I choose to the most jubilant person of myself, no matter the circumstances.

What is the meaning of life? Every person alive on this planet has a greater purpose in the grand scheme of things. The meaning of life is something inside of you, something you didn't know you had in you until one day it slaps you in the face, yells at you to wake up and gives you no choice but to listen! A person's purpose *is* the meaning of life. Your purpose might be to spread laughter, to raise your children, to invent a lifesaving drug… it might be to discover life on Mars, to be an educator or to be a leader of the lost. We all have a set purpose pre woven into our cosmic DNA, and when you find that true purpose, you will be fulfilled.

My purpose is to inspire by spreading hope, love and promise to those who are lost. I was knocking on deaths door, but fought back with optimism and a constant smile as my weapons of choice, and I won. I won. I beat all odds. My life's plan was to be thrown through the mill, so that I could emerge this different, stronger version of the woman I used to be. And that is why I chose to share my story with you, to spread love and light into your life. Take this gift, and flourish it, grow it and harbor it. Life is an adventure and you should never settle for less than you deserve and never stop exploring the beauty of all around you. Find your mantra, find your purpose, find the true you and you will be fulfilled.

Every day is an adventure in life, and every day I am thankful to be here as a survivor. There are days I struggle with the memories of what I've been through, and the severity of my prognosis - it humbles me to not sweat the small things in life. There were times in the hospital when I would stare at my hands as I washed them in the sink. I would look at them with disgust, knowing that flowing through every part of my body was

Leukemia, feeling like I was being invaded from the inside out. These are the types of memories that plague me, triggered by normal daily rituals. But these thoughts also ground me; reminding me constantly that I am now, and will always be at risk. I still keep my doctor's business card, with his cell phone number written in sharpie, in my wallet – right where I see it and can get to it in a hurry.

It's a balance of risk awareness and moving forward. I do not, and never have, dwelled on the Leukemia. I also cannot ignore it – it is part of who I am as a person. I will be holding the past in one hand and the limitless future in the other for the rest of my life – but I will do so with my secret weapons… a smile, a positive attitude and passion for life.

SHERI NOCELLI

About The Author

At the age of 23 years old, Sheri Nocelli thought she had it all; a dream marriage, two beautiful children, a comfortable home and a thriving business. On March 23, 2008 she was diagnosed with a very rare and deadly form of Acute Myeloid Leukemia which threatened everything, bringing her life to a screeching halt. After four rounds of intensive Chemotherapy and having a bone marrow transplant, she has survived the illness with her head held high.

Wife, mother, musician, artist, entrepreneur, business owner and Cancer survivor, Nocelli now celebrates her journey by adding "author" to her resume. She has made it a personal mission to share her story with fellow Cancer patients, survivors, their families and anyone who is facing a personal battle in their own life, hoping to spread her message of hope and optimism.

Now 29 years old, Nocelli currently resides in Lincroft, New Jersey with her husband Lucien, her children Adrian (10), Luciana (6) and her seven dogs. She is an advocate for Paleo lifestyle and spreading awareness of its many health benefits, especially for Cancer and other illness patients and survivors. Nocelli has dedicated her life's journey to sharing her story of survival with those in need of hope and inspiration.

Visit Her Blog for Current Updates and Extras:
Living It Up In Lincroft - www.SheriNocelli.com

For Music Including the Songs Referenced In This Book:
Lucien Nocelli Official Website – www.LucienNocelli.com

SHERI NOCELLI

Acknowledgments

There is so much to be thankful for, and so many people I am graciously indebted to eternally. My sincere gratitude which I send today and forever goes to the entire medical staff at the hospital I was treated at, you all treated me like your long lost daughter during my intensive inpatient stays. Thank you for holding my hand while I cried through your never-ending supply of needles and for always reminding me to smile. I would like especially to thank my incredible head doctor at the cancer treatment center; you never let me believe anything but survival was possible, and I look forward to torturing you many more years with my crepitus knee crackling!

Many sincere thanks to all of my dearest friends, old and new, who have been so supportive throughout my treatments and to this day; Amy "P" Gillespie, Mandi Stefanik, Maggie Dery, Kathy McGlynn, you all mean the world to me. Also to our amazing clients who I consider much, much more than that, who have all become amazing friends over the years – Thank you especially to Lisa Testa, Tracy Ilvento, the Proodian Family, Debbie and Rich Raike, Lou Forte, Nettie Matthews, Trish Lanza, Tracy Keogh, Joesphine DeVito, Caroline, Casie and Danielle Fitzgerald and everyone who has supported our family through this time and beyond. Many thanks and hugs to my crazy family; Uncle Skyp and Aunt Carole, Uncle Dicky and Aunt Bonnie, dearest Memere, Pepere who we miss every day and all of my awesome kooky cousins.

Thank you to my incredible In-Laws, Lucien and Mary Ann Nocelli for your constant love, support, guidance and for always being there for us. Thank you to my incredible mother Diane Ritter – you have always been my best friend, and are truly more than Mommet, you are my confidant, always willing to lend an ear and voice your opinion. To my father Robert Ritter who has always been my mischievous partner in crime, pulling stunts like hiding kittens from mom, making inappropriate jokes and impressions and ripping up New York City like nobody's business – you are my blue M&M. To my insane brother Scott who makes me proud every day of the man he is growing up to be. Thank you for always making me laugh like a child; just promise me you'll never go bungee jumping in Mexico, they just don't have the regulations!

Thank you to my precious children, Adrian and Luciana, who gave me a never faltering beacon of light and love to cherish in my loneliest times. Every day you amaze me with the things you say, the twinkle in your eyes and the dreams in your heart. To Lucien and Justen who are so much more than step sons – I love you both like you are my own; thank you for being my best little friends. I am so proud of the men you have become. Adrian, Luciana, Lucien and Justen - you will achieve such beautiful things in your lives, and I can't wait to see you grow into the amazing human beings I can already see you are.

Finally, most of all, my deepest never ending gratitude to my husband, Lucien, for changing my life so many years ago, and for helping me to grow every day into a better person. Thank you for your laughter, love, ridiculousness, intellect and for just being you. You never cease to amaze me in who you are and the wacky, yet intelligent things you teach me every day. You are my rock, you are my everything - you are my other half.
I look forward to discovering our future together for all of eternity as the dynamic duo that we are, and experiencing adventures to come together on this planet and beyond.